SOUND AGAINST FLAME

The Process of Yoga and
Atheism in America

Derek Beres

Outside the Box Publishing

Jersey City

Outside the Box Publishing
89 Wayne St #1B
Jersey City NJ 07302
www.otbpublishing.com

ISBN-13: 978-0-9817398-0-9
ISBN-10: 0-9817398-0-6

Cover design by Craig Anthony Miller
www.craiganthonymiller.com

For more information visit
www.soundagainstflame.com

"As a ruthlessness of opposites, the Transcendental shows through the mask of the enigmatic Master: ceaselessness of production against an insatiate appetite of extermination, Sound against Flame. And the field of the terrible interplay is the Dancing Ground of the Universe, brilliant and horrific with the dance of the god."

Heinrich Zimmer
Myths and Symbols in Indian Art and Civilization

Also by Derek Beres

Global Beat Fusion: The History of the Future of Music

Tangled Web: The Best Music Tour You Never Heard Of

A Staircase of Words, Volume One: Essays
(with Dax-Devlon Ross)

Soon to be published

Mysterious Distance

A Staircase of Words, Volume Two: Novellas
(with Dax-Devlon Ross)

To Osiris and Anula,
for being there during the process

&

To Oscar and Calvin,
who passed on to another process.

CHAPTERS

PROLOGUE

While walking through New York's West Village I noticed a large, vertically strung banner hanging from the front of a church. On it was a teenage girl staring skyward, with the words "Are You Craving More?" printed above her head. She was looking, of course, at—or should that be "for"—God, and below her feet were written the times of weekend service. The obvious implication is that this house of worship provides that extra special something that gives you what you're seeking.

More? Don't we have enough already? Haven't we realized that we don't even know how to properly use what we have, so as to make looking for more not only unnecessary, but unrealistic? Human beings, as Alan Watts liked to say, were not born *into* this world—we grew up *out of* it. We are a product of the process of existence. What *more* could we want than that? The only reason someone would crave more has nothing to do with not having enough. It's not being satisfied with what one has that feeds such a desire.

This book is an investigation into that search, and the many forms that it can take. While the title appears to focus on yoga and atheism, there is something "more" than that. Those two philosophies certainly underlie and create the foundation of what is inside these pages. But they in no way comprise the bulk of the work ... in a way. That is, this is a book written from the perspective of *jnana* yoga—the yoga of knowledge. In this way, it is a book written entirely from the perspective of yoga, but it's not necessarily *about* yoga, at least in the sense that most books on the topic are.

When we gaze into history through the filter of religion—when our religious choice dictates our views and feeds our biases of what history is—we are often consumed by our prejudices. When theories emerge that conflict with what we believe to be true, we recoil and take vengeance upon that idea. Yet how do we know what is "true" if we have not investigated the opposite of what we believe? We cannot claim to be good if we have not tasted the bad; we are never so certain to be right if we have not experienced being wrong. What is most interesting, and what will interest us in these pages, is the dance between those seeming opposites.

Some of the history contained in this work may seem new to you, or expressed differently. This is part of the design. History, like the present, is subjective. Our personal experiences will govern the way we view the world, as well as what made the world the way it is today. From the outset, I'd like to do away with two popular biases regarding the topic matter: yoga will not be treated as "mystical;" atheism will not be confined by the idea that "there is no God." Neither of these definitions expresses what these two philosophies demand.

The stories in this book may surprise the reader who expects to glance over passages of yoga and atheism. They include the African influence on Mexican culture; the Indian influence on Jamaica; cannibalism; infanticide; the Crusades; Christian mythology; and Gilgamesh. What has always interested me is the innumerable ways that humans can experience the world, and how common themes run through these experiences, even if the forms they take seem worlds apart. In essence, this work is one of comparative mythology—if we understand that mythology is not a thing of the past, but living and breathing us at this very moment. It is the unbroken thread of history that has been here as long as we have inhabited this planet.

The text is composed of three sections. The first three chapters deal with various ways that belief and behavior mingle, merge and battle. Basically, how what we say and how we act are often very different things. There are rather obscure examples of historical incidences that present the idea that history is always a matter of who is writing it, and that those writers' motives will influence (and often misinform) later generations. The stories provide a basis for belief, and how what we today know as religion has roots that are deeply covered by centuries of agendas and declarations that were not necessarily created by its founders. Nevertheless, our various takes on the eternal provide nourishment for what has grown from such soil, and offer us hope in the face of calamity, misfortune and uncertainty.

The middle three chapters are the most *yogatheistic*. They provide a general background of what yoga and atheism are, and how they have evolved into the forms that we know today. The final trinity takes a look at how these ideas provide tangible and sustainable alternatives to many of the belief systems and behaviors that modern Americans involve themselves with. There is nothing new in the presentation of these ideas, but like many things Americans assemble and fuse, it is a collaboration of forms that defines many of us today. That is, the ideas presented herein are not about finding more, but about taking what we have and making the most of it.

PART I

PEOPLING

"This feeling of being lonely and very temporary visitors in the universe is in flat contradiction to everything known about man (and all other living organisms) in the sciences. We do not 'come into' this world; we come *out* of it, as leaves from a tree. As the ocean 'waves,' the universe 'peoples.' Every individual is an expression of the whole realm of nature, a unique action of the total universe."

Alan Watts
The Book: On the Taboo Against Knowing Who You Are

CHAPTER 1

MOVING BEYOND BELIEF

Belief is a lack of experience.

I remember a female student who attended my Friday afternoon class every week some four years ago. In her early fifties, she was in good shape, extremely dedicated to her practice. She was not ultra-flexible or overly strong; she had a refined and patient approach, which always signifies someone who is using the tools of yoga as a means of sustainability and not searching out the "next great workout." When we came to postures that were a bit too challenging, she would assume another position and wait. She did not become frustrated by what she couldn't do, but rather focused on what she could—a very commendable quality. Yet every week when we came to headstand, she immediately pulled her mat to the wall, even though she never really needed the support.

After months of this, I stopped her as she was preparing for her weekly exodus from the center of the room. I told her the wall was an unnecessary crutch that she had graduated from. She replied that it was there for emotional support. She knew she didn't really need it, but knowing it was there comforted her. That's fine, I told her, but she would never have that emotional breakthrough that could occur if she stopped relying on habits—and fear is definitely a habit. I pulled her mat back and up she went … and down went she, tumbling onto her back. Then the oddest thing occurred. She began laughing. I walked over to make sure she was alright, and she continued, red-cheeked and bright-eyed. Then she told me why. In all her years of practicing yoga, she had always thought that if she were to fall over in a headstand, she would snap her neck and die. When she actually fell, she realized everything was fine. It was even kind of fun, she said. From that day forward she never needed the crutch again.

Belief is a lack of experience. When you have had the experience, there is no need for belief.

Unfortunately not everyone takes The Fall so lightly, or humbly. In fact, over the past two thousand years the idea of this Fall has created a nearly insurmountable rift between the human organism and the rest of the world, not to mention human communities with each other, and further still, the individual and the Self. The fall from grace is by no means an absence of grace, though the further away the gods moved from the everyday realities of soil, sun and water, the more distanced we felt from the rest of nature. We traded experiences for beliefs and the ground beneath our feet danced away. Soil became tile, gods became God, and religious prophets that were extremely human became extreme examples of what humans could never aspire to. Contact with anything divine turned into contact with supposed messengers of divinity, who then reminded us that they were needed as intermediaries between worlds, for the common man could no longer translate the Absolute within himself—because the Absolute was no longer inside himself. The ground of all being was plowed into an infertile field, save the memory of a chosen few who will only reappear at the end stages of the planet. And the neuroses that began to form from such thinking *are* leading to the end of something: a tipping point, a junction where the knowledge of Self is the only remedy to the misknowledge of many selves not our own. And that knowledge only comes through experience.

....

The half-cocked brow gaze over slightly glazed eyes when I tried to explain the premise of this book to friends insured the fact that I'd have some serious explaining to do. A comparative philosophy book on the practices of yoga and atheism, two systems with so (seemingly) little in common? Trying to establish a common ground between a devotional practice with images of blue-skinned, elephant-headed, flute-playing gods, and the complete opposite, the blasphemous idea of no God at all? Beyond a surface grazing—that of a South Asian spiritual practice mostly known in America as an exercise routine and for polytheistic iconography, alongside the outright denial of a Supreme Anything—there is plenty of shared wisdom. The premise of this work, and the underlying foundation of both yoga and atheism, directly pertains to the *experience* of life, not the abstraction of it.

There is little surprise that these two forms of belief/practice (or unbelief, depending on your definition) are the most rapidly expanding philosophies in our country. This is not to deny the brute strength of megachurches growing like wild weeds across the nation. (And this is not to necessitate the idea that such churches are inherently bad for us, as many atheists, as well as many sitting on the fence in the God question, put forth.) True, we are a Christian nation. There is little doubt about that. Even if we do not claim that as our faith, the forms of thought that arise in our brains have been conditioned by a specific cause-and-effect, rewards/benefits musculature defined and developed through biblical and political training. Indeed, it is impossible not to have been taught in such a manner if you have gone through the public school system. (And if you attended a private school, all the more so, as religion has a stronghold on nearly all of these institutions, as well as the majority of parents who home-school children.) Churches, it must be remembered, constructed the original educational system in America, so it is not surprising that the way we learn is dictated by theology. In many ways, this psychological underpinning is more relevant than outright belief, for when the manners in which we are conditioned stay hidden, we become prime targets for anxiety, depression, social confusion and general dis-ease.

What the basic ideological thinkers of the three major religious traditions of the West—Christianity, Judaism and Islam—have conceived is that your actions on this planet are preparations for a) some sort of kingdom of which people of your faith will lord over, and b) some form of afterlife, where a style of judgment will occur. This judgment comes in many varieties. Some maintain that you can convert to the faith and be "saved," while other sects are so bullheaded that only those born into families of their specific faith are righteous. Regardless of the degree of severity, anything done for another life beyond this one is rooted in egoistic idealism, something both yoga and atheism (at their best) aim to dissolve. To get to the roots of this comparison, which is just as much a survey of the social and spiritual state of American ideologies as it is these two specific practices, we will have to apply the wisdom of philosopher Daniel Dennett: "If we want to understand the nature of religion today, as a natural phenomenon, we have to look not just at what it is today, but at what it used to be." And this involves looking into the way all humans used to be, not just examining the doctrines passed down by a few men with specific agendas. The paths we will take may surprise you, and may not always be pleasant, but they will prove worthwhile.

Yoga, while given an Indian veneer due to its geographical roots, has been remixed and redefined in innumerable ways in its two century-plus history on American soil. Today it is believed that over forty million Americans have tried some form of yoga, and there is little doubt millions more are in tow. Yoga has successfully been transplanted from a noun to a verb to an adjective, used to describe everything from the physical *asana* practice to bread, tea, clothing and spa services. While there are many ways to dissect and explore this aged philosophical system, we will focus on two: by utilizing the tools of yoga that enrich the everyday through an appropriate understanding of the symbolic references of its mythology, and by contemplating the importance of the body (and how we treat it). We will look at these predominantly through the gaze of *jnana* yoga, the yoga of knowledge—otherwise known as the art of discrimination. I will not be confined to one time period or culture in this investigation, and will do my best to avoid the trappings of the modern yogi in this advice from anthropology professor Joseph S. Alter: "If there is one single thing that characterizes the literature on Yoga, it is repetition and redundancy in the guise of novelty and independent invention."

Atheism is, believe it or not, rooted in a similar soil. It was founded as a reaction to the political and social situations of the surrounding environment by people yearning for something deeper than the rigid and unscientific laws of religious codes. Yoga too was a reaction, a fusing of the Samkhya philosophy and an ever-expanding Vedic literature of differing schools of yoga, all of which opposed the façade constructed by religious and political leaders. Like the Buddhism that grew from yogic teachings, yoga was inherently atheistic, even if that specific term had not yet been coined. The term comes from the Greek *atheistos* and originally meant a denial of the Athenian establishment, not the flat-out refusal of a divine figurehead. Like most concepts, it began to have a universal connotation as cultures picked up the trend, and today is used in reference to anyone who does not believe in God. Unlike the agnostic, who believes that there are certain things that cannot be answered (or, put another way, that we ask the wrong questions), the atheist has no room for fluffy mystery.

The question of belief will play a major role in this book, though I want to make a precautionary note in the usage of this word compared to the term faith. The two often walk hand-in-hand, but there is a subtle, yet crucial difference, at least in the way I want to approach them. Belief is the idea that something is true regardless of proof, while faith relates to something instinctual and primal, and does not necessarily have to be applied to a god. Faith is often defined as a belief, but I want to reorient it for the context of this work. This constant default of religionists to phrases like "It just is" is why the immediate colleague to atheism, science, is in dismay over movements like those led by champions of Intelligent Design (ID). There is simply nothing realistic in their claims. It is pure, untested belief that only reflects their particular view on the world, and not the actions and habits of the world itself. As Alan Watts wrote, "The believer will open his mind to the truth on condition that it fits in with his preconceived ideas and wishes." Cloaking science in biblical creationism with no evidence does not make for good science, good religion, or even good humanity.

Let us treat faith as something necessary to the human condition—not as an untested hypothesis, but the innate ability to feel a connection to something beyond our everyday lives. More importantly, let us try not to give it form, color or taste. I do not want to label it, for there are already so many names and so little evidence that any fit the description. It is more of a connection to instinct, a sort of foresight that the experiences and the world at large are united as a process moving at the same speed and in similar directions. It is important to remember that both the words "yoga" and "religion" come from root words that mean "union." And, as we will touch upon, it is the seemingly innocuous usage of language that separates the innumerable aspects of what could be seen as part of the same process—that is, life. Words, the letters and meaning that bring us together, are equally perilous when used to divide.

What we're looking for is an understanding of the *process* of life. This is not an easy task, as it requires stripping away commonly accepted companions to the ideologies under scrutiny: dogmas and rituals, of course, although we need to go deeper than those. In order to grasp the process of an idea, the iconography and visual/emotional association must also be removed. Christmas cards, Easter eggs, mandalas, menorahs, cute little baby gods with blue skin, and sheep are parts of the manifestation of the process, but not the process itself; they are forms, not essence. We have to get to the pure process, of belief, of faith, as well as the promises that these supposedly lead to: liberation, salvation and equanimity. We need to go beyond "righteousness through Christ" and "liberation through yoga." We need to push through the verb and get to the essence, which requires a proper understanding of the symbolic meanings of rituals, and not the form that they happened to take once, somewhere else.

Let's try an actual example. One day I was dining with a fellow yoga teacher. We were planning a retreat, and before either of us committed to anything, we had to make sure that our philosophies played along well together. She told me that the foundation of her style was that the "universe pulsates with love." Her system extended out from that idea, one that she believed embodied the "true" nature of yoga. I then asked her why it couldn't stop with the "universe pulsates." Why did love have to be the definitive attachment to the universe? I reminded her that at the basis of yoga was the shadow, and that by introducing a concept (love) you by default create its opposite (hate). I suppose this is why the Buddha did not preach that freedom arises from love, but from compassion. It's a much more sane philosophy, and not so open to misinterpretation. Needless to say, we never went on that retreat.

Having decided to devote my life to the practice of yoga, there are many precepts that I adhere to. But I do not ascribe to them simply because some book told me to do so. Classic texts like the Hatha Yoga Pradipika, Patanjali's Yoga Sutras and the Bhagavad Gita are important resources to understanding the psychology and practicality of yoga. Books, however, are not experiences; they are reflections of experiences. They do not suit each person, as a suit will not fit every skin. As much as the atheism movement has lashed against the hypocrisies and tyranny of Christianity, yoga is not free from such unforgiving surveillance. The presentation of yoga in America has been bastardized in many forms, and not all of them are helpful. Like cherry pickers seeking out sweet sayings from biblical scripture, yogis are equally guilty of accommodating their needs and discarding the rest (or, as is often the case, not researching if a "rest" even exists).

Seeing a badly Photoshopped rendering of a bearded man in a white robe sitting on a cloud does not help promote the ideology of yoga, yet it appears constantly in the pages of yoga and natural health publications. It cheapens the practice, pushing forth the notion that a) there is an image to liberation and b) this particular person embodies it. An idol is an idol, and what's worse, is idle. The earth does not stop movement, and so has no need for fixed images. There is good reason that you never see images of the Buddha gazing at you with a mask of anger, yet to say that he never experienced such an emotion is to take away his humanity.

There is much good to be learned from both yoga and atheism, and like mushrooms hiding under a canopy of leaves in dark forests, sometimes it takes a little research. You have to know where, and how, to look. There are also amazing benefits from religion, even as the western model has manufactured it. We just cannot treat any of these paths as the "goal." It is in this exact seeking of a goal—of some reward or promise—that we lose ourselves, time and again. We need to be critical in our pursuit, opening our deepest held beliefs for debate, and, what's more, being compassionate in the process. Only through questioning will we uncover answers, and we may even find there's more power in the former. With any luck, over these pages some sense of the gravity of the situation will be found.

In his brief history on the subject, *The Twilight of Atheism*, Alister McGrath recounts his own religious background, which had a long marriage with atheism before it ultimately strengthened his Christian conviction. It is an informative, unbiased rendering of disbelief, although he concludes with the idea that atheism is on the outs, as outmoded forms of church are being "replaced by more dynamic forms of Christian community." McGrath had either just missed, or was not paying attention to, the rise in popularity of a few authors. Sam Harris' *The End of Faith*, Richard Dawkins' *The God Delusion* and Daniel C. Dennett's *Breaking the Spell* has become an important recent trinity in American consciousness, fueled by the underlying tension created by the Bush administration's toxic dumping of scriptural literalism across not only America, but the rest of the world to boot. If atheism is in its twilight, it is only because a new dawn awaits the dark horizon. And while McGrath's optimistic plea is rooted in a deep sense of conviction, the London resident has apparently not visited enough American megachurches, where religion and economics have so blurred that churches now *include* malls, not vice-versa, and the messages of God are no longer about salvation, but rather finding good parking spaces and getting all the money you want if you pray correctly.

Harris and Dawkins emerged as the clear stalwarts of what is sometimes touted as the New Atheism, with *Wired* magazine offering them a cover story in November 2006. Their appeal and importance is derived from a very scientific perspective: question, and get to the roots of what's going on, not simply reiterate what our ancestors believe happened and spread around as "truth." In one particularly enlightening passage in *The End of Faith*, Harris writes, "Tell a devout Christian that his wife is cheating on him, or that frozen yogurt can make a man invisible, and he is likely to require as much evidence as anyone else, and to be persuaded only to the extent that you give it. Tell him that the book he keeps by his bed was written by an invisible deity who will punish him with fire for eternity if he fails to accept its every incredible claim about the universe, and he seems to require no evidence whatsoever."

This brief summation serves as an entry point to an absurdly large amount of the religious thinking that goes on in our country. "There is no need to think about religion, it just is what we've been told, that's how it is, end of story. It worked for my parents and their parents; well then it works for me, and must be real." The problem with this thinking is that it completely denies the foundation of evolution, for the ability of life to move past what it was once was while adhering to a basic format. There is little wonder why the very concept of evolution has served as a tipping point for the religiously inclined, and why those whose livelihoods are somehow supported by the idea that an omnipotent deity designed everything are creating the friction that exists between science and religion. This tension is not supportive of anything in nature, and is the very reason scientists and scholars smack their head at the dumbfounded claims made by "believers." Museums devoted to creationism and what some consider to be legitimate textbooks are being used to educate children that dinosaurs and humans spent time together, and that fossils are God's trick into seeing whether we've been naughty or nice.

Unfortunately, many on the other side of this divide—evolutionary biologists being one major camp—have turned

the game into a cynical wordplay always one step ahead of
their opponents. While the critical premise of their work and
the importance of their findings denounce lofty claims such as
"God just is," they often offer no conclusions to their research.
They stop at complaining, at times throwing out the very idea of
faith with the bathwater. The general assumption is, of course,
that nothing in science is indisputably conclusive, meaning that
it needs widespread verification to be accepted, and is open for
further scrutiny and research and even refutation. This important
research procedure is pounced upon by ID proponents, who
exploit the integrity of science as the fundamental mistake
in evolutionary theory. They feel that an "inner revelation"
is the tried-and-tested truth, as they believe themselves to be
the conduit through which their god speaks, forgetting that
innumerable madmen have spoken similar rhetoric throughout
history. What both sides of this argument sometimes miss—
and why, in some ways, they play one edge of the same coin:
fundamentalism—is that there are real, tangible solutions that
can both promote human faith as well as further the findings of
science. This is where yoga comes in.

*N*irvana is samsara. This epoch-lasting maxim was made
by Siddhartha Gautama, the man traditionally known
as Buddha (although there have been many Buddhas
throughout time). While Buddhism is mostly acquainted
with Tibet and China, as well as Japan in its Zen/Ch'an form,
Siddhartha was Indian. There are many fascinating parallels
with Christ—he was born into one particular religious society
and ended up creating another, for one. Great thinkers such
as Thich Nhat Hanh and the Fourteenth Dalai Lama have
written books on the comparison, but for now we'll stick to
the iconoclastic nature of their findings, that something in the
teachings of their culture was not right, and that *freedom was
attainable through means other than what was advertised.* For the
Buddha, it was, as the opening statement says, that liberation is
right here in the everyday.
        In a very basic rendering of yogic theory, time is not

linear, but circular. This does not mean that life doesn't unfold
in a forward motion; they do not count backwards and such. It
simply entails that our actions are repeated over and again in a
sort of repetitive series of cycles. These cycles are called *samsara*,
and it is this that makes humans feel that they are a) in a place
other than where they want to be and b) that there is somewhere
else they need to be, or will arrive at eventually. Some equate this
with things like jobs, relationships and income brackets; others,
as lifetimes, i.e. the idea that heaven awaits the righteous after
death. Regardless of circumstances, the individual is not where
he wants to be, and spends most of his time chasing an idea that
never manifests because there is never an end to craving.

Siddhartha assigned this mysterious human activity
with the term *dukkha*, a word often translated as "suffering," but
which actually has a more specific meaning: suffering created by
the mind. It also translates as "uneasy" and "unsteady," giving it
a much broader meaning that can apply in much deeper mental
and emotional states. Even the concept that "all life is suffering"
is egoistic, as to both Buddhism and yoga the ego is what each
human needs to be rid of in order to be free. Put into another
perspective, the ego is the roadblock to understanding your true
nature, which is non-dual. This idea is a stumbling block for
people whose religions have not taught them interdependence,
weaned on a diet of good and bad, right and wrong, black and
white. People are pinballed between theories constantly, while
to the initiates of Eastern thought, life is a series of tensions that
mutually support each other. To say that something is inherently
evil makes no sense, for the idea of total good could only exist
as long as the prior lurks in its shadow. To the Buddhist, a life
of compassion is the antidote; to the yogi, meditation, which in
many ways is another form of the same.

Let us not rush ahead to the fine points. They will unfold
over these pages as, more importantly, will the idea that this is
not in conflict with many of the teachings we learned in Sunday
school (although the teacher may not have realized it). Let it
suffice for now that the lessons of yoga teach a way to be free
in this lifetime. Ironically it is only by the constant craving for
freedom that are you trapped—if it is a question to be asked

then it is not a state that has been attained. This state of freedom occurs after the expulsion of the ego (*moksha, samadhi*), in which the processes of the exterior world and that of the inner person are seen as the same thing. There is a specific rift—the idea that we are not of this world and therefore feel that we have superior control over it—that causes the predominant amount of suffering. The most we can do is understand the world and act in accordance with it. The blunt attempt to wield superiority derives itself completely from ego, and in the end it is always we, not the world, who take the blow.

(Before the green-minded environmentalist counters that the world is taking huge blows from human hands, let me clarify. The world has dealt with much more than us during its long history, and is still turning, without our input. This book is not claiming that our actions do not do harm—quite the opposite, in fact. As you will see, a healthy relationship with nature is one of the prominent focuses of this book. What I am implying is that humans suffer in the sense that they feel lost and confused. The earth adapts and moves on.)

That our emotional response to existence is not necessarily the "point" of life has long been the bane of humankind, from the most devout to the highest intellectual. We are part of the process, not the process itself. That we've given a name to the process (evolution) or tried to claim a noun as the overbearing seer of the process (God) does not detach us from it. Yet the smugness of some, claiming we are separate from it, and the ignorance of others, believing us to be judged by something outside of it, is not to be applauded. These are both forms of ignorance, and account for much of the fractioning of the human mind and, subsequently, a global-thinking community that is accepting of many shades and ideas. In this light, the space between yoga and atheism is one where individuals can complete themselves by recognizing that there is nothing to be completed, that this moment now *is* the experience of a lifetime. Of course these are only two paths among numerous others that point in this direction. As they are on the tips of many American tongues, they deserve further investigation.

That old saying "If it ain't broke, don't fix it" just won't go away. It's not surprising. People like stability: To know that when they come home from work the house will be there; that the family is healthy and happy; and that their job is secure (even if they can't stand it). Security is a most craved condition. Some may say no, what we crave is God, or some other alternate state of being. The reality is that we want what's happening to keep on happening, even if it's not exactly what we want. The idea that there is no God, or that the one that exists does not go by the name we've given it, doesn't frighten us as much as the fact that change is inevitable, including the change of our own being from life to death. Religion offers something stable and concrete, even if only in theory. We then manufacture our lives around this idea, and set it in stone as the way life is: unbroken, unfixable and under judgment.

The problem is that we *are* broken. There are many things that do not work in our culture. Instead of living up to it, we have been reverting to age-old idealism so it can "save" us. There's an extremely disturbing example of this in the documentary film *Jesus Camp*, which is an insightful gaze into a North Dakota Pentecostal summer camp sponsored by Kids in Ministry International. During one of the scenes a main character, Levi, is being home-schooled by his mother. Levi was "saved" (from what, no one is certain) when he was five years old. He plans on following his father's footsteps by being a megachurch pastor. His mother asks him two questions. The first: Did God create the earth in a few days, as the Bible says. True! The next concerns global warming, which to both mother and child is "obviously" false.

While this book had already been percolating in my head, watching this scene propelled me to pursue it fully. This interaction scared and saddened me, hearing their quibble based on sheer speculation with absolutely no desire to know the truth of the matter. It's one thing to believe that some omnipotent creature built this entire universe, but quite another to teach children that things like global warming do not matter because Jesus is coming to save the righteous, so don't worry about it. It's completely irresponsible, and dangerous to those who are trying to reverse the effects that the Industrial Age has created on our environment. Any heartfelt religion would not push the world we actually inhabit aside for the theory that another awaits. Living a spiritual life, regardless of the adjective or noun you end up using, entails being in communion with the planet. As labor organizer and editor Emma Thompson wrote, "It is the earth, not heaven, which man must rescue if he is truly to be saved."

The other thing that must be saved is related more closely than we would imagine, but for now we'll keep it separate: our bodies. We can imagine how acquiring the attitude that someone or thing lording over us would take responsibility from our backs, and create a mental rift between what we think and how we act and, by extension, how we treat our bodies. Obesity and depression account for billions of dollars in revenue to corporations pumping pills that do nothing to cure our illness, but merely temporarily relieve immediate symptoms. The fact that the three major Western religions and all of their offshoots do *absolutely nothing* in terms of coordinating the body with the soul that supposedly inhabits it is simply astounding. Atheists often state that theirs is a philosophy that promotes community ideas, yet simply stop at that statement. (Their "ideas" rarely go beyond "This must stop!") What we will interest ourselves with in this book are applicable and realistic steps of doing this, nurturing the fact that we can both strengthen our individual bodies as well as our ties to the earth without need of religion. If we are not treating our bodies well, with the foods we put inside of them or the tensions we allow to embrace us, it will be impossible to think clearly about anything much at all.

Whether theorizing over physical or geographic bodies, paradigms are quickly shifting in American consciousness. In exactly what direction those shifts are heading is debatable. Reading McGrath's tome, it appears Christianity is exploding in massive numbers. Rick Warren's *The Purpose Driven Life* has sold more than eleven million copies worldwide, and he claims on his Saddlebrook Church website that over 200,000 church leaders have been trained in the purpose-driven philosophy. In an even bolder claim, on his personal website Warren states,

"Did you know that every day 60,000 new people come to believe in Jesus Christ as their Lord and Savior?" If this number proves true, then 21.9 million people are converted annually. Like much misinformation coming from the Christian camp, there is no factual evidence supporting this. How do you even arrive at such an outlandish number? What statisticians are doing the fieldwork required to account for this many souls? Of course, if you are a Saddlebrook member, hearing Warren spout such unreliable information will immediately boost your ego. This does not change the fact that it's not real.

So while megachurches are sprouting like quackgrass, not all the statistics are in favor of a global Christ. With painstakingly detailed studies, Canadian psychology professors Bruce E. Hunsberger and Bob Altemeyer found that thirty-two percent of Americans attend a weekly religious service, while the amount of citizens claiming themselves to be fundamentalist dropped from thirty-six percent in 1987 to thirty percent in 2004. Like all polls, there are many factors determining who answers what, and none are completely reliable. Inflation and subtraction can occur on both sides. Research depends on how you phrase questions and to whom you put them forth.

Whosever favor these statistics work for, there is little doubt that religion is a hot topic. Warren and others are selling millions of books, which prove that they have powerful marketing machines behind them more than attesting to any sign of "God's grace." These leaders are eloquent and powerful public speakers that know how to rile a crowd and get their congregation screaming "Hallelujah." Yet by reading declarations like the following, again from Warren's personal site, we should be concerned. He proposes a platform of eight reasons why the Church has an advantage over business and government, concluding with: "The Church provides for God's conclusion. Since we believe the Bible is God's Word, we already know the end of history. Jesus said in Matthew 24: 'The good news about God's Kingdom will be preached in all the world to every nation, and then the end will come.' It is inevitable and unavoidable."

Doomsday speeches are too familiar. We've been hearing

them for thousands of years, and today they serve the same driven purpose as a millennia ago: distraction. They remove us from the moment, and make us fearful instead of empowering us to acquire a healthy relationship with our communities and the environment. Scream as loudly as you like, there is no "proof" or "conclusion" of God. Perhaps the actuality of the situation is a little closer to Steven Pinker's assurance that, "Ancestor worship must be an appealing idea to those who are about to become ancestors."

During my years as an international music journalist, I've come across a regular debate amongst musicians and writers: fusion. Some thought the title of my first book, *Global Beat Fusion*, incorrectly summed up the movement, as fusion implies that things are separate, where in reality they are already intact and it was only through meanderings of the human mind that things are torn apart. Hence if an Indian *tabla* player, an African *djembe* player and an American banjo player make an album, what is created is as pure a form of music as any other. I agree that any form of music made, as long as it follows the rules of cadence, rhythm and melody, is a "pure" creation. That they came together from ethnically disparate parts does not mean that the cultural epoxy between them should be avoided, however. Understanding the ethnic and sonic backgrounds of each instrument and performer enhances our knowledge of how the jigsaw was constructed, and does not mean that the sum is any less for the parts, nor does it imply that the parts are more important than the sum. The same holds true for our religions.

The idea of "one world" is pleasant, utopian. The theory underlying it is that we are all part of the same planet, and that while guns, germs and steel may have forged drastically different realities, we all share oxygen, and our bodies all rely on the proper functioning of the nervous, digestive and circulatory systems. To believe in global peace is a nice idea; our history does not support it by any stretch of the imagination. Syncretism is what people, and by extension cultures, do when coming into contact with one another, even if they started off in battle. At times the meetings are driven by fear and greed, which results in genocide, war and plundering. To deny this part of ourselves is to turn away from who, and what, we are as animals. In over 5,600 years of recorded history, over 14,600 wars have been set down on paper. During this period, there have been only twenty-nine years of war *not* recorded. The current pleas about the unification of the planet deny what we've experienced, as well as what we're currently experiencing. The idea that our planet once lived in peace is as much a farce as the notion that after we die we'll go somewhere eternally restful. It's not that either of these may have happened or could be true. The reality is they don't matter in how we handle ourselves today. We have to deal with who we are—as humans, nations and sentient beings—and adjust accordingly. To borrow from Leslie Stephen, "Dreams may be pleasanter for the moment than realities; but happiness must be won by adapting our lives to the realities."

There is the other side of syncretism, however—that which creates new cultures. As we will see, India assigned its gods with multiple roles. One of the most interesting is Natraj, the lord Shiva in his cosmic dancing form. Within the same deity exists his inclination towards asceticism, as well as his tendency to return from deep meditation to sleep with forest nymphs while his wife waits at home. The writers who penned these classic Indian tales knew that humans were multi-faceted, and that different situations called for various responses, which is why yogis are "flexible." This is the same culture that spawned the Rom (popularly known as Gypsies), a traveling group of low-caste nomads who journeyed across continents because they were never allowed to settle anywhere for too long. These wanderers made their way across Persia into Spain, where they helped form that country's identity in the co-creation of flamenco music, while others journeyed upward into Eastern Europe, where Balkan folk music was given flair with Turkish percussion. Today we take these musical forms for granted because they've been around for generations. Yet we have our own cross-cultural referencing going on, modern mythologies being born in cyberspace and on international territories the world over.

Many intellectuals put on a painful grimace when hearing of, as Ken Wilber put it, a "theory of everything." Specialization is one of the markers of our times, which exhibits a drastic divergence from, say, Asian medicinal systems, which treat the body as a complete entity, never discriminating between mental, emotional and physical conditions. While stewing cultural gumbo just to make speculative suggestions is not loaded with integrity, neither is denying the many connections that can be made with research and introspection. A multi-disciplinary approach in any –ology and -osophy is necessary, be it chemistry and biology or anthropology and philosophy. These disciplines too were evolved from older traditions, and all involve processes themselves.

It is the reunion with the physical body that was yoga's inroads into American culture. The voyage has been a mixed bag, filled with those seeking physical fitness and those entrenched in vain pursuits. The quest of the "perfect" physical body helps us understand why it has become so popular so quickly (not to mention that *everything* moves quickly in such a speeded up culture). This is contradictory to many religious traditions, which do not include any physical maintenance whatsoever, and linger in the thoughts of men as a communion with spirits. To speak of the spirit without including the body is to miss the carrier of the supposed soul. If the body is not conditioned and fit, the mind is wont to wander. Fitness comes in many degrees, hence the "sound body, sound mind" ideal. Beyond physicality, yoga is also reactionary to the oppressive conditioning of stagnant religion, which is also the obvious root of the atheism resurgence. "Recovering Catholic" is one term that many use to describe their experience searching for something beyond a conditioned and oppressive style of religion that they were brought up learning.

The gods of yoga are a polytheistic bunch of partly human forces that deal with mental and emotional states of being. There are many images, as well as many sides of the humanistic forms representing these gods. There is a central character, Brahman, who we could loosely associate with our understanding of God, though he is in no way detached from the processes of the world. He does not lord over us; it is safer to say that he comes out of us. This form of figurehead places responsibility on the individual, which is also an underlying theme of atheism. The petty ideology that "If it happens, it's God's will, and if it doesn't, it's God's will also" is seen, in this light, for what it is: a cop-out. Both yoga and atheism place this responsibility back in its rightful place, on our shoulders and in our deeds and words. In these disciplines we assume responsibility for our actions and their outcome. Whether we think that responsibility has a Sisyphean density or an angelic weightlessness is a decision each one of us has to conclude on our own. And, as we will see, our perception of the experience of life, and not the hands-free teetering of disbelief, is what matters most.

CHAPTER 2

REDEMPTION SONG

Of all the places to seek underlying themes in yoga and atheism, Jamaica would seem an odd choice. Yet if we are to get to the essence of processes, aside from whichever forms of faith they involve, there is no better place. The following slice of history has been poorly transmitted, which says as much about the media we utilize to understand identity as well as the information allowed to circulate inside that media. Processes are not bound by this or that faith, and serve as the real cohesion between traditions, not the particular form they may result in. By remaining bound by time, we overlook the process. With the way our media informs us today, it is not surprising that many people assume globalization is a recent trend and all past cultures were isolated and separate. The only way to seriously investigate modernity is to peer back at our lineages—and not only those of immediate ancestors who gave us pigmentation color, name and language. So if we want to wrap our heads around topics like yoga and atheism in America today, it helps us to see how less circulated cases of historical information can educate us. In the island of sunshine and cannabis gold we entertain our first process to see how something can underlie what appears, on the surface, unique. This story commences on May 10, 1845.

From the long distance of a clear Atlantic Ocean, the *Blundell Hunter* lands on the shore of Old Harbour, Jamaica. The ship had docked two days prior in Morant Bay, proceeding to another part of the island to transport workers—indentured servants, by name—to the Clarendon Plantation. It was loaded with a rather lively cargo, as would be proven when 261 natives of India set foot on island soil for the first time. Never again would Jamaica be the same.

An interesting article in the *Falmouth Post* stated that these Indians were immediately embraced by local Africans, themselves ancestors of men and women transported across the same ocean during slave trades. Their relationship with the colonizing British, like the Africans, would not be sympathetic or friendly. No matter. What interests us is the intermingling of these two "foreigners." As history tells it, they became fast friends.

Employed on a 54-hour workweek, the newcomers were quickly belabored with grueling field duties for meager pay. Some were brought over with promises of dynamic employment on tea farms like those in Calcutta, now disappointed to find themselves in the thick of coffee and sugar harvesting. Every true tea drinker knows the illusion of coffee as a stimulant, and while there would certainly have been converts, tea is an integral part of Indian life. One cannot, however, imagine there ever being an honest reason for loading ignorant participants on a ship to sail 10,000 miles to work under a blazing sun, six days weekly. Occupiers spin exceedingly long tales to get what they want. Alas, this is the story of post-slavery plantation Jamaica, and how almost-free labor helped build plantations after slaves became citizens.

Thing is, farm owners needed to find workers willing to work for cheap. In 1834, slavery ended, followed by a six-year apprenticeship where former slaves would basically be indentured servants. As time ran up, many natives and Africans stayed on the farm; they had nowhere else to go, and it's always challenging to inspire people to change their habits, even if they know change is the best thing for them. Yet groups of freed slaves began forming what would eventually become Nyabinghi communities, living from the soil and sun the way ancestors had, reconnecting with the mythology of land and not the forced religion of their keepers. With this fresh wave of self-assurance and responsibility occurring, new employees were needed. British-controlled India was a prime target.

It should not surprise us that the Indians and Africans became friends. After all, they were in one way or another looked down upon by big business and government officials. They were not fully "people" in the political sense of the word, so their camaraderie was a necessary cohesion on both social and spiritual platforms. In *Home Away From Home*, a brilliant look at the long and complex history of Indians in Jamaica, Laxmi and Ajai Mansingh remind us that both of these cultures were the product of "Natural Theologies," a fact that would go on to help define the Great Revival Movement on the island in the 1860s, and seventy years later, the Rastafari movement. Rastas were in many ways cross-cultural yogis, though that history is rarely told.

Today Rastas are known globally in large part due to a dreadlocked chain-pot-smoking vocalist named Bob Marley. Few images have made an impact as broad and important to liberation movements across the world as the warrior Nesta, and his music continues to be shared, explored, listened to and remixed. His entire catalog is, in a sense, sacred. There is nothing in life that is not discussed and treated in and by his music. Rural workers in deep farming countries the world over may own but one cassette tape, and it is usually by this buffalo soldier. Yet few people realize the influence India had on the movement behind the man.

Take, for instance, one of the most important figures in Rasta symbolism: Samson. Born to the sterile wife of Manoah as prophesied by an angel, he was told not to shave or cut the child's hair. The young warrior ended up killing numerous Philistines (as well as a lion, another important symbol in later Rasta theology) before being tricked by his second wife and being forced to have his matted hair sheared. His unbounded strength rested in these locks, and the act of shaving it annulled his invincibility. The Philistines then gouged out his eyes. He was eventually murdered, although while imprisoned his dreadlocked hair had returned. The symbolism meant that this great warrior, in chains and blind, was ultimately freed—his psychology had changed, and he was not captive to the forces that oppressed him. This is but one example of how external conditions might be anything but ideal, yet the state of freedom we so desperately crave is internally realized. If a man is blinded and sentenced to death and can still be liberated by reorienting his thought processes, how much easier could it be for those of us not in captivity, save by the shackles of our own minds? The importance of this mythology is in this idea, not a historical, actual person named Samson. He has lived on and come to influence generations by his bravery and courage—not because he may or may not have actually lived.

The Rastas used this figure in defiance to authority, growing their hair in what the elders called *zagavi*. We need to look no further than Hindu *saddhus* to find the correlation. These mendicants, inspired by the god Shiva, had been growing their hair in dreads for thousands of years in a style called *jatawi*. Shiva, the great paradoxical god of yoga that embodies every facet of existence in his cosmic dance (Tandava), twisted his hair as homage to snakes; indeed, Hindu artists often wrap snakes, as well as a crescent moon, into his matted hair. The snake, as we will see later, is an important symbol in Hindu mythology, representing the sacred energy of both the individual and cosmos. The kundalini energy that resides at the base of the spine is said to unfurl as a snake does. Another important aspect is its ability to shed skin. That is: regeneration.

Rebellious as they were, early Rastas did not often grow dreadlocks. The symbol of their defiance was in unkempt, wooly beards, another obvious tribute to Samson. As the mythologies entwined, and their confidence as a separate community outside of the controlling Brits grew, they began to wear their hair in long locks around the time Nesta released early hits like "Judge Not." As is the case with most movements, it took the boldness of a few groundbreakers to introduce style into their community. Samson, in prison and yet free, is a meditation on the vices of karma and the ability to stay focused within extreme oppression. In this manner his tale echoed the Buddha's ability to sit underneath the bhodi tree in calm meditation while Mara threw innumerable vices his way. Today dreadlocks are grown as a headnod to this "liberation against downpressors," but the emphasis on the Indian roots are rarely discussed.

This is not shocking. History is often at the hands of writers with agendas. If that agenda suits one particular angle over another for a varied number of reasons, details will remain conveniently omitted. The African and biblical importance is considered the fundamental root of the Rastsfari while the Indian heritage is forgotten (or never discussed). There are numerous other symbols that became so integrated into Rasta consciousness that they were attributed to the exclusive territory of Africa instead of the fusion of forms that they actually are. Another is *thandai*, a "cool drink" that Indians made from *bhang*, or *ganja*. Indians have long had a strong affinity toward sweets, and this blend of sugar, milk and marijuana was a common beverage choice. This was followed by another saddhu trait: smoking the sacred chalice. Outside of dreadlocks and music, reggae musicians are notoriously beloved for this openly admitted passion, as well as the philosophical and spiritual discourses that the mind derives from the green plant. Its 5,000-year history in the Indus Valley as a stimulant and medicine long predates the usage of it in Jamaica, making it an important introduction to what would become an autonomous society.

Besides this luxurious, albeit (now) illegal, drink, Indian cuisine heavily influenced ital cooking. The Ayurvedic concept of balance in food preparation and selection proved important to the strict dietary guidelines of the Nyabinghi (and later Rastas), which were a varied plan. For the most part it excluded chemicals, additives and preservatives, and often some (more rarely, all) forms of meat. Again the arrow points toward biblical diet in popular texts, but in reality a 2,000-year-old book with brief, rather general passages about nutrition could not have inspired the exquisite and well-spiced dishes that Indians helped create. To state that an entire nutrition lifestyle could be developed solely from a book is like believing that a physical yoga practice can be learned from flipping through a postural manual with a few photos. There needs to be hands-on education, especially if it is going to have broad appeal. One block from my studio in Jersey City sit both Guyanese and Indian restaurants, and their curry and rotis are almost indistinguishable. The owners of each restaurant may have arrived in America from different locales, yet their common thread can be tasted.

Before we delve into the psychology of why a resistance to citing Indian origins in much of Rasta culture exists, we need to look at the most critical influence they had on island life. While some African traditions may have been passed down over the four centuries since their arrival in the Caribbean, chances are this natural theology was destroyed by Christian missionaries quick to spread gospels and build churches. The easiest way to indoctrinate an individual, and by extension their culture, is to capture their metaphysical understanding of the universe. This can be done through physical intimidation and forced education, though the most effective means is through language. Africans went from having a rich philosophy that taught regeneration of existence, as well as a deep respect for all aspects of nature, into a specific form of religion that explicitly states that no matter what you do in this life, it is only preparatory for what lies after. That distinction is huge.

What the Indians brought with them, and what changed the psychology of natives, was the concept of karma. Granted, this is often translated as "what goes around comes around." This translation paints a general picture, but there's more to the story. The word comes from the Sanskrit *karman*, and means simply "action." As we will come to find out, this corresponds strongly to basic yoga philosophy. For now, let's treat it as: the actions in which you partake affect what happens to you at all moments. The distance between cause and effect may appear to occur over stretches of time, but a better way to describe it is to consider that your actions leave imprints on the present moment that essentially create who you are. When these imprints become a pattern—or better yet a habit—the individual becomes caught in a consistent cycle where cause and effect are not separate; the seed and the flower are the same. There is an elaborate scheme of past and future lives that go along with this philosophy that's not particularly relevant at this moment. What is essential, however, is that they sowed an entire internal landscape, drawn from the natural theology of agricultural cycles, to develop this idea, rather than simply stating, "Be good, follow these commandments, or else!"

"Or else what?"

"Don't question God's will!!!"

Meaning: We don't know. By watching their surroundings, the dwellers of pre-Common Era India devised a most reliable and spectacularly vivid understanding of the after- and before-life that was centered on *the life that happens now.* They had taken the physical and often brutal rituals of Vedic and Aryan culture and turned the mirror back onto their own lives to develop a system of introspection matched by few. What the Indian workers brought with them, and what empowered Afro-Jamaicans to form their own communities, was the notion that liberation was available right here, in this lifetime. To a culture bred into 400 years of mental and physical slavery, this was the adrenaline they craved. As time passed and Rastas appeared, they become bolder and more confident. To this day, the Rastafari exist on the fringes of "accepted" Jamaican society, one still listening to a national radio fueled by American R&B and Country music, and one that still clings to strains of British identity through psychological programming much the same way traces of Victorianism remain in America. As with so many movements of this nature, it is the *symbol* of the Rasta that has worldwide appeal, even if the people that are Rastas can be shelved as outcasts. Displaced at home, that symbol has found recognition across borders and oceans, in the same manner that Buddhist philosophy became integrated in Siddhartha's native India while taking root as its own form across a few mountain ranges in China and Japan.

This unintended clashing is what forms new cultures, where undirected peoples populate new regions and adapt to the circumstances in the best manner possible. As the saying goes, he who controls history controls the future. We began this tale in Jamaica for an important reason, but could have just as easily started in the Balkans, in Persia, in Ireland or America, because what interests us is the *process* by which things come together to form new things. What is of equal interest is the shadow side of this story. Why is Africa considered the saving grace and homeland of Rastas, while so little literature on the Indian influence exists? To gain insight, let's flip the story and ask why the Spanish and indigenous dwellers of Mexico give so little credence to their own African influence, one that is tremendous in their cultural derivation and yet rarely acknowledged.

There are such things as stupid questions. For a long time, I was taught to believe the opposite. Throughout my school years I heard it over and again: There is no such thing as a stupid question. Hushed snickers from unruly students became scoldings from angry science and history teachers trying to create some sort of pupil equilibrium by entertaining a lack of common sense. One of my grade school teachers would devote large chunks of time to such nonsense from students that obviously hadn't read the assignment, while one religion professor at college reiterated his point again and again until the droning put the rest of us near to sleep. They were vehement in their derision when students suggested that the putting forth of an honest, inquisitive wondering was "stupid." And I bit the bullet for all my years, until meeting Ivan Van Sertima.

A stocky Guyanese native who graduated from and went on to teach at Rutgers University, Van Sertima was the boldest, strongest professor I had the experience of learning from during all my years of study. He stood barrel-chested and lion-like at the front of seventy-some students in African-American Literature, and would give the unfortunate student who ventured to ask self-evident knowledge hellfire from the pulpit. He would not so calmly point out that the question was either a matter of ignorance or laziness, and suffer forty verbal lashes upon the unfortunate soul who was, as he would put it, wasting his time, wasting the classes' time and wasting his or her own time. Given the strength of his first and only book, *They Came Before Columbus: The African Presence in Ancient America*, this sort of stubborn but honest disciplinarianism is not surprising.

In the thirty-two years since its publication this masterpiece has never been embraced by the public in a manner befitting its revolutionary content. It stands in similar light to Howard Zinn's extraordinary *A People's History of the United States*, a scathing and enlightening view of an untold past. History is supposedly taught as objective. But as with any human topic, it depends on the lean of the teller. Just as the enumerators of Jamaican folklore have positioned a predominantly African recounting, so have Mexican historians focused on the invasion and coronation of Hernán Cortés as the dividing line in their cultural tale.

When Cortés arrived in Mexico's interior in 1519, he was perceived as the return of the feathered plumed serpent, Quetzalcoatl, and revered as a deity. His small band of soldiers ended up defeating the much larger, though ill-equipped, Mexican army, and thus began the fall of the Aztec empire. Quetzalcoatl was an older solar deity from roughly the late tenth century (though his prototypes predate this by centuries) and had, in the Mexican mind, the ability to assume different forms and shapes. The original deity was the son of a high priest named Mixcoatl, and after his death was thought to return—much like the Jesus mythology—after a series of cycles, each lasting fifty-two years. When Cortés arrived from the east—the direction of the sun—he was determined to represent the coming of a new era, ten cycles after the disappearance of the original plumed serpent king. His timing was in perfect accordance with the cyclical calendar, one that the plumed god was said to devise himself. Cortés would become infamous to the indigenous population: Due to his crew's advantage of horses used in battle, and later smallpox, Mexican population dropped from twenty million to one-and-a-half million over the course of one century.

This is how Mexico is remembered in the popular annals of North American education: through the naïveté of superstitious leaders and soldiers, their lack of technologies and medicine, and their submission to Spanish conquerors. As indigenous faiths were dethroned by missionaries and governments, and educational scriptures were rewritten to suit Spanish sailors, it is forgotten that over 200 years (four cycles prior, to be exact) before Cortés' arrival another variation of Quetzalcoatl appeared from the east: the Malian ruler Abubakari the Second, adorned in a white robe and dazzling jewels. His Mandingo traders ended up melding into the atmosphere, rather than dethroning it, slightly surprising given Abubakari's near-madness that caused him to depart from Africa in hopes of overtaking the world. Then again, long periods at sea, surrounded by the transformative element of water, have been known to change a man. It is due to this more peaceful union of cultures that the variations are not so disjointed, and to the lack of media power to broadcast these claims that the Spanish invaders eventually wiped clean the traces of an African presence in Mexico. It would only make sense, considering that by this time they were enslaving the residents of that continent to work the same lands they had already visited.

Quetzalcoatl will show up again in this book as well as, if you're a follower of the calendric system, in actual history. There is an intriguing correlation between his role as the serpent god and the yogic raising of kundalini that ties into these early African navigations. For now let us point out two relevant misperceptions that show the process of historical writing. Quetzalcoatl was a solar deity, thus his association with whiteness, and the eventual penning of his relationship to Cortés—although how "white" indigenous Spaniards are, given their Mediterranean textures and the sun and blood they share with the African countries of Morocco, Algeria and Libya, remains open to question. When Abubakari arrived he was garbed in white robes, yet in later translation the deity was supposed to be white in skin tone. In fact, older citations of the god have him black-skinned and black-bearded, which has brought into question the actual origin of Quetzalcoatl. Could an African or Arab man have been the prototype that was eventually written out of history by European conquerors?

There are many parallels between the original

Mexican rituals and those that honored Dasiri in the medieval Mandingo tribe. Both are protector deities who are honored at the beginning of their year; both pay accolades to the god through similar self-flagellation techniques and festival dances; both are the governors of their society's theory of time, and both make like use of numerology; both are honored through similar rites using trees; similar talismans and animal motifs are used to invoke these deities. Even phonetically some of the same descriptive phrases are employed. That there were not pre-European African influences on the mythology of Mexico would seem the true stretch of the imagination. The story as we know it today has been bleached by writers of a similar mindset who transformed the wooly-bearded and -haired Jesus into a wavy-textured white man—from the Middle East.

Another aspect of this puzzle relates to those who controlled historical narration. According to the educations most American children receive, Spaniards and Europeans were forerunners in nautical technology. This information is presented despite the fact that Phoenician sailors were circling Africa in 600 BCE, and Carthaginian explorers went further a century later. A certain leveraging of European childishness, and plenty of hubris, plays into such declarations of power and fortune. If these accounts, which are tattooed into our minds as reality, explain that Europeans developed these ships, and made the largest impact in the formation of Western culture—and you're told this again and again, year after year, generation upon century—this would seem obvious knowledge, so much so that it would be taken for granted. Regardless of what history tells us, knowledge is something that we quickly claim by birthright, which may account for why the indigenous dwellers of Mexico, as well as the dominant African culture in Jamaica, simply overlooked foreign influences upon their philosophies and culture. Having been oppressed by outside forces for so long, formulating any identity would be a challenge to later political and spiritual leaders, so naturally these individuals will look at the closest influence, and largest population, to appeal to. Framing history is not solely the occupation of oppressors. What's more, like the formation of any modern religion, these

scribes were piecing together their cultural remnants in reaction
to the circumstances.

Today the African influence on Mexico remains in the
shadows, although it can be seen in the curious dynamics of
their folk art—the broad noses and high foreheads of their
totems that appear so similar to those of their early Mandingo
counterparts, for one. Early altars to the plumed serpent
made use of a circle motif, placed in exact accordance to what
Egyptians were doing during the same time period. The *corrido*
tradition of Mexican music, similar in intent and purpose as the
griot lineage of Africa—men and (occasionally) women who
served as living newspapers of their culture through songs about
social, political and spiritual justices and untruths—is another
powerful "coincidence" that has lasted through the ages. It
seems curious that while Peru, Cuba, Brazil and Venezuela are
more apt to accept and integrate their African heritages, the
one country bound to the USA by land would be so hesitant.
Yet given this geographical proximity and the explorers who
exploited their country, perhaps it's not surprising at all.

It's easy to look into mass-produced books and believe
them to be truthful. This isn't an honest academic undertaking,
however; it is a particular slant by a group with vested interest.
Today many millions of people feel the same way about the most
widely published book in the world, the Bible—that it holds
incontrovertible facts, end of story. Well, the story *is* ending,
though it appears the symbols that fundamentalists claim as
historical fact are coming to fruit upon a much different tree.
How does that old joke go? If you want to make God laugh, tell
him your plans. Unfortunately, our God hasn't laughed since
pulling Abraham's tail when his beloved nearly murdered his
son. With any luck, by the end of our present journey, we will
indeed find some humor in all of this, for it is sorely needed.

In order for history to help transform our personal and
social lives, we must learn from it. If the Industrial Age
has taught us one thing, it's that too much industry is not a
good thing—a reality we are cleaning up in the form of global

warming, overtaxed soil and water shortages. When power and resources become centralized, then the further you move from the center, the further from equanimity you end up. An economic disparity of significant proportions develops, and the privilege of those with means means that the underprivileged suffer. This happens not only with money and water, but with knowledge as well. As we are in the midst of the Information Age, we repeat patterns: too much is overload. We carry the burden on our backs—literally. An estimated sixty-five percent of Americans suffer some form of stress or anxiety. We are producing intellectual geniuses who are emotional idiots, men who can configure stupendous mathematical equations yet cannot look another man in the eye when speaking to him, and women who take advantage of the wonderful technologies of birthing to ensure they can take part in life's most precious gift—evolution—and then send their children off to boarding schools and hire nannies because they are too distracted with a career to care for their own. This, apparently, is progress.

The term "world history" can be applied to the last century, at best. Before that time we lived through thousands of years of regional movement that resulted in a fusion of forms involving a select number of participants. This is not to say that that list is short. If we look at the confluence of cultures that traveled along and affected the Silk Road, or the Balkan trail, we find an innumerable amount of peoples slowly forming the identity of a broad range of land over time. Libraries can be filled with the impact that Africans, pre- and post-slavery, had on Latin America and the Caribbean, while the influence of Rom culture extending from India (and, as some believe, originating in West Africa), through all of Europe and the Middle East, is tremendous. We have barely skimmed the surface of two important, though not widely publicized, meeting grounds. There are many more cultural fusions happening all the time, both written and silent. These were introduced in this text to show how what we are taught and how cultures actually form can be different stories altogether, as well as reminding us that today's global village has been in the process of for some time.

We now sit at a crossroads where the entire history

of the world is available to anyone, anywhere, at any time (depending, of course, on economic privileges), so that we perceive what information we accept as real and what we discard has numerous consequences in who we become as a planet. We can travel and transverse the surface of all lands for an (relatively) inexpensive price, meaning that globetrotting is at least available to a large number of people, especially in higher-income countries like America. The fact remains that at the time of this writing just thirty percent of Americans own a passport, and chances are that these other seventy percent make up a large portion of those making fundamentalist claims about the nature of existence. It's easy to declare that your town comprises the totality of reality when you never leave it.

This cultural isolation is what denies any actual integration of world cultures into a sustainable and global community. The homogenizing of a few particular ideas then spreads as broadly as possible through powerful media machines, being touted as revelations while they are actually the result of very narrow thinking. If your local priest claims that Jesus is the Son of God and it works in Alabama, well, certainly it must be the same in Iraq! Would the majority of Americans support overseas wars if they had ever visited those places, had personal relationships with its citizens, experienced firsthand its art, cuisine, music and temperament? Chances are they would not. The amount of information we are privy to and the even larger amount we are not weighs heavily in the balance of perceptions. What we must do is discern between what is helping foster a global culture and what is stunting its growth.

This is not to say that we shouldn't be doing outreach, just as we should not reject those reaching out to us. We just need to separate beliefs from behavior. There is nothing wrong with supporting causes like water shortages in Africa, when you are sure the organization you financially and philosophically endorse is actually putting that money into the cause. This is fundamentally different than declaring that other countries need to submit to a Christian God or a democratic government. A proper reading of history shows how both these initiatives result in one of two paths: the exported philosophies are either transformed and infused into the existing culture (take Mexican Catholicism or American yoga, for example), or they are flat-out rejected, and wars ensue.

The critical difference between these different forms of globalization is that we can understand the need for clean drinking water on a personal, instinctual level. We know its necessity for we can physically understand what life would be like without it—or, rather, how life would *not be* without it. Religious beliefs, however, are abstract. We can think that life without God would be pointless, but this is not the case. Water is an absolute necessity, and there exists a certain healthy altruism in helping others attain it. The same cannot be said about God, although the devout will argue this point. In fact, it is this *exact* notion that atheists use as the main catalyst in their debate: There is no inherent need for God to exist for us to be altruistic individuals, to form societies and function as friendly, helpful citizens.

Before we can take sides on such an argument (if a side even needs to be taken), we must look into our collective history once more. The faithful cringe at the idea of there not being a god in the same manner that those who are sure one does not exist repel the possibility of him actually existing. Both are forms of fundamentalism; both submit to the postulation that their side is the one to be on. And both, to their chagrin, are forms of belief. What we want to discuss is the *experience* of life, and to do so we travel backwards once more. In this journey we will touch upon the shadow of light, for to deny it power is to grant it more than you would imagine possible. By bringing darkness into the light, it no longer looks so frightening, and may just help us understand who we are today a bit more.

CHAPTER 3

THE UNWISDOM OF HINDSIGHT

"The early history of the solar system predates life, although if it had happened one jot differently, there would have been no living cells. But this not our story," writes paleontologist Richard Fortey. Still, we concoct tales of creation with no understanding of what our story actually is. We're not necessarily discussing the "big picture" here: cosmic wars, divine ordeals and the like. What should interest us most are everyday events that form and shape our lives; that define our personal place in life. This requires a macrocosmic view of the microcosm, not to mention a re-reading of past tales in immediate relationship to what we are doing now. Then we can construct a better understanding of our total being. Mythology is one thing—historicity, quite another. A person's creative storytelling can be endearing as well as dangerous, depending on how seriously we are invested in the process. It is impossible to "know" a story that we did not author, and the question of whether or not it even *needs* an author is up for grabs. The assumption that it does is rooted in belief, not evidence. As Fortey also remarked, "The Universe literally made itself, nearly 13 billion years ago."

This idea is troublesome to those that feel the universe

needed to have been *made,* as in the way we tinker with toys and technologies. Religionists use the image of a watchmaker to invoke the necessity of a creator, and go to great lengths to publicize their case. The May 2007 opening of the Creation Museum in Petersburg, Kentucky, is one prime example. Some $27 million were spent on this 60,000-square-foot complex that promises to allow you to "experience history in a completely unprecedented way." Unprecedented indeed: The underlying premise is that the earth was literally made (poof!) by the hands of God roughly 6,000 years ago, and posits dinosaurs next to humans, animals that in the end just couldn't hang due to God's smiting. Complete with photographic services for children sitting atop a triceratops, this laughable example is quite sad when you realize that this is the sort of education parents offer (or demand of) their children as an "alternative" to that nasty, blasphemous creed, science.

The current debate surrounding science and creationism has set human intelligence back a few centuries. This is not to claim that science has all the right answers, or provides theological certainties. The fact remains that most scientists have not been attempting to explain God or usurp religion at all. Sure, the occasional misfit tries to "prove" that there is no God, or from the other camp, that there is. Overall, science is a rigorous discipline that helps us understand the technical and physical workings of our world, and universe—and to some, how to lead life beneficially on this planet. Fundamentalists are the ones picking fights that should never have been started. Scientists rarely step onto their turf, or out of their own boundaries, given the rigorous checks and balances in their discipline. A completely different story is told in the religious community when leaders think they are in communion with the ultimate initiator of every system. As will be noticed in the case of the Crusades, humans just need to fight about something. Now quasi-religionist factions are trying to strong-arm society into accepting backwards claims about the nature of existence without amassing even an iota of reality. Reading through the Creation Museum's website (as well as other like-minded sites) is a lesson in the lengths humans will go to in an effort to distance themselves from the actual connotation of the word religion, union. That people buy into such nonsense—that humans and dinosaurs played house together until God grew tired of the latter—is more of a crash course in marketing and advertising than anything recognizable as theology.

What is the nature of belief? How has the process of believing come to the forefront of existence for so many of us, and to such a point that it rules over everything? Why can we be scrutinizing and analytical when it comes to the words of doctors, lawyers and teachers, but not apply the same assessment to megachurch priests and celebrity self-help authors? What is it that causes us to believe one story more than another, even killing or destroying believers of other stories, as if that murder offers a hedonistic rapture of faith? These ideas will be spread across a few chapters, but let us turn back the pages of the history of belief to begin. Like the Hindu Rastas of Jamaica, we are choosing a less-publicized path. Regardless, the land of Mesopotamia is an important jigsaw in the puzzle of religious history. The origins of the God we worship today, as well as a template for the merry cast of outcasts surrounding and including Jesus Christ, can be found in the pages of this distant land. Understanding how the very idea of gods came to be shall prove most important in our journey, especially when we take a look at the mythological undertones in Christian rituals and holidays in Chapter 7.

In the distance a rumble disturbs the sunlit sky. An imposing blend of gray and black clouds swirls in the distance, destroying the peaceful ocean of atmosphere in a wrathful dance. Treetops and thatched roofs sway to this ungodly rhythm, one gaining in speed and tempo and severity. You've seen this before. As your fellow villagers pack their wares and head for cover, you pray that these rains do not flood the area again, nor destroy your simple home. There are messages in the sky; you listen closely before retiring to a single flame in the middle of a muddy enclave, and to prayers, which roll from your vocal chords sincerely and heartfelt. The rain consumes your land, and the life that you know—crops, totems, tools and sanctuary—is shrouded by chaos. The invocations you've known by heart since language first entered your life become louder, direly and necessarily climaxing as the drums of sky roll.

Or perhaps this one: A few village elders have grown accustomed to fineries, like gold and jewels and foreign weapons, as well as the fear in the eyes of subjects when taxmen make their rounds. To meet these high demands, you are obligated to maintain and farm your land and its holdings. Once, you all lived on the same plateau, your family next to these elders; you shared meals, jokes and friendship. As time progresses they built larger homes on higher beds of earth, overseeing the daily functions of the tribe from afar. Your contact with them becomes less frequent, even though their presence is felt more. Some friends ask in quiet if you'd like to retire to another land. Sickened by the growing threat of self-fulfilled leaders, you contemplate the journey, and finally concede. You abandon a life of safety under duress and enter the desert. Your gods are born. Not those of elders demanding taxes and oblations, mind you. These newborn gods are vengeful and just, and provide comfort in the middle of the quiet storm of sand and starvation.

Instead of gods, perhaps: God. The concept was developed in a similar environment, one of religious and social exile. Then again, the deity of the desert exodus represents only one take on the Big Guy. There were many more predating the Abrahamic deity, including Brahma, the overseer of polytheistic pre-Vedic natives of India. Even in the midst of all those minor gods shuffling through legendary tales, there was one in the backdrop, an unchecked supervisor that helped move things along without ever knowing exactly where they were moving. Control, the state we identify with godheads, isn't the right word. The process is organic and spontaneous. Yet with our modern gods—one of the West's great contributions to theology—control is a word we've become quite accustomed to.

Citizens of past eras partook in natural theologies, though in the moment of their founding it was probably stated simply as: natural. They maintained a relationship with the world around them; every aspect of the land was part of their overall mythology. Societies were dependent upon nearby resources and the strength of men to build shelter and partake in the hunt, as well as the strength of females to, quite literally, do everything else. Trade was slow, yet prosperous—though not to the degree that we know today. Long excursions of exploration rarely occurred, as men did not travel more than a few miles in distance; leaving the village was not necessary, at least not in agricultural communities. Hunting and gathering tribes lived differently, though they never journeyed far. They needed to save their personal economy of strength and substance, so that their well-thought wanderings amounted to distances close enough to capture game. Despite the usual advertisements in anthropology and history texts, men were not nearly as successful as woman in supplying food. The hunt provided big payoffs in protein, but the general sustenance was supplied by the "less glamorous" role of foraging and picking near the village. The journey of the hunt was always circular, as animals—like all of nature—move cyclically. As agricultural techniques became more advanced, and animal domestication more viable and less stressful, people settled into larger urban communities. Agriculture, while not of the modern farms and rows of crops we know today, was just as important to these tribes, and extends back hundreds of thousands of years—the 10,000 BCE date is a romanticized notion of plant involvement in human life. Human life has always been governed by the environment and available resources, until quite modern times, that is. Our ancestors adjusted to what was around them. In the midst of these dances their gods were constantly remixed.

To the "primitive" mind, there is no difference between the land that you live on, the weather patterns that affect that land, and all the animals and plants that grow from that land. Life as it is known is the telling of one story, each part an integral aspect of the whole, *including* the people involved. Devotion was born through the understanding of this. Some, like the *bhakti* yogis of India, developed intricate forms of worship that affected every part of life (including past and future lives),

and others, like the Aztecs, went so far as to sacrifice members
of their own race (not to mention captured men and women
during wars) to appease divine forces. There is little surprise
that ancient belief systems were integrative and comprehensive,
and included *all* forces in their philosophy. Today such systems
are called holistic and are sometimes considered to be of an
"alternative" mindset. To our ancestors this style of thought *was*
religion.

In the preface to his 2006 book, *The God Delusion*,
Richard Dawkins recalls a story pertaining to his wife. She had
loathed school during teenage years, but did not disclose this
fact to her parents until those days were well behind her. Her
mother asked why she never told them that *during* school, and
she replied, "I didn't know I could." This sentiment rings true
for many, especially when it comes to belief in God, which is
Dawkins' point. Because we are told from birth that God exists,
and told and told and told, we no longer question whether or
not it is true. In this way our metaphysical certainty is never
seen for what it really is, which is an assumption. Dawkins
often refers to the idea that in many religious philosophies,
ignorance is a heralded and rewarded quality. We are taught
not to seek an answer to the question of a divine figurehead. *It
just is.* His response: dispel the ignorance, or, as Daniel Dennett
put it, break the spell. Yoga teaches the same thing.

The means to arrival are quite different, however. What
ties them together is symbolism. In his short but important work,
Language and Myth, philosophy professor Ernst Cassirer reminds
us that mythology *is* language. Words are symbols to describe
physical and emotional phenomena, yet they cannot grasp the
essence of what those things actually are. The name of something
points the way without being the thing itself. Take for instance
the very idea of God, which is an attempt to justify the mystery
and wonder of existence with some form of terminology. The
definition of a godhead is, by default, undefined—it is described
as something that cannot be described. The term itself is inexact;
mythologies *know* that they are maps of reality, while religions
claim to be reality. As atheists argue, this stubborn term—
God—has killed innumerable people throughout time, which

is true of God itself ... if we define God as that which governs the life and death of the universe. In a rather witty aphorism on the topic, renowned unbeliever Bertrand Russell writes, "A man who commits a murder is considered to be a bad man. An Omnipotent Deity, if there be one, murders everybody."

This is a contradiction that few religionists are willing to face, even if our ancestors would concede this point. If the divine was not separate from all of the events of this world, then there could be no distance between the good and evil workings of the supposed watchmaker. The watch *and* its maker are both part of the same process. The distance between creator and created would not have manifested in the same way if we had not separated ourselves from all aspects of our gods, or God, today. Acclaimed archaeologist/philosopher team Henri and H.A. Frankfort write, "Early man does not abstract a concept of time from the experience of time." During the development and growth of our religious roots, history as we know it did not exist. Without a system to embalm language in papyrus, page or clay, oral folklore was the chosen medium for hundreds of thousands of years before the crafty Sumerians started counting sheep and writing it down. The world was a much "smaller" place, and even though this Sumerian civilization is known to have invented trinkets like sundials and decimal points, their timing was more annual than eternal, and much different than our current knowledge of billions of years of history. To better grasp this idea, let us consider a trinity of gods lurking on the planet long before the three of the Bible were remixed from this very template. Of all ironies, they come from the land of Iraq.

Well, partly from Iraq, as the story of land division goes. Mesopotamia, the lower region of which was Sumer, referred to segments of modern-day Iraq, as well as Iran, Turkey and Syria, comprising a large percentage of the most important region on the planet in terms of technological advances in agriculture, mathematics, animal domestication, astronomy and language: the Fertile Crescent, an area that covered the Levant, Ancient Mesopotamia and Ancient Egypt. Societies grew from regionalized and small bands of predominantly self-sufficient households into the precursors of modern cities, as thousands, then tens of thousands, of people became dependent on the communication and skills of a larger population. What was lost in personal relationships gained in the number of relationships each individual and household could obtain in a lifetime, something that continues to be the case in today's wireless world. With this new dependence on larger groups working for a common goal, such as harvesting factory-sized fields for food supply or reigning in hundreds of cattle, the collective understanding of the human mission and placement in this world shifted, as did the gods supposedly governing the process.

The principal deity of Mesopotamia was Anu, god of the sky, father of the gods and ultimate judge. His legacy was handed down from the Sumerians to the Assyrians and Babylonians. Not only was Anu ruler of the heavens, his name was the everyday word for "sky." By simply referring to the space between the ground and heavens, a god was invoked. Given that this land was not predominantly mountainous or covered with forest, residents felt very open and, at times, insecure in their surroundings. Besides annual flooding, which would inspire the world's oldest piece of literature, the *Epic of Gilgamesh*, citizens were totally dependent on the whims of nature. This dependence resulted in intricate sacrifices and rituals necessary to appease her forces. Over the course of centuries, Anu played many different roles, but was generally relegated to sky duties. For our purposes we will discuss his role in the Sumerian trilogy, alongside Enlil and Enki. Enlil, god of the storm, was Anu's son. (He has also been called the lord of the wind, and of the open field.) The third in this triad, Enki, was god of water, and was also tagged as lord of the earth. It's interesting that he served both roles. When we understand the symbolism in this, the picture becomes clear: He was the principal teacher and life-giver of the farming community, which used the alchemy of water and earth to sustain life.

The chain of command in importance was Anu-Enlil-Enki. There was a hierarchy, though it was not without a web of interdependence. Rarely in past cultures was one god so important that others paled in comparison. Anu was the highest law and ruled over the heavens; Enlil, god of wind and storm, next; Enki, interchangeably earth and water, completed the chain. For a society constantly relearning the trade of agriculture, it would only make sense that the principal deity was the totality of sky, while rain and earth followed— regardless of the fact that the water that fell onto the land would later be recycled upwards. In planting and harvesting, the downward moving force of rain dictated the process of life that its worshippers survived because of. The sky was clear; it clouded, and rained; soil was nourished by water; crops grew. They ate, evolved, and did it again, passing knowledge and genes to their children, who would continue this cycle after them. To ensure a successful and bountiful harvest, you had to turn to Anu. If his appetite was sated, he sent his son—who, in a very real sense, would today be considered "evil"—to nourish the land. Thus was born the idea that you must be in the favor of gods to be nourished. As historian Thorkild Jacobsen writes of these agriculturalists' relationship with the god, "He is at one and the same time the trust and the fear of man ... because Enlil is force, there lies hidden in the dark depths of his soul both violence and wildness."

Interestingly, even Enki was never considered to be purely "good." One of the pitfalls of developing this region was salinization. Irrigation streams tended to get flooded with salt, which would degrade soil over time. In the farmers' minds, this would happen if Enki was upset. Since there was no separation between the lives the farmers conducted and the actions of the planet, the disruption of the harvest fell back on them as people, not to mention their village leader. To ensure that they would be taken care of, elaborate seasonal and ritual festivities were fashioned to satisfy divinities, and the major function of the king was to promise food—he was the intermediary between sky and land, and supposedly communed with the gods. That was the basic requirement of his job description, and why he was paid so well. Human contact with these deities was definite and immediate. Their actions directly affected the response of nature, and a symbiotic relationship developed over time—a form of time that was the forbearer of our modern calendar.

Even though seasons moved cyclically, it was because of agriculture that man seriously entertained the notion of linear time. This, as one can imagine, has had profound effects on modern psychology.

Another trickling effect of this ancient idealism has continued to affect our collective psyche. It is of no surprise that these gods were predominantly male, as it was men who were considered true and full citizens. (It was predominantly men who had the ability to read and write, giving them the privilege of recording history how they saw fit.) This did not mean that women were irrelevant; they were just not accorded a high place in the social and political—and spiritual—pantheon. In truth Sumerian society extended to females many more rights than later Babylonian culture would. In some stories Anu was represented as An, and his female consort Ki was "earth." (Hence, the evolution of Enki.) Ki was the active force of both human and nutritive birth, making her a fertility goddess of skin and soil. She was also progenitor of the animal species, which called for one figure to be responsible for the recycling and assurance of all forms of life. This form of thinking offered a fusion between the developing agricultural communities and the hunting-gathering tribes that were settling. Suddenly two very different philosophies of life were finding synchronicity. Even though the hunting tribes were aware of agriculture, the sedentary lifestyle of their neighbors provided a new education. In actuality the cultural fusion of these two groups turns out to be more of a political than an ethical or geographical reality.

Mesopotamian civilization laid an evolved foundation from which even the streets of New York City can trace influences: in its vast network of people and goods, in the way a city is living and vibrant because of the excess of materials and souls that it conjures. Given the challenges of farming on nutrient- and salt-rich soil, people had to rely more on one another than maintaining single farms and smaller tribes. Their system of writing began as a way to mete out land and animal duties, as well as to keep track of taxation. Interdependence was key, and in no way was their land a vacuum. It was, in fact, extremely multicultural, relying heavily on trade from the entire Indus Valley. Being an advanced society in tool making, there was no metal indigenous to the region. As long as 4,000 years ago they had begun importing tin, copper and bronze from other nations. It would only make sense that stories of gods and things divine were traded as well. The *Epic of Gilgamesh* proved to be an early template for the Bible, as many of the ideas and divinities were borrowed directly from these mythologies. Mesopotamia reminds us that no culture is born without knowledge of previous cultures, and that the fusion of many peoples will inevitably give rise to great and evolutionary aspects of our ever-expanding network of humanity.

Though these gods may seem unfamiliar, there is good reason for acknowledging them. At the same time Mesopotamia was flourishing, a nearby culture was also making its mark: Egypt. The differences between the two are tremendous, although both were based on natural theological ideas (albeit with very grandiose visions by pharaohs). Yet Egypt has persisted and informed cultures for centuries, while Mesopotamia remains the fascination of a handful of academics. That is because today we can travel to Egypt and personally witness the rich and textured history in the forms of pyramids and catacombs, while Mesopotamia lies in ruins, covered by generations of salinization and floods. Just as these geographical considerations created the remnants of ancient philosophies, so they affected them while the cultures were thriving. Egypt's gods and those of Syria and Turkey would obviously have different qualities. A more stable kingdom will be preserved on land that is more reliable to grow and sustain humans. If you exploit and destroy the land, the gods—wind, sun, water and sky—will be angered. That is, they won't function in the way in which you have grown to depend upon them to. This is a major reason that civilizations collapse. What it boils down to, in many ways, is the ability for the culture to survive. And the way it does so is through its bones, not to mention through its literature.

The majority of cultures around the world at that time

were illiterate. Writing did not necessarily develop to capture the beauty and terror of life on page in epic scriptures, nor did it harness the yearnings of poetic love or the quests of adventurous heroes. Those tales were told orally. Villages and early cities were filled with storytelling peoples, even as hieroglyphs were in vogue. Information was passed down generation upon generation, where the mythologies and folklore of nations were stored in the minds and hearts and tongues of its citizens. In India, for example, scriptures and songs had to be memorized to the exact line, sometimes tens of thousands of verses, all the while depending on precise pronunciation, for the inflections of the voice were as important as the telling of the actual story. As bards, griots and sadhus traveled across borders, routing the first wireless tales, their verbalized literature of gods and human follies and glories was passed along, traded and redefined and continually rediscovered. Sometimes there was debate and dispute; at other moments, new gods were simply devoured, becoming part of their existing theology. It all depended on whether or not they fit into the overall theme of the gods and culture already intact.

Which brings us to one of the most insistent misperceptions in dealing with history: the "Golden Age." Also known as the Promised Land, the Land of Milk and Honey, the Ultimate Manna amongst many more titles, it is somewhere that apparently once existed, offering us entrance only if we live our lives in a prescribed manner, partake in certain rituals, or chant certain names. The Golden Age was a time when peace dominated the planet, when everyone loved and shared among their extended families, and when food and shelter were in abundance. There were no problems outside of minor everyday occurrences, which were rectified quickly and clearly. Then, there was a trigger. Something evil occurred, humans became greedy, someone killed their brother, or their father, or slept with their mother, and everything went downhill. The Golden Age rusted. Ever since, we've been trying to polish the iron oxide with prayers of peace and equanimity.

This idea, like many of our religious notions, has no actual basis, which is fine if understood symbolically. Yet this is not often the case—just take one look at the current situation in that little country between the temples of Egypt and the salinization fields of Mesopotamia: Israel. Two of the three major religions of the West exist side-by-side (with the third playing obvious cheerleader) and cannot see past the gripping chains of human ego, one that makes them both crave to "throw the other into the sea"—that is, to lead God's righteous and true creation into absolute glory by forever smiting their chosen enemy. Coat it with whatever tones of paint offer a different luster, the foundation of pride and the lust for real estate remain the same. The fight for land is the continual tribal warfare amongst sides who believe theirs to be justified by a divine figure. This is not faith; it is a perversion of cultural certainty, and unfortunately very common.

A Golden Age? The roots of humanity lie not in brotherhood, neighborly fraternity and good ol' Christian monogamy as much as they do in sacrifice, cannibalism and infanticide. We invent ideas of a perfect afterlife because we hope that will be the case, not because anything actually supports the evidence. And the only way to look ahead is to look back. There too we have contrived a prehistoric Eden—or, worse still, an intelligent design. We don't want a blissful afterlife; what we want is to continue this life forever, an ambiguous and uneventful word that is like a rootless tree ambitiously swaying from mind to tongue. Our drive towards death is thwarted by Botox and anti-aging creams, from refashioned missal passages and the gripping of rosaries between pleading fingers. No matter how dreadful or painful this life proves to be, we want to remain here more than traveling to what is beyond it, for that is somewhere we have no knowledge of, and at the very least we've grown accustomed to suffering. Never mind that age-old advice of Seneca: "Unlike life, death cannot be taken away from man, and therefore we may consider it as *the* gift of God." We reject what we do not know and turn a blind eye, even if we are all inevitably heading towards it. To truly contemplate death is to consider how to live more efficiently, prosperously and peacefully. In the avoidance of death, we avoid life.

Perhaps to trace this idea we can recall Aztec kings, who

ruled over what is often considered one of the most violent societies in the history of humankind. To appease their gods, prisoners of war as well as their own adolescents—fleshly prototypes of divinities "meant" for sacrifice—were spread over stone altars and held down by four priests, one anchoring each limb. A fifth would slice the victim's chest with an obsidian knife and rip out the beating heart. The victim would then be tossed from the top of the steep temple steps—the very same ones we see plastered on buses and billboards promoting Mexican tourism—toward an observant and eager crowd below.

The person on the altar was an archetype that would stave off angry gods. If the sun god received a blood offering of some foreigner captured during battle, or a specifically designated native whose role was as a functionary of the agricultural cycles, then he would ensure that his rays would keep shining, and replenish their crops. What neither *Indiana Jones and the Temple of Doom* nor *Apocalypto* showed was what happened to the victim *after* his or her body reached the bottom of those temple steps. In his work on the origins of culture, *Cannibals and Kings*, anthropologist Marvin Harris points out that the villagers "claimed the body and took it back to the owner's compound, where they cut it up and prepared the limbs for cooking—the favorite recipe being a stew flavored with peppers and tomatoes."

Cannibalism isn't an overly common practice in warfare and worship, but it is in no way exclusive to Aztecs. The ability to kill another for reasons of land, righteousness and personal vindication is a regular and constant human practice not relegated to any particular tribe or religion. In fact it has, for the most part, defined innumerable cultures that have graced this earth, right down to today's war in Iraq. Torture practices continue as American soldiers blare Metallica's "Enter Sandman" and Barney's "I Love You" at ear-shattering decibels for twenty-three hours a day for the caring welfare of their beloved prisoners, while American leaders establish out-of-boundaries prison systems (most notably in Cuba) not answerable to any form of diplomacy. More Iraqis have died—the majority of them innocent of any crimes—than the entire number of people killed in the World Trade Center; more American soldiers have died as well. While there were no obsidian knifes or chants made to feather plumed serpents, modern soldiers are the victims of sacrifice nonetheless, one that has much to do with Texan oil honchos as it does with the hubris and ignorance of massive political agendas disguised as religious quests. As we will see, the form of sacrifice has traveled from humans to animals to ideas, but the essence remains the same. We are still killing for our gods, which essentially means we are killing for ourselves, an unlikely paradox that is more true than even it realizes.

What interests me about Aztec history is not that humans would eat other humans. To most that is simply revolting. I'm not trying to glorify or justify it either. Yet I fully understand the symbolic nature. It is no different than other forms of sympathetic magic, like leaving grains of rice or sugary balls soaked in rose water to appease an elephant-headed deity in India, or walking thousands of miles during a pilgrimage, prostrating each step in reverence to the Buddha. It is similar in intent to throwing grains onto winter fields to remind soil that spring will emerge from Hades, or honoring the buffalo under your knife by wearing its hide after you eat its meat. Life feeds on life feeds on life, and to receive life sometimes you must offer it. What is so intriguing about cannibalism is the political nature behind it, something Harris poignantly details.

In his thorough work on the nature of dominating cultures across the planet, *Guns, Germs and Steel*, Jared Diamond points out how three factors—more efficient weaponry, the ability to spread disease and the manufacturing of steel in constructing buildings and other objects—resulted in the victories of certain nations over others. Over two decades prior, Harris had come to similar conclusions that Diamond's more cumulative work arrived at. When dealing with Mesoamerica, Harris attributes much of the savagery of Aztecs to the depletion of the ecosystem after the last ice age, one that kept what could have become a full-blown rainforest rather arid. Because of this, the ability to grow edible vegetation and domesticate animals for protein was not available.

If you want to create a dynasty there must be a system

that makes the people under you feel secure. At the very least, the most basic elements must be provided: food, shelter and protection. Without those initial promises no government can rise to power. Harris points out that Asiatic cultures in China and India had fallen to more centralized forms of politicking because of the need farmers had for water—and, with industrious dams and irrigation channels in place, rulers quickly figured out how to build empires, reminding us once again during this current time of plastic bottle mayhem that he who controls water, controls society. In Europe, where agriculture depended more on rain than irrigation, it took longer for large dynasties to take root. When they figured out what that formula was—democracy, thanks to the trading habits of the mercantile class and the social philosophies of Greek hoplites—their system ended up becoming in certain regards far more effective. Without the promise of proper rainfall, irrigation or trading, Aztec rulers ended up devising something that was definitely unique in its broad scope and yet no less resourceful: cannibalism.

What had occurred worldwide was a shift from tribal leadership to centralized dictatorship. Voluntary contributions by farmers and villagers became taxes when the government was able to store a surplus of grain, something they had not been able to do when the main form of diet was meat, which rotted and could not be ziplocked and stored in freezers. Farmlands became dispensations; land was no longer a right granted to everyone, but rather something "owned" by whoever would pay taxes and redistribute crops to the community. By becoming the main redistributors, village chiefs became kings. This trend continues in the Information Age, where the Internet serves as a major source of redistribution and third-party sales and marketing. Today you don't even need goods to make millions of dollars; simple ideas work, if properly promoted. Like how the Internet connects us today, early mythologies that were broadcast as a form of spiritual and communal epoxy soon became tools for pacifying large crowds, shaped and molded to fit the ideals of an elite group of men.

The very same Aztec community that, due to the guns and germs in Diamond's theory, would give way to a small army led by a boisterous Spaniard trying to capture land and spread religion, had developed a system of governance where the sacrificing of human flesh was a divine declaration. Before we figure out exactly why this worked, we need to court one more idea, one which involved the costs and benefits of political control, as well as touching upon another terror of the human mind: infanticide.

I have to again stress how important these events are in the shaping of modern belief. Too often we take the spiritual ideas of our parents, peers and culture as the true reality from which have sprouted all sorts of perversions. When failing to see the symbolic keys to mythologies and religions, we take our ancestral traces to be fact. That is dangerous, and quite lazy. Of equal importance is exploring the divide between what we believe and how we act. This is the greatest misconstruction regarding the contemplation and integration of yoga and atheism in our times: the rift between what we say and how we behave. We cannot believe one thing and act in complete ignorance of that idea, all the while expecting our lives to fall into perfect line with what we say it should. To get to the roots of our beliefs, we need to be aware of who developed those beliefs, and why. That takes investigation, on a personal level as well as in the realm of history.

The last thing we'd want to admit is that our religion was used as a catalyst for practices like infanticide, cannibalism or murder. Yet that has been the case for centuries. From this, numerous taboos have arisen, and the very groundwork by which modern religion has been laid remains buried in a collective and unconscious history that most refuse to face. In the shedding of the darkness of our past, and in the lighting of a clear path to what informs us today, we can understand exactly who we are with a bit more clarity. And who we are is not the "end" of evolution. Richard Dawkins makes a great point when he suggests that the idea of evolution does not imply that there is an end point to the process. Chimpanzees were not "made" to become humans, nor were prior *homo sapiens* just waiting for us to arrive. The study of our past, however, does have an important role. With conscious and rigorous self-reflection we can learn more about ourselves and our kind, even if the stories haven't taken place on immediate soil. While it is true that the path to self-realization is internal, the outside world is a reflection of what we believe and how we live. The more options we consider in formulating that landscape, the more complete we are as people and cultures.

Much of this confusion stems from our believing that the laws and codes of our—let's put extra emphasis on *our*—religion are divinely ordained, even when history teaches us that they were treated as tools for kings and presidents. Today nothing has changed. Romanticizing the social and spiritual past is common. We'd like to think that any minor infringement on the human spirit would always pale in comparison to the glories received by the faithful individual. I'm not denying that having a positive outlook can have a major influence on one's life. It's just that to do so is a serious discipline and takes a lot of time, not to mention courage. Merely labeling yourself this or that and then forgetting about the actual and real applications of that faith is not going to cut it.

Even if we consider them written as harbingers of an enlightened age, our scriptures sure do have a lot of paganism and folklore. In the Hebrew tale of Nimrod, infanticide takes a prominent role. The king had been astrologically informed that a boy would one day be born to overthrow his religion, which effectively meant his political rule. Nimrod ordered every male baby to be killed, a decision that cost the lives of 70,000 young ones. Abraham's mother, frightened that she would lose her baby, fled the city and hid in a cave until the birth of her prodigious son. When it turned out to be a boy, Abram, she was relieved that she did not have to let him be killed by the government. Instead, she wrapped him up in a blanket and left him in the cave, leaving his fate to "God's grace." (It's easy to see how our own lack of responsibility is dictated by such a reading of this story. Imagine a mother today doing the same, and question how lenient a judge would be in this case of abandonment.) As the mythology goes, God sent Gabriel to nourish him with milk.

In Genesis 10-11, Nimrod and Abraham are born seven generations apart, meaning that they would never have met. This story is obviously a later tale concocted around the Tower of Babel, the wicked anti-religious device Nimrod installed before his reign of terror was subdued. Here you have a good-versus-evil tale centered on a wicked king and the holy father of modern religion, with infanticide obviously pointing toward unrighteousness. This is a mere snippet from the moral codes that this and other religions have developed, using a supreme deity as the decider of human fate through the instrument of mortal men. When Abraham proved victorious over Nimrod, Judaism claimed the land of Canaan, and monotheism destroyed the polytheistic heathens. It is a prime example of a political agenda that would cause any real estate agent to giggle with excitement.

Infanticide has very old roots—we should not romanticize our ancestors. We have better health care now than ever, even if our pharmacological dependency is outrageous. Birth control is readily available; whether we choose to use it is another story. But the ability to control pregnancy is advanced enough so that today we can decide whether *to* have a child, not hope we *don't* have one. This was not always possible. In times past, forms of birth control included pounding a woman in the abdomen after sex, violently massaging the uterine region and even repeatedly hopping on a wooden plank placed across a woman's belly until blood spurted from her vagina—things you're not going to see on a PBS commercial. In these grueling ordeals, oftentimes not only would the placenta be evacuated, but the woman as well. Condoms and pills are comparatively gentle, and much more effective.

What's so interesting about Harris' thesis is that birth control and—if those methods proved ineffective—infanticide were evolutionary tactics to keep society at a certain population. Political dictatorships have tried different methods, to ward a more publicized end. Over and over, a theme emerges in the varying lengths a society will go in order to keep its members "in line." These efforts do not have to be conscious, though they most often suit the party in control in some manner. Let's face it, men are not going to *not* have sex if the village leader says they are in danger of overcrowding. Village leaders were men, most of the time, and many of these societies were polygamous. As is the history of our species, women have suffered immensely for the plight of men. During the Paleolithic period, in fact, infanticide rates may have been as high as fifty-percent in aboriginal Australia.

Given the focus that modern society places on the family, I find this fascinating, even if it turns out that it is the idea of the family, rather than the actual family, that's most prominent. When rare cases of infanticide appear in American media—and they do—the mother is instantly dubbed a she-devil. This practice is not just relegated to an "ancient" people. A tactic called overlaying still exists, where a mother "just happens" to lie on top of her child while sleeping, smothering him or her to death. To combat this problem, foundling houses were set up in London in the 1750s, where parents could drop off their child, no questions asked. During a five-year period, over 15,000 children were deposited. Given this surge combined with a lack of proper nutrition and funding, only one-quarter survived until adolescence. In France, the numbers were even more astounding. In a ten-year period in the 1820s-30s, over 336,000 children were dropped off. Nearly ninety-percent of them died within their first year.

While BBC's Planet Earth series captures a giant Panda bear going to extremes to nurture her young on a poverty-stricken diet of bamboo, most animals are not as protective and endearing as humans are of their offspring. Yet it took us time to learn this practice, and family is of crucial consideration in cultures that can afford to take care of its members, as well as those that cannot; many will suffer starvation to make sure a loved one is fed. Perhaps childrearing with such rigor is beneficial in the long-term, as a cared-for child will want to procreate and offer the same, and so on. This moves us beyond the scope of DNA and into morals, which is a sticky place for scientists and religionists alike.

There have been arguments that better technology,

economy, and healthcare lead to more childrearing, from both medical standpoints (a lower mortality rate) and cultural ones (the wealthier, the happier and more abundant). In certain countries the reverse is true. The more one has to devote time and energy to work, as in a country like America, the less time for childrearing we have (hence a plethora of drugs to ensure a female's fertility well into her fifties). There is no clear and discernible answer to this, as certain religious sects purposefully procreate as much as possible to extend their family, while others do so simply out of the sheer drive to reproduce, as well as the love of sex. No matter how it's phrased or justified, procreating is exactly what our genes "want" to do. Some cultures feel the need to dress it up and make it an act of God, while others do it naturally.

As Jared Diamond points out in *Why is Sex Fun?: The Evolution of Human Sexuality*, our habits are not the norm in the animal kingdom. For the most part, no animal is so self-conscious as to need to do it in private with the lights out, and few animals other than humans do it for sheer fun. The idea that sex is being practiced when women are not ovulating is another rarity. From the standpoint of the rest of the animal kingdom, *we* are the freaks, not the dog humping the neighbor's porcelain statue. Yet it is fun to us. The notion that it should be done just for procreation is ludicrous. Some desire drives this urge in us, one that Diamond attempts to weigh in light of evolutionary biology. While certain religious practices seek to quiet and (self) control this urge, only the absurd ones attempt to stop it altogether, never realizing that what is banned will only pique our curiosity that much more. Taking cues from other species also offers insight into our own distinct feelings on what is considered by some to be life's most sacred, and by others life's most taboo, event. The fact that the most basic human urge toward evolution is stunted by religious demands points toward the fact that religion is used, once again, as a political and social tool. Of course we can't imagine eating our friend or killing their baby when you can drive to Wal-Mart and pick up dinner on the way to the soccer game. Still, these were very real occurrences when the religions we today call the ultimate truth were being developed, and their echoes are heard in the curious phrasings of political and spiritual leaders, even when clothed in different garb.

When our personal actions are dictated as the blueprint for how all humans should act, and when we simply dismiss our previous actions as primitive and of no significance, there will always be a reaction. *All* religions are created as a reaction to something, be it an oppressive governing body or the oppressive forces of the unpredictable outdoors. Natural theologies, at least, attempted to remain as fluid as the life witnessed in every direction, never clinging to permanence, for everything is always in transition. If anyone has any doubt of this, simply visit a major city and find an area not under construction, or some transportation system not being fixed. Even closer to home, explore some area of your life that you feel is not undergoing a similar construction, be it of your home, family or emotions. Or try this simple exercise. Stand up, close your eyes and lift one leg a few inches from the ground, and try to keep it suspended for one minute. Observe the chaos that ensues in your ankle and leg. Our physical bodies are representative of the process of existence, because we were born into this process. Our bodies are symbols of the world, long known to many spiritual traditions. What seems simple with our eyes open, like lifting one leg a few inches, tells a completely different story when our vision is removed—or, to put another way, when we turn to our unconscious. All these examples highlight the Buddha's most basic principle: All life is transient. This applies not only to life as a macrocosm, but to the daily moments we experience as well.

The challenge of history is recognizing that we are making it every day, never free from the occurrences of the past. It is only by understanding our past that we are liberated. This is the lesson of religious prophets. At the core of their teachings is the message that we have to understand the venerable principles and apply them to our times. If we continue to romanticize and idolize their persons without integrating their words, the message is lost. Today we are not suffering the political-disguised-as-spiritual dictates of cannibalism and infanticide, or many other human horrors that our kind has encountered before. We have entirely new beasts to slay. Old patterns are reformed by political and religious leaders who grasp the essence of language and psychology and use it for their own gains. It is well known that our media is being restricted by the agendas of terror-waving cowboys who use the image of God as the righteous judge behind their cause. This pattern is not new, but because we are living through it and not reflecting back on it, we think it cannot happen to us. We have our excuses ready-made: We've learned from the past. This time it's different. They wouldn't do such a thing.

But things don't change; circumstances merely rearrange. We are not in good shape as a nation. In the course of a few years we have been turned into a fearful, suspicious citizenry afraid of tipping the scales in any direction. Every day when I enter the New York City subway system, if I'm not having my bag checked by three police officers or the National Guard, I'm listening to the constant drones over the platform speakers: "The New York City Police Department encourages you to be vigilant in your pursuit in reporting anything suspicious." Look at the language: Vigilant. Pursuit. Report. Suspicious. Terrorists are not really being addressed. This is the creation of a psychology, one in which we don't trust one another because we don't trust ourselves. This kind of seemingly subtle verbiage will continue until it doesn't need to be subtle. When we finally turn to reflect, we find that all the freedom we believed inherent was part of the illusion.

All of our philosophies are in some way reactionary. Atheism was a social response to constrictive political situations. So was, as we shall see, yoga, as many principles were developed when the rituals of the Brahmin caste became a little too rigid and self-righteous. The community that lies at the heart of these and all traditions remains focused on the relationships of individuals working together for a common cause. Yoga was part of the individual's journey into himself, while atheism was often concerned with more external goals, yet the meeting point where inner and outer worlds converge is where the philosophies unite. There is much to be learned from both, as, in the words of Howard Zinn, "It is as if a whole nation were going through a critical point in its middle age, a life crisis of self-doubt, self-examination." This is the America we live in.

Doubt is a powerful tool when used to clear away the rubbish inside one's mind and heart. Constant doubt is a dangerous pattern, though, one being fed every time we are told to watch out for unattended bags on a subway, or peering on our neighbors to ensure nothing "funny" is going on. There is nothing funny about this, though. Citing George Orwell's *Animal Farm* in her book *The End of America*, Naomi Wolf points out that our current government is employing tactics that serve "to make the other animals lose their ability to trust their own judgment." And they're not doing it by brute force in the way we've read about in textbooks. It is much more subtle, which makes it that much more dangerous. By appealing to our desires and making us suspicious of anything or anyone that is not cut from the normal grain of what American society is "supposed" to look like, our citizenry has been molded with a Pavlovian clay. The seeking of pleasure becomes a narcotic. As media critic Neil Postman pointed out some years ago, comparing another Orwell classic, *1984*, with Aldous Huxley's *Brave New World*:

> What Orwell feared were those who would ban books. What Huxley feared was that there would be no reason to ban a book, for there would be no one who wanted to read one. Orwell feared those who would deprive us of information. Huxley feared those who would give us so much that we would be reduced to passivity and egoism. Orwell feared that the truth would be concealed from us. Huxley feared the truth would be drowned in a sea of irrelevance. Orwell feared we would become a captive culture. Huxley feared we would become a trivial culture, preoccupied with some equivalent of the feelies, the orgy porgy, and the centrifugal bumblepuppy. As Huxley remarked in *Brave New World Revisited*, the civil libertarians and rationalists who are ever on the alert to oppose tyranny 'failed to take into account man's almost infinite appetite for distractions.' In *1984*, Orwell added, people are controlled by inflicting pain. In *Brave New World*, they are controlled by inflicting pleasure. In short, Orwell feared that what we hate will ruin us. Huxley feared that what we love will ruin us.

After comparing these two authors, it's hard not to draw correlations between Huxley's warning and the current state of affairs, the promises of liberation by presidents and the guarantee of eternal and financial security by megachurch pastors. Their pledges sooth us because they're want we want to hear, even if that does not represent what is actually happening. We live in a world of belief and recoil at the idea that we may not be the chosen ones. These false pledges by marketing masters assume many shapes and sizes, and they have proven themselves to be extremely good at employing the services of the Big Guy. The pharaohs of yesteryear *are* our presidents and priests. Their echoes can be heard tumbling through the ages, changing frequency, and yet never losing steam. Make us believe we need certain things, and then devise a plan to make us fear losing it. We'll risk our actual freedom for the manufactured version. Huxley was right: What we love is destroying us, even if—especially because—that love is really desire in disguise.

To get to the light at the end of the tunnel we need to pass through the shadow that that light creates. Denying the shadow takes a toll on the minds and hearts of a species. It is this denial of our totality that results in the fragmented factions of numerous religious, cultural and political beliefs, resulting in a diversity that is anything but celebrated. Our media has grown so rapidly that each of us has become a reporter of some sort. Like Wolf suggests though, we need to be innovators in the field, not mere commentators. It is problematic that every time we discuss freedom or God we need to invoke the Bible or the Constitution. We need doctrines we can relate to, ones signed and sealed during this age, that use the wisdom of past works while updating the story even as the cycles remain the same. We need to experience the history of now, to recognize false faces on television screens and overblown shouting in pulpits (or stadiums). We must support each other in a global community and get over the idea that our small section of this vast world represents infinity.

An understanding of how belief and behavior can merge so that what we believe is no longer an abstract idea lies in developing a complete theology. That theology in turn supports our personal, social and political views, not to mention any thoughts we may devise regarding the numinous. If we do not absolve the karma of our ancestors—one rich in the practices of sacrifice, cannibalism and infanticide, both real and symbolic— we will continue to partake in these rites, often never realizing that's what we are doing. There is no separation between our shadow and the light we crave—we never really "leave work at the office." Our work involves every aspect of who we are; the person who enters their home at night is the same walking on tiled floor during the day. Recognizing this is part of the practice of integration, of the union that the word religion denotes. To integrate this discipline into our lives, we now turn to yoga.

PART II

THE YOGATHEIST

"The old differences separating one system from another now are becoming less and less important, less and less easy to define. And what, on the contrary, is becoming more and more important is that we should learn to see *through* all the differences to the common themes that have been there all the while, that came into being with the first emergence of ancestral man from the animal levels of existence, and are with us still."

Joseph Campbell
Myths to Live By

CHAPTER 4

THE PLIGHT OF PROTO-SHIVA

When one studies a spiritual tradition, there are generally two significant entry points: a physical common ground and a required reading list. Many of us are born into a tradition, and later decide to continue with it, seek out another, or none. Leaving aside the psychological tendencies towards believing the religion of your parents to be the "correct" one, these two things—a church, temple, mosque or yoga studio, which is a meeting place to commune with like-minded individuals, and sacred texts, poetry and doctrines—define the experience of that tradition. I want to focus on the second.

In my yoga teacher training course we were required to read three texts: the *Bhagavad Gita*, a small section of India's masterwork, the *Mahabarrata*; *The Textbook of Yoga Psychology*, an intense and scholarly translation of Patanjali's *Yoga Sutras*; and *Anatomy of Movement* by Blandine Calais-German. All are excellent works. I've seen quite a number of reading lists from other training programs and often find these as the main texts. I'll sometimes see a few other classics, such as Iyengar's *Light on Yoga* and the *Hatha Yoga Pradipika*. The incredible scholar Georg

Feuerstein is referenced, yet bafflingly his works are rarely used as textual sources. (We did read an article by him, though his thirty-plus books are essential reading for teachers of any tradition.) I've never seen Mircea Eliade's *Yoga: Immortality and Freedom*, Jean Varenne's *Yoga and the Hindu Tradition* or Robert Alter's *Yoga in Modern India: The Body Between Science and Philosophy* used, referenced or discussed. In my conversations with many teachers, they are often ignorant of these important works.

More than yoga-based texts, however, I've seen no trace of books on the history of Indian culture in yoga studios and schools. This is not exclusive to yogis. Some Christians think that the only book worth reading is their bible, and do so over and over and over again. The people involved in spiritual traditions often promote this behavior. Exhausting a limited body of scripture of one system is supposedly the way to learn and integrate it into your life. Yet this form of study creates blinders as to the actual history of that religion. The culture and time which births a tradition is as relevant to understanding that tradition as its texts. These books are the work of one or a few men, so it is not surprising you will read biased and at times sexist remarks under the guise of spirituality. God is a man, after all. That perplexes me even more when I see women referencing "him" as frequently as I do, so removed from the goddess have we become. To really know a religion, you must at least have some sense of the nation that created it, for the behavior and actions of that culture are the very essence of the scriptures that resulted. Today masterful works of mythological leaning are classified as science fiction or new age. Why then do we feel that similar works written thousands of years ago are actual, factual truth?

Over the last two chapters you've read about cultural movements in Jamaica, cannibalism in Mexico and infanticide in France, three things you probably were not expecting when picking up a book on yoga and atheism. What I'm calling your attention to is a synthesis of beliefs—not necessarily what we believe, but *how* we believe, and why we believe what we do. To not question your belief is to promote ignorance, what yogis call *avidya*. (*Vidya* is knowledge. Adding "a" to anything in Sanskrit denotes its opposite. Hence the opposite of knowledge is ignorance, or even better: unknowing.) Numerous comparative philosophy books accomplish tremendous feats in merging religious traditions. Both Thich Nhat Han and the Dalai Lama have eloquently strung together an unbroken thread between Jesus and the Buddha. Even these works, however, do not dive into the actual societies that created these mythologies. Without that knowledge, you cannot claim to know the reality behind the tradition. (Both Han and the Dalai Lama know their traditions exceptionally well. I mention their work in this context as points of reference to highlight a different approach to comparative literature.)

I've been in too many classes where teachers discuss the "ancient" roots of yoga, how this incredible movement we're about to experience has been handed down unbroken for 5,000 years. Indeed, the "goal" of yoga remains the same now as it was then: liberation. How this idea manifests has taken innumerable forms over that 5,000-year history which is both longer and shorter than that. If this is a confusing statement, we are entering the paradoxical and intricately detailed practice of discrimination, which lies at the heart of jnana yoga—the yoga of knowledge. As the great Romanian scholar, Mircea Eliade, wrote, "If the word 'yoga' means many things, that's because Yoga *is* many things."

My intent with this short book was never to exhaust the philosophy of yoga. Indeed, these are only words on a page; it is the *experience* of yoga that is truly worthwhile. Yet we can use words as a road map to help us along the way, or, as I like to tell my students, we should treat yoga as a blueprint to build our personal architecture upon. Everyone will have their own idea of creating these structures, even though we use the same source, much like the incredible diversity of the planet shared by a global cast swapping DNA. For the rest of this chapter we will focus on what the history of the culture that created yoga was like, and in Chapter 6 we will explore the movement that evolved it into the form we practice today.

In 1922, a team of diggers with the Archaeological Survey of India unearthed what would be referenced as one of the earliest cosmopolitan cities in history. The remains of Mohenjo-Daro reside in modern day Pakistan, part of the once-burgeoning Indus Valley Civilization (also known as the Harappan Civilization) that flourished between 3000 and 2000 BCE. While the region is invaluable in tracing the social architecture of South Asian culture, the site is still largely unexcavated nearly ninety years later. What has thus far been found has made a huge impact on our understanding of Indian civilization.

Despite its seemingly small role in the scope of archaeological digs, with each site offering tiny clues into pre-Aryan Indian culture, these digs are providing the archaic blueprints for what could have been the first planned cities in the world. The two dominant sites usually associated with our urban past—Egypt and Mesopotamia—dwarf any one of the Indian digs in scale and scope. Yet taken together, all of the minor sites comprising the ever-expanding Harappan cities have displayed a far-reaching attempt to create a giant network of smaller suburbs that stretched hundreds of miles across. While two major digs in Sind and Panjab are the crème of diggers (and even these do not reveal a wealth of material), a myriad of sites extends throughout Pakistan, India, and nearly into Iran. Unfortunately these regions suffered the same fate as Mesopotamia, at the mercy of numerous deluges and salinization. What archaeologists have discovered, however, is that the foresight of elder architects and their kingdoms match our modern world in ways that even vain pharaohs couldn't realize within their own kingdoms.

Harappan civilization dates back to roughly 3000 BCE, giving modern yogis the "5,000-year history" they often reference. The Mohenjo-Daro dig produced an earthenware seal depicting a cross-legged figure surrounded by wild animals. This image became known as "proto-Shiva," the earliest known idol of the Lord of Yoga, as he is known in one of his many aspects. As described by historian John Keay, he is a "big-nosed gentleman wearing a horned head-dress who sits in the lotus position with an erect penis, an air of abstraction and an audience of animals."

Here we must face a challenging dichotomy: that which lies between scholarship and faith, academia and belief. Keay, one of the foremost minds piecing together the history of India's land and thought, admits that this seal could very well depict Shiva. The image matches what the blue-skinned deity is known for: the lotus position is the "seat" of yogic meditation; he is the erotic god, as well as the creator/destroyer, renowned for carefree romps in the forest with *apsaras*, so the erect penis would be fitting; the "air of abstraction" fits the soft-eyed *drishti* that the yogi develops with meditation; he is associated with numerous animals, and speaks with them in the forests—his son, Ganesha, is the result of his relationship with elephants. The horned head-dress could also signify this ongoing dialogue, although as he is depicted today, there are two main images in his dreadlocks: a crescent moon, a symbol of femininity as well as the dark side of his destructive aspect, and snakes, a major image in yoga due to the its correlation with kundalini.

With all of these parallels, it is easy to see why the yogi would instantly make the association. But Keay brings up two important points. The first, that "the chances of a deity remaining closely associated with the same specific powers—in this case, fertility, asceticism and familiarity with the animal kingdom—for all of two thousand years must raise serious doubts, especially since, during the interval, there is little evidence for the currency of this myth." The second, somewhat related, is that "we have no idea what part religion played in the lives of the Harappan people."

I find the second point especially relevant. Regarding the first, it is true that it is difficult to ascertain proof that the coin represents Shiva. Most likely it could be, as the name "proto" implies, a version of what would become Shiva. The fertility and asceticism connection is a rather interesting one that we will return to. That agricultural and animal imagery would be employed together is not surprising; the ascetic aspect is something altogether different, and would not be a major aspect of Indian spirituality until another two thousand years had passed. Faith aside, you cannot blindly assume that this *is* Shiva, or a prototype of him, and then claim that if he was idolized at that time, then it must mean yoga was a part of their everyday life. That sort of statement belittles the integrity of history by attempting to mold this one coin to fit into an entire chronicle of contexts that the speaker wishes it to.

Now, regarding the religious aspect. Most of what has been discovered at the Harappan digs, besides a few statues and seals, are utilitarian objects suited for survival and not belief. Keay is correct in his assumption that there is no proof of religiosity. Yet what I'd like to put forth is that that fact is not necessarily important. Whereas yogis sometimes make blanket statements without doing the math behind the equation, scholars sometimes rely completely on the archaeological and physical evidence without giving enough consideration to the culture behind it, which can be equally dangerous. Not that Keay is in any way attempting to undermine tradition; he's being honest with the evidence. But there's something more than the physical that underscores the practice of yoga. Shiva is the perfect figure to contemplate this idea alongside, so here we will undertake a brief gaze into the yogic tradition before reentering modernity.

Today there are two main questions asked in regards to the topic at hand. The first is, "Do you practice yoga?" Assuming an affirmative, the questioner will put forth, "What type of yoga do you do?" The respondent will most likely name one, or a few, of the formats popular in the West: Vinyasa, Hatha, Kundalini, Bikram, Power, and so on. On occasion you will find someone state one of the more interior aspects, such as Bhatki, Karma or Jnana, which are not specifically physical exercises but still integral to the practice.

When questioning about someone's faith, it is often put forth thus: "What religion are you?" Unsurprisingly, you will rarely hear these questions reversed, so as if someone would ask, "What type of yoga are you?" or "What type of religion do you do?" The assumption is that yoga is something one *does*, while religion is something one *is*. Yet it is perfectly possible to *be* yoga and *do* religion. The one who has dedicated a life to yoga knows this, and integrates yogic philosophy into every aspect of life. Going to the gym or a studio for a ninety-minute class is merely the introduction, and while that too has major benefits, it is just one aspect of a complete system of being.

That's why there's no better representation than Shiva, the playfully destructive deity subsequently known as a yogic master. So great is his power that after a major flood, which caused many important objects to be lost at the bottom of the ocean, Vishnu incarnated as Kurma, a tortoise, and churned up the waters so that what was lost could be recovered. Both *devas* (gods) and *asuras* (demons) wrapped the giant snake, Vasuki, around the mountain that Kurma created with his shell. They then played tug-of-war with the snake, causing the waters to churn and free the lost objects, including the precious elixir amrita, and Lakshmi, goddess of fortune and beauty.

No good mythology is complete without a bit of badness. The asuras simply wouldn't have taken part in a struggle if there were nothing in it for them. Unlike Pandora, whose box contained only one positive quality for humans to benefit from—hope—this ocean released a bounty of treasures with only one negative. Unfortunately it was a poison so terrible that the human race would be wiped out had it spread. Shiva ran to the rescue, drinking the poison and holding it indefinitely in his throat so that everyone else could delight in the pure waters. This is how Shiva gained another nickname, Nilakantha, coming from *nila* (blue) and *kantha* (throat), and why in most symbolism his skin is the color of ocean and sky.

Mythology is a system of symbols, useful only if decoded and integrated into one's life. The Indian myths are rich with beautiful and textured folklore, and Shiva is certainly one of the biggest stars. In this tale alone we find numerous important insights into a wealth of information. Yoga is a practice of balance, which is why both gods and demons would have partaken in the liberating dance of destruction going on underwater. The kundalini energy that lies dormant at the base of everyone's spine, awaiting the proper meditative frequencies by which to be awoken, is depicted as a coiled snake. When the devas and asuras—here representing the two *nadis* (energy channels) that wrap around the spine—dance, the snake uncoils and frees the aspirant of delusional knowledge (avidya). The left and right nadis are *ida* and *pingali* respectively, and the central channel, *sushumna*, is the spine. When the *chakras* are purified the snake awakens, and unfettered by the tight muscular and mental energies that inhibit free movement, samadhi is achieved.

Yoga is a practice of purification as well. The sacred energy travels from the base of the spine to the crown of the head through the practice of *pranayama*, intense breathing exercises. When Kurma kicked up the waters, everything was not essentially "good." The yogi has to face his or her deepest self and all its baggage to move forward and be liberated, and this is rarely a pleasurable experience. The poison that arises is oftentimes the exact cure needed, but if the yogi is not prepared to deal with this, it can be seriously damaging. Thus: the arrival of Shiva to drink the poison. In asana practice, this is known as *kumbhaka*, the restraining and holding of breath at the level of the throat. Shiva's skin turned from white to blue after this episode and, like the great yogi he is, he never complained about it. This new colorful pigmentation is symbolic of his intense yoga practice of *tapas*, purifying actions that clear the aspirant's body and mind. He was humbled at the opportunity to serve humankind in such a way, using his powers to sustain life. He gave of himself for the greater good of humanity.

Yogis will always choose reality instead of bickering between good and evil, for it is part of the path to understand that both qualities are aspects of one story. If Kurma had only churned up goodness from the oceanic depths, what relevance would the story have to us? It would no longer be a reflection of the world we inhabit; it would be a fairy tale. This is why Shiva is the most dynamic of gods, representing the totality of possible experiences in this world, and not an authoritative and domineering schoolmaster lording over every action. Nobody likes a demanding and uncaring boss. Sure, it's great to have someone disciplining you, yoking you to your own inner processes so that there is no great rift between what you think and feel inside and who you are outside. But a dispassionate, judgmental lord who controls every aspect of your being is a rather sterile and not very enticing prospect. Shiva has none of these qualities. As Wendy Doniger points out in her intensive survey of this deity, *Siva: The Erotic Ascetic*, he appears much more often in both aspects of his persona than as either all good, or especially evil. Even the play on words in the subtitle hints at this. One of the first rules of asceticism is chastity, and yet Shiva is often seen conducting forest orgies. It is this refusal of adhering to any one specific trait that makes it possible for him to govern the dance of the universe.

"The myth makes it possible to admit that the ideal is not attainable," she writes. Take, for example, modern yogis claiming this to be a 5,000-year-old practice. In the Mohenjo-Daro dig were other telling artifacts, including the half-burned bones of sheep, goats, and cattle found in the kitchens, as well as those of elephants, camels, pigs and water buffalo. This is important to those who claim yoga to be a strictly vegetarian endeavor. Not only were those animals being eaten—down to the last cow bone—but they were being sacrificed as well. Some speculate that animal sacrifice became ritual because of the guilt that hunters-gatherers once held about having to constantly kill their game, leading them to devise a way to make divine offerings of the remains a means to both alleviate said guilt and to keep game plentiful. Others have commented that the sacrifice is a way of showing thanks to the Great Spirit for allowing them to be fed. Whatever the reasons, the birth-death-rebirth motif has been part of the process long before a tiny proto-Shiva was preserved.

Vegetarianism is part of ahimsa, non-violence. To partake in *himsa* (violence) is to disrespect the very life you depend upon. Those who involve themselves in such dealings can expect their actions to be returned, be it in a form similar or otherwise. This process informs their karmic repertoire, with each violent action causing further affliction. By not killing you are increasing the chance of a peaceful coexistence with all forms of life. This has become a creed to modern yoga, though this was not always the case. Far from it, actually.

Yoga was a practice of warriors—not the sage poses we embody in physical classes, but real, actual bandits and pillagers, as well as men who had to fight to maintain their villages from invaders. India had long been a ritualistic culture, and Olympian precursors such as chariot races and mock battles were part of the seasonal cycles. Religion was confined to the Brahman caste, which made it essentially the practice of an economic and social elite. It took a matter of centuries before the mythologies and folklore became integrated into the general populace, thanks in part to the frustrated work of ascetics who were so fed up by the disparities of society that they journeyed into the forests, often naked and without food or shelter, to ease their internal suffering. It would be their display of fortitude that inspired the general population to realize that spiritual freedom was always at hand, even if they could not perform the extremes of asceticism themselves.

Over the course of the ninth to seventh centuries BCE, the priestly caste compiled a series of scriptures, the *Brahmanas*, which transformed the actual physical rituals into disciplines of the inner state. This was no easy task for the *kshatriya* caste, comprised of warriors who were intent on inflicting harm as a means to salvation. There still exists a romantic notion of a peaceful and spiritual India, before the "invasion" of a nomadic group that may have originated in Russia, Germany, Scandinavia, or otherwise. Over a period of centuries the Aryan peoples became integrated into Indian life. Their traveling mythologies became incorporated into local ideology, comprising the basis for what would, centuries later, become Hinduism, as well as influence Jainism, Sikhism and Buddhism. Having been travelers for so long, their spiritual notions were played out on the actual battlefield, not in silent temples contemplating the inner meaning of battlefields.

Over time a body of literature developed that was, at first, not literature at all. It was song told in story form. We live in a culture dominated by the idea that the meaning of a word is more important than the sound that saying it produces. That is because most of our education revolves around looking at alphabets splayed across white pages, as you are doing now. The sound of each word is silent inside of your head; it is only being heard if you are reading aloud. Mythology and spirituality did not begin with writing. It was told through the human voice. Being that this form of communication predates even language, the pencil-less authors of the original tales of the Vedas were master orators.

The West has this tradition. Take Malory's *L'Morte d'Arthur*, for one. Like much medieval English prose, it was written in a style called *amplificatio*, meant to be read aloud more than in silence. The rhyme schemes and annunciations *were the meaning*, not the meaning of individual words forming the spectrum of thought. This is a challenging concept to those who, like myself, have been educated in a manner that states that a thesis must be complete. In yogic philosophy nothing is ever finished. No body of work is so comprehensive, no idea so singularly relevant, that it upends every other philosophy. Continuity—not completion—is key.

In *The Great Transformation*, Karen Armstrong writes, "The visionary truth of the Rig Veda stole up on the audience, who listened carefully to the hidden significance of the paradoxes and the strange riddling allusions of the hymns, which yoked together things that seemed to be entirely unrelated. As they listened, they felt in touch with the mysterious potency that held the world together." Holding the world of India together was upheaval, in the forms of rigorous village debates and attacks of nature by way of monsoons and floods, all of which informed their spirituality. Like the later code of Japanese samurais, Indian warriors became enlightened through dying a violent death. This is not a correlation to the current (and false) meaning of jihad—a word that originally denoted an inner alchemy, not a fundamentalist payback. Soldiers did not necessarily *want* to die; that idea would go against everything biology has taught us. It was just that if they did happen to come to such a fate while in service to Indra, there would be a place for them in the afterlife. We have to speculate if this was the actual feeling of the warrior, or merely advertised by their superiors as part of the job.

As the *Brahmanas* began to be crafted and circulated, some semblance of what we associate with yoga today was birthed. During the period between 900 and 800 BCE, the notion of ahimsa took valid currency. It was also then that certain rituals which had been confined to the Brahmans were being utilized by the lower castes. The practice of purification by fire did not need a seasonal declaration or temple; it could be done in the middle of your living room. Seemingly small acts like these segued into becoming what we now consider to be the greatest asset of yoga: the ability to transform yourself by concentrated mental effort. This is not to say that sages had not come to similar conclusions before this time. But this was a social trigger that allowed everyone to attain higher states of being during the formation of these templates of yoga theory.

I do not mean to sound like these times "were meant to" evolve to yoga. Chronology certainly has its important points; I find the steps by which yogic ideology became my personal path to be absolutely fascinating. I cannot even guess what yoga will look like 500 or even 5,000 years from now. Very likely scribes mentally typing on internal computers which can instantly email all their associates will regard the year 2008 as a "step" toward becoming what they are. That is part of the process of evolution. If there was one essential quality to yoga, then and now, it will remain as such for time immemorial: the continual development and refining of presence.

This refinement occurred when the gods were taken out of the sky and put into our hearts through personal and communal ritual. With an entire culture empowered by the ability to conduct daily rites, there was no need for the divine to be removed from everyday existence. To connect with this inspired source inside, aspirants would conduct the "three breaths," a harbinger to pranayama. Mantra chanting grew from this practice, where the devotee would repeatedly sound the names of divine figures and ideas, consciously putting themselves into hypnotic states that *were* the gods themselves. That's right: Just as the sound of words was divine, so now through breath and chant could the yogi attain similar status. Throughout the past of every religion, east and west, the words "breath" and "spirit" have been synonymous. It is our immediate and continual connection to the world we share.

We may have left Shiva, but he did not leave us. The

blue-skin deity was never an actual man who walked around conducting orgies and drinking poison. He was never a man at all; he was created as half the equation of Shiva/Shakti, the dual male/female pair who represented the totality of the universe. Everything masculine needs its feminine counterpart. The reason Shiva was so flexible and diverse is because human beings are flexible and diverse, when not diseased with fundamentalist ideologies. The gods were meant to be nothing other than our internal states of perception and emotion. When read (or heard) to be actual persons, the symbolism is lost. The importance of ritual evolving to inclusion in the homes of everyone canceled out this false notion that a "chosen" race (or caste) could study and partake in religion. Like any other culture promoting those ideas, it is a bastardization of the teachings if they are used to keep the elite, elite. The power of Shiva and all other gods—and even God—arises when the concept is digested inside of your own heart and mind, when you are able to act as they do and not just say what they may have said.

The yogis devised simple practices, like chanting OM, the *bija* (seed) mantra that is thought to express the entirety of language. When chanted, OM allows yogis to mimic the supposed tone of the cosmos, an idea that would influence Pythagoras when he returned from his studies with Indian mystics to create his "Music of the Spheres." The figure OM represents the four states of consciousness one can attain: *jagrata*, waking; *svapna*, dreaming; *susupti*, dreamless sleep; and *turiya*, which transcended them all and cannot be expressed in words. It is represented in the OM figure by the empty space at the upper right corner, and in mantra by the silence that follows the sound. Within the cessation of sound and thought lives the divine, and to tap into it is to recognize that short space between inhaling and exhaling each breath. The cultivation of breath retention is an important aspect of meditative practice, as it promotes this state.

These gradual and not-so-subtle practices and symbols deepened with the spreading of sacred texts, such as the *Upanishads*, a numerous collection of texts that translates as "to sit down near to." Each story revealed knowledge as if one were sitting next to a master storyteller. To comprehend the inner meaning of these tales took a certain suspension of disbelief. Not that anything contained within them was unbelievable; what needed to be relinquished was the purely rational, logical form of thinking that continues to dominate educational systems. The balance between the forces that Kurma kicked up takes an extreme devotion to discipline. The states of being the yogi sought were not unlike a deep sleep, which was not a forgetting but rather a reminder of the possibilities of unified consciousness, in which the practitioner and the divine were merged and shared within every breath. Death, the state of being that was once honored through physical violence on the battlefield, was now another aspect of the process of living that could be insinuated by way of deep meditation. To tap into the creative and dark energy that is death is to be enlightened, for the knowledge that death is not to be feared is the greatest a yogi can realize. If one no longer fears death, only then can one live fully.

It is here that the system we know of today as yoga began to emerge, some 2,400 years after the salt-heavy funeral of proto-Shiva. Anyone who's ever read Patanjali's *Yoga Sutras*, a collection of two hundred aphorisms considered to be the original "yoga textbook," knows the intensity of philosophy involved. It is part of the Samkhya tradition, a word that means "discrimination," one which greatly influenced the practice of jnana yoga. Here a system was developed that led a full mental assault on the mind, the sort of paradox India is so revered for: the mind is the carrier of thoughts, and thus it would essentially be attacking itself. By turning the mind back onto the mind, liberation could be achieved—which is probably why one of the translations of this process is "blowing out." Samkhya recognized the universe as run by two distinct ideas: *purusha*, which was pure intelligence and infinite consciousness, and *prakrti*, which are the innumerable manifestations of purusha.

Purusha, like the Tao, cannot be named or even be discussed. As soon as you offer a definition, you've missed the point. There were three states (*gunas*) one could exist within: *sattvic*, *rajasic* and *tamasic*. Only when an individual resided in the sattvic state, which took plenty of purifying, could they hope to join the ranks of the *jivanmukti*, "one liberated while alive." Every individual is involved with *chittam*, considered the first manifestation of prakrti. Divided into two categories—cosmic and individual—it is the personal chittam that each yogi has to transform during her life through a series of intense austerities, or tapas. "Indeed, tapas may well be the oldest element of Yoga," writes Georg Feuerstein in *The Essence of Yoga*, connecting it with earlier Vedic sacrificial rites. Today this idea is common in asana classes, where various *kriya* techniques such as "breath of fire" are thought to "burn away" chittam, or past karmas. In the Samkhya system, this could also be done by pure and focused concentration known as *ekagrata*.

"Not only does a yogin suppress evil tendencies; he understands them and burns them totally. Otherwise they may shoot forth again if he postpones their complete destruction," writes Ramamurti S. Mishra in *The Textbook of Yoga Psychology*. Early yogic techniques were intensely therapeutic and mindfully detailed. One did not do a few postures and then assume he or she was "freed." Liberation has never been a state one thinks one is in. If it is a debate, it has not happened. While there is a progression of states one exists within, this does not mean there is a strict linearity. Here we get to some of the most complicated ideas of this philosophy, for they undermine everything we've been taught in a Judeo-Christian culture, including Mishra's usage of the word "evil," which would not have denoted something so much sadistic or malicious, as it would ignorant.

Our languaging often limits us. Words *are* philosophies. How we use and express them dictates how we experience the world and each other, not to mention ourselves. This, more than any external deity, is the force that yogis rein in. Even though all prakrti are forms of purusha, this does not mean purusha "created" prakrti. As Armstrong writes, "Yogins did not believe that they were touched by a god; there was nothing supernatural about these experiences. Samkhya, after all, was *an atheistic creed* [emphasis mine] and had no interest in *devas*. Yogins were convinced that they were simply developing the natural capacity of the human person."

Both Samkhya and yoga were concerned with a full understanding of the individual; with his or her place in the universe; with the universe's place within our bodies, thoughts and emotions. There was no separation of forms in the comprehension of life-as-process, which would make any form of divinity unnecessary—we were part of it, it was part of us. Since purusha is both eternal and unspeakable, and beyond the realm of ordinary speech, why bother discussing it? Words would never drive into the core. This is akin to the famous dictum of a circle whose center is everywhere and nowhere. Much better to focus on what can be transfigured and mutated, purified and refined: the self. By coming into the knowledge of this, the Self is realized. The fragments between the individual and cosmos are dissolved; every external act has an internal correlation, and vice-versa. We physically manifest the external world through the direction of thoughts, words and deeds. The process is one.

To be clear, Samkhya was not yoga, but heavily influential to its development. For centuries they ran side by side, two of the six orthodox philosophical schools in India. Patanjali would not script his *Sutras* until the second century BCE, so we still have four hundred years of exploration to go. Both of these traditions grew out of the Vedantic schools, the oldest "revealed" scriptures of the culture. As we have mentioned of older Indian spiritual quests, knowledge of the Vedas was controlled by the Brahmanic caste. As Samkhya and Yoga philosophies evolved and offered techniques to everyone willing to undergo the disciplines, they were woven into one another, especially by the words of Patanjali. Yet at the outset Samkhya was again atheistic, as practitioners felt the polytheism of older scriptures was distracting. Then and now, yoga continues to, at least on the surface, display theistic tendencies, relying on the idea of many gods involved in the eternal pantheon. It takes the yogi time to move beyond the external referencing of these gods and understand their internal meaning.

In either case, both systems offered aspirants liberation by their own willingness. The path to get there may have been slightly different; what glued them together is karma.

Derived from the word karman, which means "action," the
concept of karma has become a ubiquitous and at times
meaningless coinage. You hear statements like "Oh, it's your
karma that caused that" and "Karma is going to get you," as if
a philosophical idea about the energetic nature of existence can
be a dastardly boogeyman waiting underneath your bed—or
worse, a judgmental God peering down from the heavens with
thunderbolts and bibles. From the ultimate to the mundane,
cheery batistas write "Tipping is good for your karma" on
jars in hopes of simultaneously arousing some inner guilt and
alleviation—a very Christian thing to do.

The seed for each future action is embedded in every
action. This is part of the Indian theory of time, which, as noted,
is not linear. The world was never "created" in the sense of some
all-powerful deity winding its springs and letting it rip. Motion
was always in movement, and there are different chapters of the
same story that sometimes overlap. Karma is this overlapping,
but it is not something that judges the tale. This is why the yin
and yang sides of the famous Taoist symbol each contain a
section of the other—a little white in the black, and vice-versa—
as well as why the totality of life as displayed in that symbol is
contained within a circle, and not a straight line or box. Take a
look at a Christian timeline and it starts somewhere, and ends
somewhere else. Never mind that none of us has ever seen the
beginning of that line, nor can we prove an ending is imminent.
Yogis are not concerned with what could be or could have been.
They are concerned with what is.

As previously noted, early theories of time were built on
the cycles of nature. During the agricultural cycle we witness
two major occurrences: the recycling of the seasons and the
codependency of all living things. The soil does not "create"
crops. It is a matter of seed being dropped from living plants,
which are needful of soil, water and sunlight. There is no one
thing that decides whether or not a plant can grow. The forces
are woven symmetrically, which is why no Indian god is ever
really "better" than any other; they all share roles and duties.
Such is the case with our lives, reflective of the seasons that
ebb and flow year after year. As the practice of ahimsa took

root and spread widely, people realized that harming someone now would create harm upon their own person at some point, in this life or the next. If all things grew and died and were recycled, then it must be the same for human beings, giving rise to the concept of reincarnation. To think otherwise would be to extricate our species from the rest of the world—which is *actually* what other religious traditions were beginning to do with desert exoduses and declarative deities.

According to Georg Feuerstein in *The Yoga Tradition*, earlier proponents of Samkhya considered there to be an "essential identity between the individual or empirical self, called *budhyamana* or *jiva*, and the universal Self, called *buddha* or *atman*." Yogis saw a rift between the transcendental Self and the numerous layers of ego that the individual could exist within. This rift continues to this day, where yogis meditate on the chakras in an attempt of raising the internal kundalini above the *sahasrara*, or crown, seated just above the top of the head. When this energy is raised—the chakra system serving as a symbolic guide to accessing various emotional and mental states—the "blowing out" occurs, and any trace of dualism that exists in the mind dissolves. The codependency of the universe—where everything weaves in and out of each other and no one thing creates the other, but all constantly create everything—is realized. The individual self is recognized as part of this continual process of life, and fear of death or suffering is absolved, for they too play necessary roles in this mythology. While the path to achieve this state is long and arduous, filled with uncertainty, confusion and strong-willed discipline, the yogi eventually understands she was "there" all along; it was an inner fine-tuning that was needed. As the old Buddhist maxim goes: after you cross the river, leave the boat behind.

All life, therefore, is *lila*, part of the cosmic "play" being orchestrated by no one, yet experienced by everyone. Even being ignorant of the play is part of the unscripted script. No image has come to define this game more than Natraj, a variation of Shiva in his incarnation as Lord of Dancers (also known as King of Actors). During his dance, Natraj harnesses and releases five qualities: evolution, preservation, destruction, illusion and salvation. When considering this theory in terms of actual, physical actions, he is responsible for these, among other innumerable facets of existence: the death and life of soil, the destructive monsoons and life-giving waters, the perpetual Ferris wheel of souls incarnating in human bodies. Indeed, every act of dissolution and emergence can be considered the work of Natraj, for he is not so much a "he" as the full embodiment of the natural forces of life and death. And he does not decimate and build kingdoms or continents alone. As A.K. Coomaraswamy noted in *The Dance of Siva*, he destroys "not merely the heavens and earth at the close of a world-cycle, but the fetters that bind each separate soul." When hindrances and chains in our personal lives are overcome, that too is an act of Natraj's dance. The beauty of this performance is that it can happen at any time, for anyone willing to step onto the floor.

The main fetter that stops people from dancing is ego. This is one of the most common insights known to us, yet the usurping of said ego is the most challenging task imaginable, and why yoga is considered a serious undertaking. The fight begins with the very languaging: "Oh, there goes my ego again," as if it is separate from the "I" that referred to it. When we consider the ego to be removed from ourselves, we offer our minds the opportunity to believe that *it is* separate from us, and therefore we can pretend that it is not affecting us. The link between yoga and atheism which we've been slowly uncovering resides in this very instrument, one which battles itself without even knowing who it is fighting, or what winning even entails. To continue this story, we need to look at the hero.

Joseph Campbell's entire career was a lesson in circularity. His first major work (he had co-written two other books by this time), *The Hero With A Thousand Faces*, was published to critical, yet not popular acclaim in 1949. He spent the next thirty-eight years defining the role of the hero in numerous contexts, until the posthumous publication of *The Power of Myth* in 1988. It seems unfair that Campbell would not live to see the legacy he would leave behind. While revered and respected by those who knew his work, the term "hero" and the field of comparative mythology would not hold the general public's gaze until mere months after his death.

In *Hero* he investigated the recurring motifs of the hero, found in an individual raised in a society or culture that had some form of deficit—be it spiritual, social, physical, or any combination thereof. In each scenario something was amiss. There was an unnecessary war, or the citizenry had strayed too far from the ethical norms and needed to be readjusted, fine-tuned. The hero steps in. He or she could be a local doctor who helped mend the fabric of a small village, or someone who would come to enjoy worldwide status as a physician of the soul, such as Buddha, Jesus or Mohammed. By wrestling with their own inner turmoil and battling wily and slippery demons, the hero returned from his journey with medicine, most often in the form of a story or scripture, one which healed those who heard it.

This is basic knowledge: Leaders don't teach through demands, but by behavior. If you want to show someone how to live an upstanding existence, live that way yourself. Talking about how one should live and then exhibiting different manners is not fooling anyone. The hero is the one who fully embodies their inner state so that no separation between what he thinks and who he is exists. Anything other would be a neurosis—to say one thing, and act in a completely other manner. It is not surprising that yoga has become so popular in America, where the idea that the hero is always someone higher (economically, socially, spiritually) is predominant. But instead of embodying the hero, we have contrived hero worship, which in the past was known as idolatry.

The hero myth displays certain basic patterns, regardless of where it was conceived. As Campbell points out, "If one or another of the basic elements of the archetypal pattern is omitted from a given fairy tale, legend, ritual, or myth, it is bound to be somehow or other implied." He goes on to state that by finding the omission of other patterns, you are given an insight into what that culture or time is lacking. Without irony, this sort of *negative theology*—to figure out what is going on by inspecting what is not—is part and parcel of yogic philosophy. Campbell knew this quite well. His Indian journals were published posthumously as *Basksheesh & Brahman*, and he held a long fascination with Indian iconography and philosophy.

When discussing the ego, it is oftentimes negatively, as if it were only something to battle and overcome. As mentioned when discussing the mind turning back upon the mind during meditation, so it is with the ego: It is the very instrument that defines the journey we are to take as we aspire to fully working with it. I prefer to use this terminology—working *with* it—because, again, to say it needs to be defeated or usurped is to imply that it is a foreign invader attacking from without. How much better it is to work *with* rather than *against* something that is, essentially, us.

In his mind-dizzying survey of existence, *The Origins and History of Consciousness*, Erich Neumann, a celebrated student of Carl Jung, uses the image of the uroboros (the mythological snake that devours its own tail) to discuss the stages an individual takes to becoming conscious. Starting with the gestation period inside the womb, and using the image of the Great Mother side-by-side with an individual woman, he states that it is the development of the ego that comes to define who we are as people. Within this development one begins the hero journey. To view the ego as an external evil that should have "never been there" is to miss one of the most primary points of yoga: to deal with what is, not what should or could be. By embodying this idea, what "is" and what "could be" again become merged in an internal and emotional alchemy. Interestingly, Neumann writes that, "Man's task in the world is to remember with his conscious mind what was knowledge before the advent of consciousness." This statement reminds one of Plato, who wrote, "Searching and learning are, as a whole, recollection."

This is no easy task. Our first inclination is to say that it defies linearity, but that too implies that chronological time is the only direction in which time can move. Remember, we're dealing with philosophical systems that were developed alongside natural theologies, prior to the advent of Judeo-

Christian influence. What does "natural" imply, though? How is any religion or belief unnatural if it is the product of the human mind? The differences are in custom and ritual. Later religions relegated their rites to churches, mosques and temples, while our first connections to the world were with the world itself, not constructions of it. Our architecture speaks much about the frame of mind of the builders. It seems rather impractical and unnecessary to build closed-ceiling artifices to worship the sky, when a simple walk outside would be a lot more "natural."

How does one acquire this knowledge before knowledge began? Such an undertaking requires working within the realm of the archetype, and involves "losing" the ego which we have taken a lifetime to create. When the dissolution of the ego is described in yoga or Buddhism, the translation is thus: To dispel any thoughts or ideas that may lead to the conclusion that you, as an individual, are separate from the rest of the universe. What this means is that all of your actions affect yourself, as well as everyone else, equally. To do violence to another is to do so to your self; the spreading of compassion offers like results. Better to develop the latter if you hope to live an equanimous existence. Each individual act leaves a form of karmic residue behind. Yoga offers techniques for ridding yourself of undesirable traces, those which stop the ego from recognizing its true, original nature—one that is a part of, and not separate from, everything else.

In his classic book *The Wisdom of Insecurity*, philosopher Alan Watts discusses how anxiety, so often declared as something to be destroyed, is also a tool that helped early man learn how to survive in the wilderness. Our selective fitness would have adopted behavioral methods conducive to securing shelter and protection from the elements, and from other animals. The energy developed (including anxiety) was a form of tension that helped us evolve. The body does not always differentiate between good and bad stress; people cry when overjoyed, and can suffer panic attacks when completely calm. Like all other emotional responses, it is in first the understanding, and then the balancing of them, that we glean what can prove crucial in the long journey on the path of self-realization.

Yet people feel victimized instead of responsible for what their life has become. Even disdainful acts, such as robbery and bigotry, exhibit karmic traces. While you may feel yourself to be the unwarranted recipient of a ghastly joke, there is always another form of psychology available for adoption. As Watts writes, "The difference between 'I' and 'me' is largely an illusion of memory. In truth, 'I' is of the same nature as 'me.' It is part of our whole being, just as the head is part of the body. But if this is not realized, 'I' and 'me,' the head and the body, will feel at odds with each other. 'I,' not understanding that it too is part of the stream of change, will try to make sense of the world and experience by attempting to *fix* it."

It was Siddhartha Gautama, that inspired Indian sage, who remarked that there is nothing broke, so nothing to fix. Of course, to reach this realization he had embarked on one of the most famous folklores in history. When his time came about, the religionists of India were seeking an ideal that, as Karen Armstrong writes, "was no longer merely to refrain from violence, but to cultivate a tenderness and sympathy that had no bounds." Watts, one of the foremost scholars of Japanese and Chinese spirituality, always reminded listeners during lectures that when Buddha stated that all life was suffering (dukkha), that did not mean that we were "meant" to suffer. (Notice the implication in the language of there being a predestined plan for us.) As we recall, dukkha is suffering created by the human mind. And if the mind created it, just as the mind creates God, so it is entirely possible to uncreate the illusion.

It seems a truism that once a religion is indoctrinated, it stagnates. Our understanding of modern religion is based on both a response to a pre-existing one, as well as a comparison with others. The schools of Samkhya and Yoga developed and merged when a stifling Brahman caste and their violent tendencies were too much to bear, a move that subsequently took power away from their gods and into the citizen's own hands. Buddhism later responded to the overbearing scholars of these two systems, which were involved in self-defeating feats of unnecessary physical and mental strength instead of appealing to a broad population. Gautama knew these practices well; he studied in Vaishali with two expert yogis, Alara Kalama and Uddalaka Ramaputta. While he learned much, he felt that there was not enough penetration into the psychology of the aspirant. To engage in pranayama and meditation would calm the seeker only while engaged in the actual practice (although the knowledge acquired in such a state could be transferred when out of it). Yet the Buddha had no interest in quick fixes. He was after something that would sustain him for life, which he found in the transformation of his total consciousness through a moral and psychological outlook which seeped into every facet of his existence. This is true of the devoted yogi as well.

Totem worship can be dangerous; biblical prophets raged against idolatry. There is good reason why. There are two famous images of Gautama lasting to this day: the serene, poised monk seated in lotus posture, and the jolly fellow holding his belly while laughing. Because the latter is the predominant imagery, we expect that this was how he always was. After enlightenment he probably did maintain composed states indefinitely. Yet there was a lot of work to get to that point, and this did not stop him from being forceful and demanding of his pupils. He warned them that nirvana, or "blowing out," would not be instantaneous but rather, slow and arduous. The folk stories involving him being seated under the bhodi tree and becoming enlightened in one evening are an accelerated recapitulation of what took years to accomplish. Even after attaining such a level of consciousness, the work did not stop. His discipline would only have become harsher, and there are texts that reveal him to be both impatient with students and demanding of crowds.

When he did feel himself to have reached samadhi, Gautama did his best not to become dogmatic. Because his path took one form, it almost certainly meant that a student would take another. He could draw a blueprint, but the building of consciousness would have to be erected within the hearts and minds of each seeker. Most importantly, he would lead students away from unnecessary questions, such as "Does God exist?" Abstractions would be of no use; he was pointing them deeply and intensely inside of their own experiences of life, not of anyone else's. Surely people would combat his outlook, but as

Armstrong wrote, "his rejection of God or gods was calm and measured. He simply put them peacefully out of his mind. To inveigh vehemently against these beliefs would have been an unskillful assertion of ego."

While the dating of Buddha's life is uncertain (estimates range from 566-350 BCE, not quite an accurate degree), Indian history does become more reliable around this time. Early Buddhists were meticulous with their papyrus. Thus, much of what we know of this era, at least in written form, comes from journals and scriptures. That Buddhism would not take root as a national spirituality is indicative of Indian history, which for the most part was an oral culture anyway. In one of the more interesting social parallels, numerous versions of one of India's greats of literature, the *Ramayana*, appeared over the course of centuries. When today we read these massive texts and decode their symbolic structure, we are often awed by the detail and significance of how the people interacted politically and culturally. As is always the case with history, it is important to know who was, and is, telling it, for when uncovering an artifact thousands of years old, we cannot simply assume we know the context in which it was written. Writers today have agendas; we should think no less of those who birthed us.

The Vedas are the oldest known writings in the Indian canon. The word *veda* means "knowledge," and these texts are considered to have been revealed truths from gods, not devised or tainted by the human mind. This was a romantic claim at best, since gods, from what we understand of them, do not have need for books. The next two major works followed much later. Both the *Mahabharata* and the *Ramayana* are epic tales continually referred to by students of modern Indian spirituality. While these are indeed classics, an important point is raised by John Keay which I have not heard examined by yoga teachers who constantly cite them: "Basically the Vedas and the epics portray the concerns, and celebrate the exploits, of a society consisting almost entirely of well-born clansmen."

The same concern arises when people talk about the equality of "every man" in the Constitution, written during a period when Africans, women and most anyone of non-

European descent were not considered people. This does not detract from the important teachings embedded within these rich texts. Their messages shine through regardless, and have been applicable ever since. If they did not reveal information that could be utilized by future generations, they would have been left behind. What is important to remember, however—something we will return to when discussing the Bible—is that picking-and-choosing passages without regard for the totality of the work is self-defeating, and dishonest. "Legitimising monarchial rule, in India as in south-east Asia, was the *Ramayana*'s prime function," Keay continues. One cannot pretend that the foundation of many scriptures does not display similar intent. Then as now, politicians understand the importance of doctrine in maintaining power, and the means by which they take to stay in control are not necessarily pleasant, or immediately comprehensible.

We do not need to have been around in the time of the *Ramayana* to instinctually grasp its political undertones, or how this work of literature would have affected general society. We are living it now. This is where the essence of mythology resides—in its ability to be relevant thousands of years removed, in nations undreamed and far away. For mythology introduces us to the universality of the human condition, and reveals how the patterns of yesterday become the habits of tomorrow. Existing in a time and culture that is determined to speed itself through inordinate amounts of cycles in one lifetime, we forget that evolution is a slow process, primarily uncaring of our desires. So when the current political administration wages war on Muslim countries by using God as a rallying cry and as an essential point of reference for our righteousness, we are witnessing the same style of human thinking that would have led scribes of old to immortalize leaders and their mindsets. Their karma is being worked out through ours.

Subsequent additions to the term karma appear in the *Bhagavad Gita*, a small chapter of the *Mahabharata* which has been adopted by yogis as a primary source, due to its universal appeal and the friendliness between the formerly stiff lord Krishna and the famed archer Arjuna. The *Gita* lists three types of karma: *sattvika-karman*, an action performed without care of outcome; *rajasa-karman*, actions performed for the result of pleasure; and *tamasa-karman*, any action done with absolutely no moral or ethical regard. Krishna instructs Arjuna in the highest idea, karma yoga, which is an ethical lifestyle in which everything one does is an act of devotion, with no regard for the fruits of success. This notion has come to define the "goal" of yoga, in that it is ideal to live every moment as an act of sacrifice for a greater good.

This is, however, only a template. Eventually "good" and "bad," as well as having any "goals" whatsoever, disappear. To do yoga for a particular reason is missing the primary point of being able to live simply for life itself. We will see in the closing chapter that this does not mean that life is meaningless—quite the contrary. But we do have to reflect on the idea that "what you do comes back to you," for while this is but an underlying theme, the phrasing makes it sounds deterministic, and even pessimistic—more like a fairy tale, where life is as we fantasize it to be even though our demands may prove impossible, than a mythology, where life is as it is and we adjust ourselves according to the nature of it. When you are able to exist every moment with a heightened sense of presence, and that moment alone represents the total focus of your attention, you are able to suspend the moment, and hence any action involved within that moment. Since enlightenment is often idolized in the image of various figures in seated meditation, we forget that to be enlightened is not something that only occurs while still and in silence. It is a continual state of being that demands as much discipline as any other form of employment. Being suspended in such a state, there is no longer any actor separate from the action. The process is being processed as one continuous moment, not comprised of numerous separate entities that happen to share space at that particular junction. The entire world can be observed when the individual is present within himself. It is a state where one no longer seeks more of anything, and can remain calm and focused even when the direst state of chaos surrounds him.

This is where the ego dissolves, as it were. When you

consider yourself removed from the events around you, your actions will continue to accrue karma, be they positive or negative. To paraphrase from the Buddhist tradition, when one becomes as an observer observing the observed, there is no more accrual of karma, for the yogi has nothing for it to "stick" to. Accrual can happen mentally (*samskara*) or physically, manifesting in the form of sickness, disease or muscular tightness, stopping the proper flow of *prana* to and from vital organs. One of the genius aspects of yoga is that while some things are rooted out, the spirituality is never removed from the body. Even if the hundreds of asanas we practice now were not part of the early yogi's daily routine, they were still physically active. They understood that thoughts have effects on the body, and movements affect emotions, all in an intricate and complex system that defines who we are. Purifying tapas were practiced to cleanse the body, thoughts and emotions, as they are all aspects of being, namely, human.

Through tapas, pranayama, meditation, and behavior one could surpass the three states of karma (sancita, prarabhda and vartamana), which represent respectively, the karmic seeds waiting to fruit, that which has come to fruition in this lifetime, and that which is to come in future lives. This brings us to one of the most intriguing nuances of Indian philosophy: reincarnation. We are exploring a culture that knew both the hunting-gathering lifestyle, as well as intensive forms of agriculture. Their gods, like the Mesopotamians, ruled the cycle of seasons. Destructive tendencies were paralleled in failed crops, and any abundance was homage to fertility. This was the psychology of the culture. It only makes sense that when Arjuna was understandably vexed over the prospect of killing his cousins and friends in an unjust war, Krishna would reply, "As a man abandons worn-out clothes and acquires new ones, so when the body is worn out a new one is acquired by the Self, who lives within." That is, after all, what the harvested foods that nourished them—who they were—did.

The alternate idea to this form of thinking dominates modern life, that of humans being created and placed inside of an already functional world. This is more a psychosis than an actuality. We are part of the process of nature. Today our sciences and technologies, as our mythologies did in the past, are accentuating the experience of life through story. Myths were past attempts of "figuring us out." Biology, chemistry, and physics are no different. That the double helix and caduceus of old is now a DNA strand is just another parallel we've drawn. It does not detract from the magic of our lives, especially if we treat terms like "mysticism" as the natural manifestation of unrestricted human potential and not as an abstract hypothesis of impossibilities. At the same time, by exploring the physical similarities common to all humans—by realizing that everyone goes through physical, mental, and emotional challenges that are not different then our own—we lessen our demands of others in adopting specific belief systems and lifestyles. Just because the town preacher screams false righteousness from the pulpit about our hometown being an Edenic paradise, in which life there is exactly what the entire world should mimic, we do not have to fall for the claims.

Falling for it is, arguably, part of our karma, since that idea encompasses every action made. This is not a negative idea, however. As Mircea Eliade wrote, "Universal suffering has a positive, stimulating value." The more one suffers, the more freedom is desired. Each of us has expectations based on past experiences, and when what we want to happen does not, or when something completely unexpected befalls us, our reaction is that of having a sense of gravity weighing down on us, oppressing us with pessimistic thoughts and broken hearts. When Gautama set out on the road to Magadha to take the vows of renunciation, he was certain that something beyond suffering existed. Little did he know it would bring about a preeminent change in psychology and not merely the conscious hardships endured by twiggy men holding their arms above their heads for twelve years until the muscles atrophy in supposed devotion to the divine. As Eliade also remarked, "Suffering is universal; if man knows how to go about emancipating himself from it, it is not final." After his enlightenment, the Buddha spent the remainder of his days teaching the same message: Your karma can be absolved. You can be liberated from the bondages created by the mind.

This too is the yogi's intention. While Gautama may not have practiced the asanas common to us, or chanted Sanskrit hymns, he used the sheer strength and integrity of his being to overcome any disparities from past karmas. Upon "arriving" at his liberation, he understood that no other human could achieve such a state by doing exactly what he did. They would have to follow their own path, as they had their particular karmas to absolve. There were techniques available to everyone, though, that could be applied to every situation, and by adhering to them, the individual would be acting in accordance with universal truisms that led away from suffering, and toward union. They are not painstakingly detailed like the ethical, dietary, and emotional demands made by many religions. Gautama never planned on Buddhism being a religion at all, and was simply creating a field book to help others on their journey. Later commentators would develop exceedingly intricate and unnecessarily extravagant lists of precepts. This would not have pleased the Buddha, who was content with the universality of the ideas behind his Noble Eightfold Path, namely: right view, right intention, right speech, right action, right livelihood, right effort, right mindfulness and right concentration. What "right" meant continues to be debated until this day, but for men like Gautama, the answer cannot be put to paper—the definition appears through that challenging balance between discipline and instinct, and cannot be predetermined until one experiences the moment itself. This is the integrity of cultivating presence. What we can be certain of is that compassion must play the central role in each of these eight actions. By following that one principle, the "rightness" of each thought and deed becomes clear.

That the Buddha's legacy did not uproot and remix Indian culture in the manner that it would in countries north of the Himalayas is par for the course with the constant social and spiritual maneuvering of the country in which he was born. As Keay notes, "In the history of what used to be called 'medieval' India, the key words are 'fragmentation' and 'regionalisation.'" Unlike most countries or regions in which one king, president or governing body controlled the land, taxes, and theologies of that area, very few rulers held power over any large tract of land, or for too long a duration. This made the implementation of one specific ideology difficult. It is basic knowledge in America that to be president you must be of some form of Christian background. The nuances of religious belief may shift from person to person, but the overriding and underlying theme has been the same since this country was "founded." Not the case in India. Until the British conquest in the latter part of the eighteenth century, there was no sense of an actual national identity. Even today, since the Partition in 1947 (and the subsequent Partition of Muslim-ruled Pakistan in 1971), that phrase is undefined in many respects. The term Hinduism applies more to foreign understanding of their identity than to internal certainty.

Even if Gautama's legend would not leave the imprint in India that it would in China and Japan, the very principle he rigorously espoused has common ilk at home: neti-neti, "not this, not that." This idea can be clearly seen through the lineage of Shiva, especially when ol' blue skin's union with the god Rudra in the third century BCE merged the Samkhya ideas with the yoga practice in very interesting ways. In this manner, an atheistic school integrated gods as symbolic representations of inner states exhibited in the human being. This practice continues today, where Sri Natraj is the most ubiquitous motif in American yoga studios. This particular form of Shiva does not appear until the tenth century CE in Tamil, however, nearly thirteen hundred years after the aforementioned fusion, and nearly four thousand after his prototype was crafted. Still, the underlying principle was always intact: to go beyond the boundaries of dualistic thinking, to contemplate the universe and our role within it as one continuous process, free of the psychology that stamps labels of righteousness and defilement on everything. "The specific identity of the Lord in question," writes Armstrong, "was less important than the fact that he had become accessible in meditation. The yogin knew that this god existed, not because of a set of metaphysical proofs, but because he had seen him."

This form of seeing is an insight received in meditation, or contemplation. Shiva's mythos encompasses the total possible situations an individual can encounter in life. What has both frightened and endeared him to devotees is that he can easily choose any route offered, many times choosing the warpath of destruction. This is part of the cosmic lila that is his dance floor. One day Shiva visited a group of sages in their forest huts, who proved ignorant of his true identity. They cursed him, first with a hungry tiger. Shiva skinned the cat alive and wrapped the skin around his midsection. Next came Naga, a giant serpent. Again, he rebuked their petty attempts at harm by wrapping the snake around his neck as an adornment. Last came a vicious dwarf, which Shiva stepped on. That dwarf is symbolic of the ignorance of these hermits in not recognizing the deity in his full splendor. When you see an image of Natraj on that little man, he is stepping on Muyalaka, ignorance, or to put it another way, squelching the forces that stop an individual from reaching liberation.

In his upper right hand, Natraj wields a *damaru*, the drum that represents time and creation. Infuriated by the boisterous hermit sages, he began a cosmic rhythm that destroyed everything. In his left hand flames arise, symbolic of both destruction and creation. All the gods from on high came to watch the display known as Tandava, Natraj's dance. Essentially this is the same thing the Buddha experienced underneath the bhodi tree. To create an enlightened being out of yourself, the ignorance inside of you must be destroyed. Every stitch of clothing and adornment on Natraj are keys egging the yogi on toward understanding the nature of the universe, one that exists beyond the boundaries of good and evil. Duality, that strange fruit a woman named Eve tasted in another garden mythology, is the disease that keeps each of us from comprehending our true nature, one that is balanced between benign and sinister forces. Shiva, through numerous incarnations and various guises in the however many thousand years since his prototype was carved, has maintained his secret wisdom through a yoga as evolutionary as the technologies of each time could devise. Today he continues his cosmic dance a half-world away, and the message—that the universe is a balance of good and evil forces that are both necessary for the dance to continue—remains the same.

CHAPTER 5

THE FIFTIETH SECOND COMING

One of the biggest frustrations that author Sam Harris faced after the publication of his first book, *The End of Faith: Religion, Terror and the Future of Reason*, was his immediate association with a collective known as the New Atheists. Time and again Harris points out that he did not mention atheism once in his book, to no avail. He has continued educating the public as to the inherent danger of the very word—how it is self-defeating to the growing community of people who do not have faith, at least as we understand it in the religious sense. The following point, offered during a lecture at the Atheist Alliance in September 2007, is a summation: "Atheism, I would argue, is not a thing. It is not a philosophy, just as 'non-racism' is not one. Atheism is not a worldview—and yet most people imagine it to be one and attack it as such. We who do not believe in God are collaborating in this misunderstanding by consenting to be named and by even naming ourselves."

His plea is not without reason. A self-proclaimed non-partisan group called the Discovery Institute has been pushing Intelligent Design into public schools through an initiative they call "academic freedom." Their basic platform is that evolution is but one concept, and children should be offered alternatives. They pimp textbooks by authors who do not identify their work as creationist in an effort to avoid any messy political situations. (The mere mention of creationism will most often be thrown out of court immediately.) By engaging with scientists and creating debates where none existed, organizations like Discovery are giving the public the appearance of there *actually being* a debate. Crafty maneuvering. Under scientific scrutiny these claims stand no chance, which is why they appeal first to the public-at-large, where science legalese does not hold stock. They are basically engaging in maya—the illusion—knowingly, and milking the cow for all it's worth. In fact, it would not be a stretch to say that they are willfully creating the illusion for their own gain. The danger, of course, is that people are buying into their supposed controversy.

Harris has also argued that a danger with the term atheism is that there is no name for people who do not believe in other things, such as unicorns, werewolves or Republicans. Nor is there any proof that the Flying Spaghetti Monster does not exist—in the same way that those who employ reductionistic means state that there's no way to prove that God does not exist. Harris shows how you can essentially argue this point with *anything*, and that arguing that God does not exist because you cannot prove it is frivolous. His underlying creed in *The End of Faith* is condensed when he writes, "If religion addresses a genuine sphere of understanding and human necessity, then it should be susceptible to *progress*; its doctrines should become more useful, rather than less."

Many decades prior, mythologist Joseph Campbell addressed the same issue. He felt it necessary for religion to evolve with every generation, to keep up with the mindset of technology and society. A religion that fails to do this prevents the people who adhere to it from moving forward, culturally, mentally and emotionally. While the foundational ethics of an elder religion can be applied to modern times, to put forth strict observations of traditions thousands of years old is implausible, especially—and this is where Harris, and authors like Richard

Dawkins and Christopher Hitchens derive their strongest points—when the totality of those passages is not respected. The picking and choosing of certain scriptures, conveniently molded when fitting into the curious agendas of religious groups, is what proves most unnerving.

When you step back from a tradition and see how it interacts within the general sphere of society, and is not bound to the beliefs that a particular figure is identified as being The One, unfortunate contradictions are blatant—and we are not discussing the paradoxical play that gods like Shiva partake in, either. There's a world of difference between dancing among the sides of duality in an effort to become enlightened versus being stuck in an arrogant display of supposed religiosity. The three major monotheistic traditions all derive from the same root—Abraham—and two of them share the same book, while the third pays respect to that book, but think they have a better one. The two that share one book have divided it into halves (well, the second religion did; the first has no need of the second half), continually picking and choosing what fits their itinerary from those divided sections. The whole ordeal is an infinite regression where no peace will be known, for it is not in the nature of debate to know calm. This is nothing new to these religions; it has been part and parcel of the package since inception.

We will peer back at some very important developments in this triad in a moment, so we can trace the origins of our modern friction. The following story is much more recent. The 2007 documentary, *Jesus Camp*, is an insightful and frightening gaze into the Kids on Fire summer camp in Devil's Lake, North Dakota. Led by Evangelical pastor Becky Fischer, the film hit home for me just how far away from reality we allow our beliefs to lead us. As much as I'd like to think this is an isolated case that just happened to make it onto screen, the sad truth is that it is this exact thinking that underlies and informs a good deal of American religion. It is a simple example of allowing that deceptive state of mind—avidya—to shadow the light that has been revealed.

One of the film's main characters is twelve-year-old

Levi, a boy who claims he was "saved" by Christ at age five because life wasn't offering him anything substantial, and he was craving more. Quite an example, certainly, of where Becky Fisher's personal crusade of enticing children into the faith derives: "They are so *usable* in Christianity." Levi's case is not surprising in the Evangelical camp—forty-three percent claim to have been saved before age thirteen. Evangelicals make up a quarter of America's Christian population—roughly eighty million people. Throughout the documentary many incredible claims are made, such as one man's rant against abortion, where he alleges that one-third of the children's friends were not here tonight because they were murdered by their parents. How, exactly, a person who was never born could have been present in the first place deserves a leap of faith, and these believers take plenty. When Fisher is not telling the children to never make "heroes out of warlocks," for if Harry Potter was around during the days of the Old Testament "he would have been put to death," she's praying over microphones and Powerpoint presentations in an effort to dissuade the devil from performing the mischief he loves to do during sermons. For her to denounce J.K. Rowling for supposed pagan worship and then perform the exact same form of idolatry is astonishing. Yet nothing is as disturbing as what follows.

Like many children of fundamentalist families, Levi is home-schooled, predominantly as a response to the public educational system not teaching "alternative" sciences like Intelligent Design. Mothers take the duty into their own hands: Seventy-five percent of home-schooled children in the United States are Evangelical. While sitting at the dining room table reading from the "textbook" *Exploring Creation With Physical Science*, his mother presents Levi with a question: "One popular thing to do in American politics is to note that the summers in the United States over the past few years have been very warm. As a result, global warming must be real. What's wrong with this reasoning?" Without irony, she does not inflect the final line with the toning of a question, but rather as a command, which would more appropriately require a period instead of a question mark. Humor me. Levi's response: "It's only gone up .06 degrees." Mother: "Yeah, it's not really a big problem, is it?" Levi: "No. I don't think that it's going to hurt us." Mother: "It's a huge political issue, global warming, that's why it's important for you to understand…" Levi: "Is evolution too?" Mother: Stutters. "Not really, so much." Levi: "Creationism?" Mother: "It's becoming one now. What if you had to go to a school where they said creationism is *stupid*, and you're *stupid* if you believe in it?" Levi: "Uh…" Mother: "Or what if you had to go to a school where they said evolution is stupid, and you're stupid if you believe in it?" Levi: "I wouldn't mind that." Mother: "If you look at creationism, you realize it's the only possible answer to all the questions." A moment later she asks if he had come across the part where the textbook states that science "doesn't really prove anything. It's really interesting when you look at it that way."

Interesting? Keeping your children at home to "teach" them principles like this is damaging the integrity of people who devote their lives to making sense of the environmental disasters currently at hand. Removing yourself from the world with the belief that Jesus, or any such prophet or god you may believe in, will make everything all right is taking the very idea of personal responsibility and throwing it out the window. At the present moment we have serious issues to contemplate and, more importantly, take action upon, for if there cannot be a global religion now, we will certainly form one when serious dangers (and not the literary threats of past writers) are raging war *on us*. We've done an exceptionally good job at killing one another for tens of thousands of years. I do not propose that this will end anytime soon, but one thing is certain: It would be a shame for us to awaken to this fact when we're all scrambling from situations that are truly beyond our control, like the sun spraying cancerous fireballs or oceans filling into the gaps of subway stations and streets. Global warming and other environmental topics are issues that these groups claim they need to see to believe, yet their entire belief system is built upon something they will never, and can never see.

Many religious people have a better grasp of the symbolism, rather than the literalism, of their tradition's teachings. As evidenced in this documentary, or by the onslaught of feel-happy drivel guaranteeing a return of the savior in book and CD form, Fisher's sermons are *exactly* the psychology dominating public policies and philosophy in America—the idea that something is going to come and make everything perfect. It is not a huge leap to understand how this carrot in front of the horse's mouth inconspicuously blends into the education system and corporate office, where students and workers receive constant promises about the "next big thing" that will happen to them. The staircase, however, never stops. This form of thinking, and lifestyle, promotes two mental/emotional states. First, complacency. If Jesus is coming, why should I worry about anything? He's going to arrive soon, kill all sinners and remove every last Internet pornography site. Second, it downplays personal and social responsibility. No note is taken on filling up the SUV with extra octane; it's OK, Jesus rides a chariot of fire. In the same breath, it promotes the idea that someone else is going to fix things, be it the government, the town church, or whoever else can repair what I cannot. Another disturbing scene during *Jesus Camp* is when one unnamed woman brings out a life-sized cardboard cutout of George Bush and commands the children to bow to it while speaking in tongues. This is a great example of how we pass our personal failures on to the nation-at-large, as well as the figurehead sitting atop the throne. If this isn't false idolatry, I don't know what is.

I completely understand the argument that some will make—that many religious leaders have good intentions and focus on creating positive change in their community. But I pose this question: Are they promoting change for the benefit of humanity and the planet, or to promote their own brand of godliness? Important distinction. If one has to pray that others of foreign skin and tongue will one day "come around" to the fact that Jesus is the savior, or that Allah is the most holy, and so on, are you really hoping for a better existence? Or are you simply praying that once everyone becomes like you, you will no longer feel threatened by everything and can live happily ever (and often forever) after?

I have stated that the largest danger of belief is that it removes you from experiencing life in its full and rich complexity. When the opportunity of experiencing life in its total and complete oneness is taken away, life is a series of events unfolding into ideas that never actually manifest, and why we feel disconnected from everything around us. We will look more closely at the psychological strains this sort of thinking places on the individual later. For the time being, let's return to the foundation and implication of atheism by taking a look at how this non-believing belief became forever indoctrinated as the antithesis of everything that should be, simply because it offered the possibility of what actually is.

It has been argued that when humanity lost contact with ritual, the violence associated with war became more prominent in our psyche. Displacement is certainly possible, though remember our rituals were also violent, inspiring those in Vedic India to turn ceremony inside out. Violence has never *not* been a part of our kind, be it against neighbors, other species or the environment, not to mention our bodies and minds. Deity worship throughout the ages has revolved around death and murder, the underworld and resurrection. Practices that did not focus on a godhead (Buddhism, Taoism and certain branches of yoga) are rare in that they did not include violent competition in their daily life. (Although the Buddha did perform great violence upon himself, in the forms of fasting and body mutilation, during his quest. He would later renounce those as unnecessary.) In Buddhist literature you never hear of meditation as a tool for conquest, or how to properly assimilate a foreign culture into your social expansions. Just like when asked about the existence of God, the Buddha would most likely have deferred your question as irrelevant—if you were asking about the ultimate nature of things, that is. Forms are not essence, even if they do reflect it. The three monotheistic religions that have come to dominate us very much concern themselves with violence. If a percentage of their prophets and adherents have promoted ahimsa in some regard, the reality of their missions and explorations have accomplished anything but.

Religions have produced a cornucopia of beautiful relics, from paintings and literature to churches and philosophy. In whatever form it has taken over the millennia, religion has comforted and assured individuals and their communities that everything is going to be all right, even when it's not. This is where complaints regarding religion stem from: it conjures false hope. To the faithful, that sentiment sounds pessimistic. Yet it was such knowledge that Buddhists and Samkyha philosophers recognized to be an escape from dealing with issues at hand. To contemplate future gods and heavens is to run away from the moment. To wish for something that may very well never be is to fall victim to disappointed expectations. If you are hoping for something and it does not occur, the undisciplined mind will blame the external world instead of its own expectations. This is nothing new. Numerous wars and conquests have been waged over that very idea. In fact, we are living through one at the moment, put forth by a very old battle caused by a triangle of bruised egos and vain demands for power and resources.

While the origins of Islam were not, as so often supposed today, violent in nature, the pacification and overthrow of various governments in India and the Middle East often resulted in skirmishes and battle. Yet we have no right to judge the Muslim world because various stages have exhibited hostile ambitions—this is a crime every nation has been (and many remain) guilty of. Islamic culture, while ready from the moment of inception to spread their religious creed, was not inherently barbaric—reactionary, to some extent, but rulers did not live by the sword as much as by their word. Many adhered to Mohammed's pledge of peaceful negotiations (as long as it was not threatening to Islam), one that he exercised when signing the Treaty of Hudaybiyya, allowing Muslims to journey to Mecca without warfare. For centuries after, even upon overtaking foreign territories, Muslim leaders did not force conversion on their subordinates. Their Christian counterparts, on the other hand, were much more vindictive. Throughout different centuries and leaders both of these faiths had their own insecurities, dealing as much with politics and land as with faith. Yet today we regard Islam as savage on so many levels, which is unfortunate, and unwarranted. While fundamentalist groups do clutter the American-focused media, the rituals and pledges of the religion are beautiful and have left behind a brilliant legacy of writing, music and art. The roots of our misunderstandings, however, are not surprising. As Karen Armstrong points out in *Holy War*, the Christian view of the Muslim world began with "a crooked mirror image of Western deep-rooted feelings of inferiority and a projection of Western envy."

We generally view life as two separate processes. The first is personal and immediate, where we live for daily wages and nutrition, shelter and family. We become accustomed to routine and follow it through until we either find another, or it evolves into something else, or we change the routine entirely. It is the daily grind, the hustle—how we make our careers and homes and, essentially, define ourselves. The second is the "grand scale." For many, gods and religion fall into this category. There is some cosmic story that happened or will happen, and we are merely biding time until it manifests. When a religion remains separate from daily life in such a manner, we feel disempowered, and allow the workings of the universe to continue with their own regard, leaving us to worry only about the tasks at hand. We may have some small weekly service, maybe even scant opportunities to integrate a few lessons of our religion into our day-to-day, but for the most part a separation exists between the cosmic and the community.

It's hard to decipher when this trend took over, for it may have always been the case. From whatever artifacts we have of ancient civilizations, it does seem clear that religious life was central to the workings of society. How deeply it affected each man and woman we can never truly know. The educated minority who left behind traces, of course, would cause us to assume religion was *extremely* relevant. Priests and rabbis claim the same today, though we can plainly see how many people it does *not* affect. What does seem clear, though, is that for centuries gods and goddesses arose, or evolved, in pairs, to complement the dual nature of reality. At times everything was divine, or at least touched by this or that spirit. Very often the substance itself—rock, soil, water, wind—*was* the divinity, not a product of something else "creating" it. It was not until the advent of the God of scriptures that a definitive rift between mankind and the divinity was so oppressively made public.

While no finger can properly point to one particular movement or man, we do have a story that has helped promote this separation: the mythology of Abraham. Somewhat of a proto-gypsy himself, the man once called Abram most likely led a nomadic life, guiding a small tribe from Mesopotamia toward the Mediterranean. He settled in Canaan with his Hebrew-speaking community, eventually purchasing land in Hebron, now the West Bank in Israel. His pilgrimage was not conducted out of mere curiosity—he was commanded by one of the local gods, Yahweh, to move to Canaan, for he would rule over a nation and his followers would call this land home. The rest, of course, is history: Abraham became the father of not one, but three, religions. While he is normally associated only with Judaism, as different figures came to dominate the landscape of Christianity and Islam, his revelations were what created monotheism as we know and love—or disdain—it today.

The irony, of course, is that Abraham was not monotheistic. He lived and traveled around a pagan world. There were other gods, most notably El, as well as Marduk and Baal. The monotheistic God we associate with these religions would not have been Abraham's. This god was more of a support system, an internal guide who even assumed human form, much the way Krishna appeared to Arjuna in the *Bhagavad Gita*. For a while they had a friendship, until one day Yahweh made a rather unsettling demand of Abraham: He must sacrifice his son Isaac to prove his devotion. This is also not uncommon. As we saw, human sacrifices at the request of gods were part of the process of ensuring healthy crop cycles and fending off droughts. Abraham thought it odd, being that he had received a promise of leading a great nation, that now he had to kill his first-born. Alas, he consented. Until the moment that his knife was unsheathed did this god tell Abraham that he had been, well, pulling his leg. Isaac's name, after all, means "laughing."

Seeing that Abraham would do anything for Yahweh, this deity was certain that this man could lead a nation—an interesting paradox, since as an omnipotent godhead, you would think he would have known if Abraham was the right man for the job in the first place.

In this example we can understand the foolery of Indian and Greek gods, forever stumbling through the constantly shifting universe. They too were subjected to the whims of an unpredictable cosmos. Yet today we no longer treat our gods, more specifically God, as a laughing matter. The very idea is blasphemy. To Abraham and the people of his time, when the gods were part of their daily life and could be persuaded with favors and occasional human meat, it would make sense that they too could joke. Even if the requested sacrifice of Isaac was not a laughing matter, but rather a serious test of one man's devotion, it still shows a manipulative side of a deity who would come to be known as entirely separate from the rest of the world. And if God could partake in human games, then he must have a pretty diverse bag of tricks, which leads us to another aforementioned misperception regarding Islam—spreading religion by the sword.

After the death of their prophet, Muslims went on a public relations campaign as yet unrivaled in the history of the world. They spread their religion quicker than any other faith during a time when Internet connections and airplanes were hundreds of years undreamed. Yes, there was violence and bloodshed—no religion has escaped this, and I'm not arguing that their hands were free of murder. Yet when they attempted to invade India, there was a curious reaction: miscomprehension. As John Keay writes of their task, "The peculiar nature of their mission—to impose a new monotheist orthodoxy by military conquest and political dominion—was so alien to Indian tradition that it went uncomprehended." It is safe to assume that a quest of this nature, put forth at various times by all three monotheistic traditions, received a similar response wherever it went, which inevitably added further fuel to missionary fires.

When you study history with a personal bias toward a particular faith or nation, slanting stories to fit into what you want to believe, two consistent and constant recurrences appear. First, the initiators often have good intentions—most often for their own tribe—and want to witness their divinely inspired messages touching the furthest corners of the planet. Second, these good intentions are subject to whatever form of martial forces exist, as well as the general population (sometimes the two are combined), who translate well-meaning ideas with an indignant righteousness that can be summarized as such: You're either with us, or against us. This demand of the current American administration has been going on for nearly a millennium now, since that auspicious day in 1095 when Pope Urban II launched what would later be known as the Crusades. Be it for a feeling of spiritual validation that your version of a god is righteous or for blatant political positioning of resource and power, the voraciousness of human pride in conquering societies is relentless. We have never known anything else. The promise of land proclaimed by Yahweh to Abraham in Genesis remains a calling card even today as Jews try to retain Israel for themselves, a right they believe is fully indigenous and inherent.

We cannot look at that battle in terms of Judaism and Islam alone, however. I have heard it said that the Jews and Palestinians have always fought, and will always continue to fight, that it's in their blood to do so. But that is not true. The current state of Israel is not the result of a millennium of battles between these two faiths. Just as yoga is not an "ancient practice," the fighting between these religionists is a product of the twentieth century (albeit with deeply embedded roots). These seeds of discontent were not sown by Jews or Muslims; Christians scattered that grain. One of the first biases we are taught in school is that European civilization was the crowning achievement of culture and created most of what today we refer to as modernity. The luxuries and technologies molded and sculpted by their hands are what have given us the world we inhabit. In reality, Arab and African cultures were far superior in craftsmanship, philosophy, medicine, and all other forms of human endeavors we now equate with "primitive" societies. It was this very bias that occurred as the first wave of invaders from Europe entered Arab territory to find developments superior to their own, in technology as well as something which really crawled under their skin: faith. Arab architecture devoted to the cosmic was astounding. Instead of sharing these tributes to the sacred, Christians waged war.

The peasants and knights who went on their first Crusade were not necessarily on a pilgrimage of battle. They truly believed that it was their divine right to return to the land of Jerusalem, the very place where Jesus was crucified and resurrected. Because this Son of God had walked that piece of earth, Christians, his true followers, had every right to claim the property in his name. They saw the Muslims inhabiting it as part of the wave of unrighteousness that had spread since Jesus' death, manifestations of the great evil that it was now a Christian duty to defeat. Given that these pilgrims sincerely believed God intended them to go there and reclaim his land, they did not, at first, expect to have to battle for Jerusalem. They merely expected to arrive and take ownership of it.

Realizing, however, that the journey would require a bit of brawn, ol' Pope Urban changed his game—although, of course, he would have said that God changed it and he was merely conveying this important news. He used a piece of biblical wisdom to his own end, reminding followers that those who left their homes in the name of Jesus would be repaid a hundredfold. This egoistic rendition of karma worked. When he commanded them to bear arms, an act that was previously forbidden in peasant armies, he introduced a physical and psychic violence that remains to this very day. Unfortunately for them, the very first attempt never made it past the Hungarians and Turks. As can be expected, something was amiss in God's plan. Therefore, these first Crusades were renamed the "Peasant's Crusades," because God would have never let his true army be massacred. Church officials and chroniclers disowned the entire spectacle. Soon the plight was redefined by *The Song of Roland*, a ninth century French tale about an attack on Charlemagne. Christian leaders took this as a cue to instill holy virtue in their newfound army, and what would become listed as the official First Crusade commenced.

All along their trail we find instances of pride, most notably upon their arrival in Constantinople when they jealously encountered the much more advanced Greek civilization. This envy, and their leaders' promises about eternal salvation and the glory of God, fueled them into victory at Nicea, boosting their morale after a long and tortuous trip. They pushed on to Antioch. Arriving there in October 1097, they were dumbfounded to find an ancient church dedicated to St. Peter, now serving as a mosque. Their divine mission was once again sparked. They *had* to reclaim this city in the name of the Holy Father. It was here, during the direst of famines, that they deemed themselves the Army of God. The crusaders were kept at bay for nine months, considering it a divine test to see if they could truly persevere. Again they turned to scripture, relating past sufferings to their own, and knowing that only through such suffering could they be liberated—quite a different take than Siddhartha had, yet in some fundamental sense they understood there was a way beyond suffering. Their path, however, was not a withdrawal of the senses in an understanding that everything in the universe is related and balanced. Theirs was one steeped in dualistic ideology: they were righteous and Muslims were evil. Rumors of famine-stricken crusaders eating Muslim flesh in an attempt to survive abound, a tale of cannibalism that would repeat itself throughout the centuries at different times. They were engaged in the ultimate sacrifice and would not be stopped.

There is an important reason why Christian soldiers won the battle of Antioch, beyond the mass hallucination that supposedly occurred when fighters saw visions of angels fighting alongside them, slaying the wicked. It was the same ideology that helped them to attain, however briefly, Jerusalem, and in some ways relates to a Jewish minority governing Arab-dominated Israel today: the tendency of thinking in complete dualism. While this was not part of the gestation story of the Bible, as we will discuss later, the picking and choosing of passages had allowed the faithful to determine war to be a divine decree, and that only by total victory would righteousness prevail. None of the three monotheistic religions would escape this ideology, and many still hold it as true today. What the

Christians had on their side was not ultimate glory, but the ability to be so stubborn that their unity in pride allowed them to conquer a much—and this is where Western history books fail us— gentler Islam.

If a Muslim leader is truly following the dictates of the Koran (and there have been both faithful and treacherous), when a treaty is proposed it should be signed. There is an embedded flexibility to their social relationships. European Christians were not accustomed to anything of the Arab world, be it nutrition, weather, surface conditions, customs or philosophies. It is a very human occurrence that distance allows prejudice to develop. Because their religion "worked" at home, they assumed it would "work" everywhere. Yet apparently it was *not* working. Religion by its very meaning is supposed to "unite" or "bind" together. While it is true that it bound these soldiers on their perilous quest, and that their psychology towards this end helped them win seemingly impossible battles, we have to ask ourselves: If your religion is not binding the entire human race, is it truly working? It was common in prior times that when cultures clashed, the other side was not treated as human. The downtrodden were a bastardization of the species, or a lesser form of it. Muslims were not men and women to the Christians, at least not to popes and politicians, many of whom governed by satellite. What happened next would shock all of Europe and infuriate kings and priests.

When people come together and recognize each other as people, and not merely as mass ideologies, paradigms shift. Fueled by the initial fire of Antioch, Christians killed some 40,000 Muslims in Jerusalem in two days. God's holy war was justified, and from that day onward violence was canonized in the Christian religion. Ironically, many of the pilgrims were worse off in this new land than at home, well before the illusion of a religious motherland (which in many ways was a political maneuver to acquire more territory) governed their psychology. Some left, but those who stayed realized that Muslims were actually human, doing the same things as they: surviving, raising families, being educated, praying, and so on. After the initial shock of conquest wore off and people had to integrate,

Christians began intermarrying and a new culture formed. This scenario is not unique to any single city along the Crusades. The people stirring up reasons for war are rarely pilgrims, those forced to settle into places of discomfort. But when you are in dire straits, castes and classes no longer hold the same degree of meaning. While this settlement worked for these new neighbors, stories of their blasphemy spread around Europe. Those who had never visited the Middle East were horrified, and once again an unholy predicament presented itself. The purity of the crusaders was being tested, and they too had to be liberated.

For the next half-century, with varying success, Europeans set off on annual Crusade. For the Christians, these holy escapades were their *raison d'etre*. To the Muslims, however, it was simply a matter of colonial exploitation. It took them some time, in fact, to even realize that Christians instilled a religious purpose to their attacks. In Islam, characters like Satan existed, but occupied the same part of the cosmic sphere as Natraj in India—he was part of the process, not a definitive evil that only God could dispel. There were no absolutes; Christianity is unique in this vocation. It was not until 1146 that the leader Nur ad-Din began to formulate the idea for what we today know of as a jihad, realizing that for his Arab population to regain its former prominence, such a bout of faith was necessary.

It is crucial to remember that Christians believed themselves to be on a righteous mission. On the flip side, regional natives were so blown asunder by the attacks that religion played less and less of a role in their lives. Their confidence was shot. Early jihads had little to do with religion. The attacked wanted to be respected, to have their land back. The jihad was a defensive, not offensive, maneuver. Today we recognize the word in connection with the events of 9/11, and consider it to be a form of retaliation, one that conveniently allowed the American government an opportunity to strike on the defense. But it was *never* a defensive maneuver, which makes you wonder what the American government's role was in the first place. If it was truly a purely Muslim preemptive strike, then it was by a sect, and not the soul, of the religion. Our media set up a brilliant smokescreen in assuming that Muslims live in an undignified and violent world. They do encounter violence, but seen from a distance we can never know the inner workings of that or any society. Still, the mediaplex in cahoots with the government has assigned the Muslim faith with the archetypal character of Satan. Given the very old roots of this form of thinking, tracing them back is not difficult, except for those still clouded in smoke.

During the Crusades, Muslims transformed from being perceived as inhuman agents of evil to becoming mere tools for the liberation of humanity by Christians—not exactly the best offer of promotions. Like any power trip, once they had control of Jerusalem, the crusaders wanted more, because more never ends. With their enemies pacified, they did the only next step possible. They turned onto themselves. Jerusalem was *the* holy city, so the Christians in Greece must be living blasphemously. The Muslims had become perfect scapegoats for the invaders to work out their violence and sexual repression on, and all other manner of emotional and mental issues. Christian mandates began pouring in, and the inner factions waged verbal warfare with each other regarding who was conveying the "true" messages of God.

Nearly ninety years into the occupation of Jerusalem, the Arab world finally produced a leader courageous enough to organize the right sort of resistance, yet cordial enough to do it without bloodshed or slavery. In 1187, Kurdish political and military leader Saladin entered Jerusalem and reclaimed it for Islam, a move that lasted until the early twentieth century. As soon as the city was secured he stopped any unnecessary killing, and allowed Christians to leave with only a minor tax. He did not, as his adversaries had done, plunder and pillage needlessly. Most unique about this reclaiming was the Jewish immigration into the land after 1187. On their dogmatic warpath, Christians had, not surprisingly, ostracized Jews. They had murdered their savior, and were every bit as despicable as Muslims. When Christians were ousted, Jews felt safe to enter—one of those ironies you can only shake your head at.

Today we assume grudges are long-standing; it is our

nature to believe them to be ordained. Yet even more recent religionists have sought unity first. In the early twentieth century, when Zionists pushed forward into Jerusalem on their "Conquest of Labor," there was little plan for violence. Vienna native Theodor Herzl wrote an enticing treatise entitled *The Jewish State*, calling for his people to have a land of their own. Mere decades before the empowerment of Hitler, growing anti-Semitism sentiments in Europe made men like Herzl wary. In contemplating where this Jewish state would be, his first choice was not Israel, but Uganda, which already had a small and devoted African-Jewish community. Herzl was disappointed by fierce opposition from his colleagues, who seemed hell-bent on Israel. He would die in 1904 at just forty-four, thirteen years before his fellow Zionists secured support from the British to establish a national home in Palestine. A year after the declaration, Jews were outnumbered by Muslim Arabs, 512,000 to 66,000. They were nearly outnumbered by Christian Arabs as well, who were only 5,000 less. Yet their "conquest," when seen in light of the spirit, was not of warfare. The word for labor in Hebrew, *avodah*, also meant religious worship. They arrived in Palestine to reconnect with their agricultural past, tilling soil and planting crops, and to pour their devotion into the actual, and not imagined, land. That fantasy would grow in time. Unfortunately, the mythology of Cain and Abel was always one of betrayal and power, and as the Zionists began to demand political sovereignty, Islam responded. They would not give up the land they had lived on for centuries because of some biblical claims about a man named Abraham owning this territory. They too were promised this earth.

It made sense: Muslims were also a product of the Bible. The revelations of Mohammed were never in contradiction to that book. He was illiterate and only knew the stories by hearsay but nonetheless, from the little he knew, he was able to utilize the spirit of the words in conjunction with his own society's predicament. In reality, his story is so similar to Herzl's that it's shameful that the two "sides" cannot see past their own hubris to understand their commonalities. In the prophet's native Hejaz, tribal warfare was rampant. As brother fought brother, social unity was impossible, keeping them subservient to the more unified forces surrounding them, such as the Persians and Byzantines. Like Abraham, Mohammed had a desert vision, and Allah, the principle deity of the land's pantheon, spoke to him. Instead of pointing to Abraham's legitimate son Isaac, Mohammed found solace in the story of his other offspring, Ishmael, who was born to Hagar, his concubine. Just as the (almost) sacrifice of Isaac secured what would become the Jewish nation, Ishmael and Abraham's building of the Ka'aba, a shrine to Allah, was the seed that eventually sprouted as Islam. After Mohammed's death, his followers, and the Sufi heritage that derived from the Koran, occasionally borrowed stories like this to decorate their mystical tendencies. Of the three Abrahamic religions, however, Islam remains the most pragmatic and functional, as the entire revelation of Mohammed concerned the real and tangible plight of his people to succeed, both politically and socially.

These ideas are tough to wrap our heads around in a country that, first and foremost, has been monotheistic since its European founding, and that today uses jihad—a word that originally meant "struggle" and had nothing to do with war— as a catchphrase to keep suburbanites scared of turbaned men and shopping at malls. I cringe at the oversimplification of that statement, one derived from effectiveness, not falsity. We hope that our religious leaders offer us something of the supernatural, but we must always remember they are flesh and blood as well, subject to the same desires and illusions as the rest of us. And what the above tales remind us is that religious power and political power have never really been separate, even if in America we claim that a separation of church and state exists. On paper they may claim to be apart, but their psychological tendencies and understanding of the world remains married.

Government functions on one basic assumption: the simpler, the better. The stories they concoct to create heinous folklore are astounding. The bottom line remains, though; it is a matter of power. If God is the word that will cause you to submit your beliefs, money and conviction, so be it. If that word were Yahweh, the divine would have a different pedigree today, while retaining its hypnotic power. Over the course of thousands of years a few men and women have devoted their lives to the unity of their communities, to the struggle in overcoming forces natural and social, to stand up for freedom. That *that* valiant effort has been so vainly bastardized is appalling. The reality is that unknowingly many of us remain polytheists—not to external deities, but to our inner, conflicting and transitory emotions. Before getting to that, we need to understand why someone would choose not to believe in God, which turns out to be just as political and reactionary as the reasons others do believe.

R ight around the time when the inner voyagers of India were retranslating physical ritual with a newly minted emotional and psychological alchemy, the great philosophers of Greece were playing table tennis with words in an attempt to become immortal through oration. To the Greeks of antiquity, "ideas" did not have the same connotation as they do to us today. They were "forms" and "essences." Through language, one took part in the same process as life itself—one stunningly similar to the underlying theme of mantra in India. In fact, there are many close parallels between the philosophies of Socrates and Plato to Samhkya and Yoga. Yet before either of these men was contemplating the spheres, men like Anaxagoras were calling the sun "red-hot metal," not the god it was purported to be, and Xenophanes lambasted Pythagoras about his cosmic philosophies, to bring him back to the earth with his fellow man. Anaximander created the first map of the planet, and even postulated the first known theory of evolution, stating that our ancestors resembled fish and that we grew from marine life.

Democritus, a contemporary of Socrates, wrote an essay entitled "Concerning the Gods," in which he admitted that he could not discover any firm basis for whether or not the gods of the Greek pantheon actually existed—an agnostic view more than atheistic, certainly, but still an early criticism during a time when famed gods ruled Olympus. Critics prior to the Common

Era ranged from making nonchalant theatrical asides to full-blown assaults on theology, as well as inciting an intellectual movement that cost Socrates, for one, his life. Charged with blasphemy for denying the existence of the gods (though his more obscene crime was questioning democracy), he was forced to commit suicide by drinking hemlock. The very word atheist is derived from this time period, when the term *atheistos* meant "one who denies the traditional religion of the Athenian establishment." To this day atheism remains a response to some form of accepted theology, very often entwined with the political climate of the culture. That is certainly true of today's movement in America, even though, as psychologist Steven Pinker remarked, atheism "is defined by negation—an unwillingness to swallow certain beliefs about the supernatural—and has no content on its own."

After the death of Socrates, critics continued their political/religious writings and lectures against governing bodies. For the Greeks, language was the closest that one could come to divinity. In the same vein as the effervescent strains of mantra yoga, debate and the written word were the very connections to something "beyond," which, depending on with whom you talked could mean "within." While contemplating a military problem, Socrates is reported to have stood motionless for an entire night while pondering—a form of silent meditation that resonates with the jnana yogi. His greatest student, Plato, also utilized language in an effort to reach higher states of consciousness. Of his inquisitive nature, Karen Armstrong writes, "We moderns experience thinking as something that we *do*. But Plato envisaged it as something that happened to the mind: the objects of thought were living realities in the *psyche* of the person who learned to see them." This would hold true in many of these philosophers' views of what, exactly, the gods represented: embodiments of ideas as witnessed through the process of being human. When regarded in such light, gods were progressive and emotional forces that could alter our experience of reality, thereby altering reality itself. When removed from the internal structure of man and kept locked in shrines and books, these forces no longer had any power, because they were idolized. The idea of atheism was created *against* a ruling body that insisted the gods or God are inaccessible except to the privileged, broadcast by those whom happen to be so.

Much of European (and subsequently American) culture built its foundation upon the knowledge and philosophies of early Greece. Of course, it is always a matter of picking and choosing, for the theories of their most renowned thinkers remain discussed, though rarely implemented. Democracy, which "began" in Greece (forms of it existed in India centuries prior), is the style of governance we currently practice in America. Today, as then, many remain skeptical that it works for the benefit of the broader population, not to mention the individual who seeks freedom. That the same underlying themes of today's war in Iraq, as well as our tendency to cater to the upper economic class, traces nearly two-and-a-half millenniums back is testament to the Greek notion of time, which, again like the Indian, is circular. As historian Norman Cantor wrote, "While many Greeks ... thought that history moved in circles, repeating itself infinitely, the Jewish idea that each event was singular and proceeded along a straight line had a great impact on European thinking." This new psychology—linearity over circularity in our understanding of time—is a major reason we lost the magic in our lives. Living became something that began and ended with no thread tying birth and death together, and thus the supposed overseer of the process became a judge, instead of being part of the process. This is the misfortune of monotheism.

In his book *The Twilight of Atheism*, Alister McGrath considers modern atheism to have emerged in France during the Revolution of 1789. At that time there were three estates in which the general population could exist within—essentially a caste system based on economics. The first contained the aristocracy; the second, the clergy; and finally, the middle class. (Like many countries at that or any time, members of the lower class were simply disregarded as people.) The churches focused on the two top estates, either ignoring or denouncing the third. This paved the way for atheism, which, as McGrath points out, is not so much a declaration that God does not exist as it is a rebellion from the popular notions of God. If the ruling classes wax poetic about the divine and are also in control of all the resources, there's little surprise that the masses would be disillusioned. As he writes about France's neighbors, regarding the emergence of atheistic thought, "The English experience suggested that nobody really doubted the existence of God until theologians tried to prove it. The very modest success of these proofs led many to wonder if God's existence was quite as self-evident as they had once thought."

Whereas McGrath, a professor of historical theology at Oxford (and former-atheist-turned-Christian-scholar), feels that atheism has seen its heyday and is heading through the out door, I cannot agree. He does an excellent job of elucidating the past few centuries of atheistic thought in America and Europe, and concludes by stating that fundamentalists, especially those bound by political motives, and *not* necessarily everyday religionists, are to blame for the negative associations with theology which arise in its wake. "When religion starts getting ideas about power, atheism soars in its appeal." How he fails to realize that current religious figures are still engaged in the same power struggles as centuries ago is unnerving. Unfortunately his summation is victimized by the same linear idealism that Cantor mentions, and while he is hopeful that modernity will produce a more flexible Christianity, I find his optimism hard to share. It's easy to pretend that the home team is going to win. If atheism is a response to unstable and unfair politicking, and further meshed with the disguise of religious symbolism, then there will always be pundits ready for battle. While the shadow of belief does not have to be disbelief or outright dismissal, there is a certain level of discrimination that rationality provides against the dangers of blind faith. Although we've seen that, in many ages, notions of divinity are essentially beyond language and understanding, flatly stating that it must mean it represents *this* or *that* is not going to help create a broader understanding of what it takes to build a sustainable human community.

This conundrum strikes the heart of one of the most disturbing phenomena of modern belief, and is where atheists get fodder for their philosophy. The Gnostics may have entertained visions of aliens implanting God into our stratosphere, but the lengths we've gone to in our imagining of the cosmic drama are quite frightening. The following example is a recent example of Pope Urban's mass illusion planted and grown on American soil. *The Book of Mormon*, a supposed translation of "ancient gold tablets" excavated in upstate New York by Mormon founder Joseph Smith in the 1820s, is seeing a print run of 15,000 copies—*a day*. In this epic battle between the Lamanites and the Nephites, Jesus is, of course, resurrected ... in the Americas. In fact, the man was reincarnated here specifically to set up his church over one thousand years *prior* to Columbus' landing, which is rather odd considering that no Native American folk tales offer prostrations to this heroic Son of God. In Smith's book, this very soil is obviously the top choice of all lands in the world. And undoubtedly, when Christ returns for a third visit, he will do so in the *exact* location of the *original* Eden discussed in the Bible: Independence, Missouri. From there he is to lead the next chapter of humanity in a crusade of righteousness as lord of ... Jackson County, Missouri. Smith, while held in a makeshift jail by dozens of pissed off Christians before being murdered, had claimed that Jesus was coming before the end of the century—1900, that is. To this day his followers still believe that heaps of gold await them in the Dream Mine in Utah, to be discovered when God is ready to make his final move. There are currently over one hundred million copies of his book in print.

When I hear arguments claiming that the details of these works are irrelevant—that what matters most is a sense of socially embodying Jesus's message, and not the rhetoric espoused by believers—I recall these stories. In fact, I have heard them with my own ears on numerous occasions. For years during my studies at Rutgers University I worked as a monitor at Robert Wood Johnson University Hospital, making sure suicidal patients did not try to escape, or repeat what had landed them in the ward in the first place. From these usually depressed and lonely souls—for these conditions were much more prevalent than actual mental disease—I heard tales of alien gods and modern prophecies. They too were keepers of the Word of God, and I have absolutely no doubt that they fully believed every word they spoke. Some orated with such conviction that, had they been adorned in a black robe instead of a white gown with blue flowers, they very well could have inspired hundreds, thousands, tens of thousands to believe along with them. They were eloquent, poised and rational. They retold fables and folklore with stunning accuracy. And, time and again, I came to realize that what they wanted was not God or some fatal apocalypse to wipe unrighteousness from the face of the earth, but ears to listen to the words their hearts were trying to speak. Life had, in some way, not lived up to their expectations, and instead of questioning their own behaviors and thoughts they looked outward for signs of salvation. In the process, they extricated themselves from society—be it through drugs, alcohol, gambling or good ol' depression, until they were so utterly alone that the only place they could turn to was purely of their own imagination. They borrowed the symbols of the religions they knew and practiced and bent them to fit into the shape of their own life. I also have no doubt that in their version of the story, Jesus would return to New Brunswick, New Jersey, to set up his kingdom within the borders of Middlesex County.

A few hundred years is not a long time in the scope of human evolution in particular, not to mention the overall evolution of the world. To think our more recent ancestors would not have suffered similar bouts of loneliness and miscomprehension would be to overlook an important aspect of the human psyche. We really don't change as much as we think, which led Indian sages to consider the idea of reincarnation: how the spirit of humans, and not the physical body, repeats itself over and over until we consciously make a decision to evolve. In this philosophy is an openness to the rhythm of the world around us, while the above mentioned—from the Crusades to the suicidal—are focused on one particular form of the world. They convince themselves that this form is the end-all of the essence, and tune out or deny that other forms could have relevance.

This is not comprehension of a symbol. It's a perversion. As Sam Harris points out, "The danger of religious faith is that it allows otherwise normal human beings to reap the fruits of madness and consider them *holy*." Certainly many of the supposedly ecstatic conditions described in prior times would today be diagnosed psychiatrically: hallucinations, multiple personalities, hearing voices in the dark, seeing apparitions and people forming out of inanimate objects. This is what spurred Benny Shanon, a professor of cognitive psychology at Jerusalem's Hebrew University, to conclude that there is a great possibility that Moses was drunken on the hallucinogenic acacia tree during his revelations. His 2008 article in the philosophy journal *Time and Mind* related his mind-bending experiences with ayahuasca to the religious icon's insights into the nature of existence. This does not deny any correlation with the "mystical" experiences that are possible when an overwrought nervous system deals with shifts of perspective, lucidly described here by Gopi Krishna, a man who, upon raising kundalini during meditation, suffered from many years of a near-fatal illness: "Like the vast majority of men interested in Yoga I had no idea that a system designed to develop the latent possibilities and nobler qualities in man could be fraught with such danger at times as to destroy the sanity or crush life out of one by the sheer weight of entirely foreign and uncontrollable conditions of the mind." That yoga is advertised today as blissful, peaceful and exotic is unnerving when reading such passages. Yet it also brings into question the psychological nature of the "religious" experience. Can we prove that Krishna was touched by divinity any more than Joseph Smith or crusaders blessed by sword-yielding angels? No. But we can judge them by what they did *after* acquiring knowledge during the experience.

I am not trying to dissuade mystics. There are many occurrences unexplained in this world, and the overly confident bravado of rationalists also misconstrues important aspects of existence. The major difference between Krishna's experience and that of fundamentalist-oriented religionists is that his occurred during meditation and brought him, after some time, into a state of equanimity and compassion, two highly sattvic qualities which are not constricted by either side of a dualistic perspective. He then became a spiritual counselor and lecturer, promoting an open-minded understanding of the tricky balance of forces in this world, not to mention pushing for a life of compassion to all beings. When dealing with ego-laden issues, however—as with Smith and others—the visions promote one or another side of the total process, which makes it more of a declaration than a true insight. In the same way that Christians, Jews, and Muslims considered battle victories to be symbolic proofs from their respective takes on the same God that they were righteous, losses suffered on the other side were to be considered as clear indications that God had ordained these too as stepping stones toward eventual victory. In this constant battling of egos there will be no peace. Nothing propels the vindictive spirit like a damaged ego. Nothing pushes forth humans to the brink of death like fear of humiliation. Centuries after Buddha gave a clear prescription for humility and Taoists used, literally, toilet humor to stop adherents from overthinking the nature of existence, the tri-fold group of monotheistic clans were doing anything but turning the other cheek. If the experience cannot be integrated into a sustainable, universal theory, then it was not effective on the individual who had the experience.

It is not hard to see how disempowering this is, or how dangerous it makes one who thinks they are divinely ordained. Tyrannical dictators and modern presidents truly feel that they are being called by a higher power to install their particular brand of government around the world. The actuality of such installations is not divine, but egomaniacal, regardless of whether a few friends surrounding you pat you on the back and smile. This is what we see in our major newspapers watching the American administration crowded together proclaiming why the war in Iraq is a necessary step for worldwide democracy, even if it was one of the major reasons our economy plunged and thousands of families lost soldiers to the ides of battle. This is a real-time example of what, in historical terms, seems to happen instantly because we jot a few years down on a textbook page and the event appears to have been so clean-cut. The effects of any war are never immediate. To get an indication of how it happens *as it happens*, how a government slowly crumbles and stumbles until its power is so weak that something else wipes it up, we only have to gaze around us this very day. It's always harder to see when stuck in the middle again.

I wish I could pretend this commentary *only* pertains to our administration's bloodthirsty reign in the Middle East. The problem is that a government is only as powerful as its citizenry allows it to be, and by the looks of it, our mental health is not well. If it were only our president using the totemism of the Christian God as an invitation to spread a very specific form of democracy, then the crisis of forced globalization could be held in check. Yet it's the breadth of the population that's buying into his crusade that's truly disturbing, all the while using, as history dictates and warns us against, God as justification for our exploits. We can discuss this on grand scales, like wars, or we can look a little closer and investigate how our everyday education leads us to accepting the microcosm for the macrocosmic truth. When we approach it in this manner, we realize there is no one to blame but ourselves.

With all the wonderful technologies and scientific breakthroughs of the past century, the actuality of a Golden Age is realizable now more than ever. The notion that ancestors had "the life," when in actuality they survived with less shelter, food, healthcare and protection, is small-minded. An entire world to be explored and experienced, through our media and vast transportation networks, lies at our fingertips. Yet only thirty percent of Americans, a people endowed with privileged tourist access to almost anywhere on the planet, have passports. Just as we assign our children with a religion without ever asking their permission, we raise them on a travel itinerary that includes Disneyworld and the Mall of America—not to mention lower Manhattan, to witness firsthand the dangers of Islam upon this Christian land. No wonder we confuse myth for mythology.

Most frustrating in this compounding of misperception is the Intelligent Design movement, an initiative that received verbal support from George Bush in 2005 when he announced that it should be offered as an "alternative" approach to science education (read: evolution) in classrooms. Never mind that we are still using history textbooks that claim Columbus "discovered" America, a myth propagated by adults who really should know better. No job is worth lying to children. The underlying premise of ID is that a God created everything perfectly as it is, in order that humans may serve him. To be fair, there is a certain flexibility depending on whom you talk to. Some proponents give credence to evolution, although, of course, humans were not the result of mushroom-chomping chimpanzees (if you would have asked Terrence McKenna), but rather specially placed here with the molded clay of God's hands. The deeper you travel into Middle America, the more baffling the definition becomes. Certain segments of the ID clan go so far to say that the earth really began with Adam and Eve, is only a few thousand years old, and that things like dinosaur bones were "planted" here by God in another act of tomfoolery akin to Abraham's test of Isaac. Or even worse, those very dinosaurs were in the garden with Adam and Eve and died out quickly to make more room for humans. If we "believe" that dinosaurs existed before Eden hundreds of millions of years ago, then we have fallen for His trick and are not truly righteous. Sadly, these forms of "education" are actually working, as Daniel Dennett suggests in *Breaking the Spell*: "According to a recent survey, only about a quarter of the population of the United States understands that evolution is about as well established as the fact that water is H20."

I find it more than ironic that the Intelligent Design Network's website boldly claims that "certain features of the universe and of living things are best explained by an intelligent cause rather than an undirected process such as natural selection," when that statement is about as undirected as imaginable. Natural selection is anything but misdirected. Evolution is so easy to understand, on some fundamental levels, that fellow scientists shook their head in dismay at the simplicity of Darwin's theory when he put it forward. Natural selection implies that the features of an organism best suited for the environment in which they live will survive, while what is superfluous will fade out. This can be actual physical components of a species, or the species itself. That latter fact is what troubles humans, who like to believe we are the crowning achievement of God's master plan. This is the motivating factor behind the massive PR campaign that fundamentalists put forth in their dogmatically disguised sciences. The notion that *we* are transitory is ungodly. In the same breath, the political incentive backing their rampant media is easy to grasp. As Leonard Susskind, professor of theoretical physics at Stanford, wrote, "A well-respected scientific community can be a major inconvenience if one is trying to ignore global warming, or build unworkable missile-defense systems, or construct multibillion-dollar lasers in the unlikely hope of initiating practicable nuclear fusion." So the advertisements of such a god, or intelligent designer, are two-tiered: A government installs a system by which its people feel entirely subservient and safe with whatever knowledge is put forth through their media in order to capitalize on their own interests, and as a sign of good faith to their kindness, North Dakota housewives teach their children that Jesus is a-knockin' and Al Gore is the devil.

And it is exactly the media, in whatever form the current technology has allowed, that helped create such visions of divinity in modern America. Whereas once the fairy tales of bards and regional folk stories about evil spirits would have sufficed, today it is the visual spread of virtual culture keeping us spiritually affixed. The Christian climb and climax has been a long road indeed. In 1797 our government signed a treaty with Tripoli (modern day Libya), declaring that the United States was in no way founded upon the Christian religion. Nearly a century later, the Supreme Court declared we were fully a Christian nation. This flip-flopping is not surprising, given the constant political seesawing between who we want to appease and when. Thomas Jefferson certainly had his own say on the future of the country, when in 1804 he cut-and-pasted four different bibles into his own "relevant" Testament of Christian faith called *The Philosophy of Jesus of Nazareth*. (Nearly two decades later he would trim it down as *The Life and Morals of Jesus of Nazareth*.) At the time, Jesus was not the central focus in churches, and Jefferson felt the man's image needed a little pre-Botox facelift. His country did not have the religious roots that we claim today. Many first-wave immigrants were fleeing political persecution that was under disguise of religion in the first place, and had too much to worry about in the tilling of soil to focus on the supernatural. It wasn't until the early nineteenth century that religion really took off. In the period between 1800 and 1850, Catholicism went from a small membership of 50,000 to one million. Methodist congregations grew from 65 in 1776 to 13,280 in 1850. Other factions grew at similar rates, keeping time with the movement from an agrarian society to one in the boom of the age of industry.

"In what was quickly becoming a market-driven society," writes Stephen Prothero in *American Jesus*, "preachers in the early nineteenth century were forced to compete for souls not only with other preachers but also with secular pleasures of the camp and the city. In this way, preachers entered the world of entertainment, tailoring their performances to not only the eternal truths of the Bible but also the shifting desires of a fickle public." Religionists became increasingly aware that to keep church membership up (and tax-free status legitimate), they too would have to evolve—in a directed manner, of course. Responding to a 1906 essay by William James, which called men to wage something heroic instead of war, Washington Gladden and Walter Rauschenbusch founded a social order dubbed Kingdom of God, one focused on the mythic figure of Jesus. We can only guess where the current Army of God had their influence—probably, as the Kingdom of God did, from mythic tales of the Knights Templar and other crusaders. Around this time preachers everywhere were defining and redefining Jesus to fit their needs, crafting his image in the range of anything from an untouchable and ultimately holy Son of God to your best friend, always at hand. At times, Jesus could be the rebellious spirit battling pagan spirits and prideful governments, while at others he was the pacifist par excellence. That is, he was shapeshifted into as many entities as Shiva, flexible for the moment and comfortable within the seeming paradoxes of existence.

Two efforts solidified Jesus as a celebrity, fully fusing the entertainment and media worlds which religion was trying to conquer. In 1925-6, Bruce Barton's *The Man Nobody Knows:*

A Discovery of the Real Jesus topped bestsellers lists, making
the Jesus icon accessible in an increasingly capitalistic and
corporate environment. The book was concerned as much with
the politicking of business as with the religiosity of this prodigal
son. With Jesus selling oodles of books—a trend that continues
today—an obscure graphic designer named Warner Sallman
forever changed the trajectory of Christ in 1940 when painting
his opus, *Head of Christ*. The image remains the most widely
used interpretation of Jesus, donning millions of prayer cards, t-
shirts, buttons, plaques, and websites to date. Sallman continued
to paint hundreds of very Eurocentric versions of the Christ
figure throughout his life. This is a big part of what has afforded
twenty-first century Americans the bigotry of what is known as
the "White Jesus," a physical impossibility already cited in the
Bible when proclaiming to make no graven images of the divine.
If Jesus truly were the Son of God, himself at least part (if not
fully) holy, then the creation of his image would be considered
blasphemous. On top of that, his complexion was certainly not
ivory-cheeked. This is just one of many contradictions which
remain both overlooked and unaddressed.

Yet Jesus, as God, remains extremely pliable, which
is a major critique by atheist and skeptic camps—as well as
individuals who take advantage of things like common sense
in their sensibilities. It is rather difficult to make a claim about
an eternal, all-powerful and -knowing cosmic force that is
essentially unknowable, when that very theory is at the whim
of popular opinion or your mood that day. Now the same
technologies that helped blast the white Jesus across the world are
being used to promote ID and its lackluster textbook, designed
for adolescents and teens, *Of Pandas and People*. Using verbal
cues from biology and anthropology, the writers bend integrity
to match the platform of their peers. As evolutionary biologist
Jerry A. Coyne summarizes, "ID is simply biblical creationism
updated and disguised to sneak evangelical Christianity past
the First Amendment and open the classroom door to Jesus."
Again, the thought is painful. Tens of thousands of Americans
are risking their life every day trying to secure oil pipelines
for a few men who, at most, do an annual PR campaign to the

desert and talk about how righteous they are from the safety of their ranches. Their version of the numinous is self-serving in every facet. How anyone would fall for a God so brazenly being touted as the ruler of the American people is beyond any comprehension whatsoever.

Plenty of people have stopped falling, however. Sociologist Phil Zuckerman points out that many people who do not believe in God also do not resonate with the term "atheist." Translations of the divinities mean various things to various societies. He points out in a detailed study that this unnamed group of nonbelievers can be considered the fourth largest collective in the world, behind Christians, Muslims and Hindus. By his estimates, there are between 500 and 750 million people falling into this category. Like many others, he finds a ternary correlation between economics and mental stability, and with belief, writing, "societal health seems to cause widespread atheism, and societal insecurity seems to cause widespread belief in God." Where food and shelter is scarce, belief is strong, while the inverse is true for more stable countries. I agree with this to an extent. For many, faith does indeed become more of an issue if and when life is not treating you well. At the same time, this does not explain the vehement religiosity of Americans. I would have to argue that the second part of this equation—not economics, but mental stability—is a factor. Their fears do not derive from scarcity. They are projections born and instilled through the process of acquiring objects. Few people who are financially comfortable are truly carefree regarding their monies, or they would readily offer up the majority of what they have if called upon. God then becomes the protector—not of the world, but of a particular way of life. If you live in Jackson County, Missouri, and adhere to Smith's supposed visions, then in your mind that region is a blueprint of what heaven looks like. (Although few Mormons actually live there anymore; they were booted out some time ago.) Anything that threatens your region will cause you panic and distress, even if—as evidenced around the country by the World Trade Center incident—it is nowhere near where you live. God becomes *very* important if you're in danger, regardless of how much money you do or do not have.

A religion is only as useful and realistic as the response it raises from the general society, not by the hopes of a few men writing books and giving lectures about it. We've spent hundreds of generations split between belief and behavior, with very little common ground shared between them. When the occasional brave soul arises to take on that challenge, it is by the integrity with which they live that they truly inspire us. At the moment, I see plenty of it through the struggles of my close friends in New York City and around the world, in the constant dedication of artists and business owners working in the organic foods and sustainable health and clothing industries. They do not invoke the name of a deity in their efforts, but do it because they care—for their community, society, and the state of the world. They have made conscious decisions to better the world, and passionately and whole-heartedly devote their time here on earth to help crate a sustainable reality for future generations. In the process, such devotion can only intensify and deepen their appreciation of living, of life.

Unfortunately, I cannot find a trace of such devotion in what has become the wildest United States election process in my thirty-three years on this planet. The entire media spectacle has been focused on a small number of issues, and is playing out like a popularity contest more than anything with political trustworthiness. It is truly sad to see grown adults focusing their time and money to undermine others with childish commercials and name-calling. And, of course, the invocation of religion has been a major sticking point among them all. One of the greatest observations that Sam Harris makes in *The End of Faith* pertains to this, when he points out that the only thing an American presidential candidate has to exhibit is a belief in God, especially evidenced in December 2007 when Mormon candidate Mitt Romney gave an elaborate speech about the universality of (Christian) faith, and opponent Mike Huckabee responded by making a television ad reminding us that the most important thing to remember during Christmas is the celebration of Christ (as well as denying evolution). As Harris writes of such media hounds, "They do not have to be political scientists, economists, or even lawyers; they need not have studied international relations, military history, resource management, civil engineering, or any other field knowledge that might be brought to bear in the governance of a modern superpower; they need only to be expert fund-raisers, comport themselves well on television, and be indulgent of certain *myths*. In our next presidential election, an actor who reads the Bible would almost certainly defeat a rocket scientist who does not."

Still, a religion would not—*could not*—survive if its symbols did not matter to us. Even the staunchest atheist lives through the use of symbols, even if it is simply the fact that they speak, for words are symbols of external substances and internal contemplations. How we employ these symbols is evidenced in what and how we believe. In Chapter 7 I will look at important symbols of monotheistic religions that we can use without having to claim that we, ourselves, are imprisoned by the oppressive dictates of this or that club. For now I'd like to end with a story, before returning to yoga's influence in our time.

One afternoon I was eating lunch in a Jamaican patty shop in midtown Manhattan. Before beginning my meal, I bowed my head momentarily with eyes closed to give thanks for this food. Within thirty seconds of digging in, two youngish men walked over and excused themselves for interrupting. They had noticed me praying, they said, and wanted to let me know that their church is right around the corner. They were intrigued, as they rarely see people praying in public before a meal, and thought I might like to attend their services.

I asked them why they thought that I was praying "to" something. They didn't understand. The simple fact is, I wasn't praying at all. I was giving thanks, certainly, for being healthy, for having a job that afforded me to eat good Caribbean food, for being alive. But when I think that I have to give thanks "to" something, I have to question the process. Isn't simply giving thanks enough? And if I were to pray, cannot prayer itself sustain me? Why would I have to pray "to" some fixed idea of something I'll supposedly never know? As mentioned earlier, natural selection works on a very elemental principle:

the simpler, the better. As human beings are part of the process of existence, making us part of the process of this selection, why do we need to complicate things with proper nouns? Something fixed will not remain forever, or very long at all. Verbs, however, are where the real integrity of language exists. By staying involved in the process, and not stopping permanently at this or that residence, we are doing the most natural thing imaginable: living. I'm not sure if they got the meaning, but they did get the hint, and left me to my lunch.

CHAPTER 6

INTEGRATION IS GLOBALIZATION

"Integration is meditation and meditation is integration," writes the great yogi B.K.S. Iyengar in *The Tree of Yoga*. The revered teacher knows this well. His book *Light on Yoga* remains the "bible of yoga" in the West. First published in 1966, the illustrated guide is the teacher's tool of choice in understanding the anatomy, alignment, and effects of each posture. Nearing his 90th birthday, he still writes, tours and teaches regularly, especially relevant because it was actually illness that brought him to yoga in the first place. During his first months of life he suffered from influenza, and by adolescence he had been stricken with malaria, typhoid fever, tuberculosis and malnutrition. There are few examples of overcoming circumstances to find freedom more profound than those embodied by this man.

Reading his books, and practicing his slow and exacting science of yoga, the student quickly learns how important it is to understand the total human being. Unlike the more widespread aerobic and heat-drenched practices, Iyengar's sequencing and ideology are unnervingly slow. That's the point. His recovery from all those physical maladies was not instantaneous. At age fifteen, six years after the death of his father, Iyengar moved from Belur to live with his brother-in-law, the yogi Tirumalai Krishnamacharya, in Mysore. There he learned self-healing techniques as prescribed by this elder man, though the experience was anything but pleasant. Krishnamacharya was a disciplinarian responsible for helping to create a number of diverse forms of Hatha yoga. Being related to him, Iyengar often felt slighted; when strong enough to teach, he accepted a position in the far-off district of Pune, partly to escape the demanding attitude of his relative. To this day he remains faithful to his deceased guru, though also recognizing his temper and intellectual hubris. Through this disciplinarian relationship he learned the principle of neti-neti, dealing with a heavy hand that could also be comforting and healing.

Immersed in the therapeutic aspects of yoga, Iyengar developed and implemented the breath-focused and physically refined style of Hatha that we know today. While his form is much different than the gymnastic Vinyasa and Ashtanga yogas, it is precisely *because* it is harder to hold a pose for two minutes than to fly through twenty of them that makes his science so challenging. In one of its translations, the original form of the word Hatha equates to "violent." The basic idea is that you are structurally changing your body to cause transformation from the inside out. The intense heat of tapas, drawn up by a meditated focus with pranayama, is much more effective when holding postures for extended periods of time. Hence, the original meaning of asana, "seat."

Having taken his unhurried practice to Pune during a time when yoga was not particularly popular, there Iyengar remained until a seemingly chance encounter with violinist Yehudi Menuhin altered the course of his life, not to mention the West, forever. During their first meeting Iyengar only had a few moments to spare before running to an appointment. He told Menuhin, who was tired from the rigors of international touring, to lie down. Iyengar touched a few points on Menuhin's body and sent him into a deep sleep for over an hour. Upon awakening, Menuhin described the experience of a trancelike state that he had known only when hearing a Bach interpretation, and quickly became a devotee. He invited the yogi to spend the summer as his personal teacher in Switzerland in 1954; Iyengar accepted. This journey, covered substantially by local media, opened the door for Hatha yoga in the West. Menuhin, immortalized for introducing the West to the music of India via his superb collaborations with sitar player Ravi Shankar, helped bring the culture to America in more ways than are normally footnoted.

Menuhin is one of the millions of people that have succumbed to the insight and healing energy of Iyengar. The style of yoga that bears his name is often an entry point for beginning students due to its emphasis on alignment and the use of straps, blankets and blocks—tools often useless in more aerobic forms. For my own practice, Iyengar was and continues to be crucial. Even though I most often study and teach Vinyasa, I practice "gentle" yoga for therapeutic reasons. I began to study asanas after suffering a broken femur, collarbone and ankle, the last one two times, all on the right side of my body. Spending nearly a decade visiting chiropractors, orthopedic surgeons and podiatrists, being told time and again that all I could hope for was maintenance and not a cure, my own path in yoga was forged due to injury. I understand Iyengar's plight on a very personal level, as well as appreciate the mythological motif of the hero being introduced to his journey because of an injury. So while I'm usually the youngest student in that particular class by one to three decades (and most often the only male), my clarity and focus is often heightened more than through a grueling and tiresome Vinyasa class. Obviously, all styles have benefits, or else I wouldn't teach the more rigorous form. I digressed to this personal tale to highlight a point that a former capoeira teacher once mentioned. In discussing the difference between the exacting science of Angola versus the flaring and fast *modern regional*, he said that if you can do it slow, you can do it fast, because you'll know exactly how to move. The opposite is rarely the case.

While Iyengar is still going strong, his first teacher, Krishnamacharya lived to be 100. He was recognized as the greatest innovator in modern yoga upon his passing in 1989, and is responsible for teaching four of the world's most renowned teachers, and their styles (Iyengar, Ashtanga, Sai and Viniyoga). From an early age his father encouraged a discipline of yoga postures in his daily routine. Having been told that the family had descended from a ninth-century yogi named Nathamuni, at sixteen he claimed that this sage appeared before him and sang the verses to a lost book of yogic wisdom, the *Yogarahasya*. A lifelong path of yoga was certified by this revelation, and the boy went on to attain degrees in philology, music, divinity and logic. While at university, he was instructed to seek out a teacher named Sri Ramamohan Brahmachari. For seven years he studied with this Hatha yoga master, learning a supposed three thousand postures. After his apprenticeship, he returned home to a life of poverty. Unlike today, teaching asanas was by no means economically sustainable. He drew in students by showing off extraordinary feats of his body in public, such as holding his pulse, stopping cars with his hands, and lifting heavy objects with his teeth. While these were not in any means the aims of yoga practice, he needed to get people interested in the little-known discipline. He resorted to practicing a certain form of trickster mythology, in which the teacher has to demonstrate something that the discipline is not, in order to draw students in to learn what it is.

Other yogic aspects have held India over during the course of centuries, most prominently bhakti yoga. This devotional aspect would come to play a large role in Krishnamacharya's teaching, in which each breath was to be considered a meditation on God. In 1931 he was assigned to teach at the Sanskrit College in Mysore, his first full-time occupation in yoga. The arrangement didn't work out as well as the headmaster had hoped; the elder man was personally inspired by the therapeutic aspects of yoga, and wanted this teacher to succeed. Students, however, had a different take on the man. They found Krishnamacharya too rigid and demanding. But instead of disbanding the class, the Maharaja offered him the school's gym to open his own *yogashala*. This room would become the playground from which every modern form of yoga would emerge.

During his years of poverty, one of the few students he taught—every morning before school for three years, in fact—was Pattabhi Jois, arguably the most well known figure in modern yoga outside of Iyengar. Jois is credited with creating the rigorous Ashtanga-Vinyasa system, which he developed alongside Krishnamacharya from a fusion of classical yoga, gymnastics and Indian wrestling. Most of Krishnamacharya's students were young boys. Thus an energetic, flexible and aerobic workout was required to keep them both mentally and physically engaged. Over time it would become known popularly simply as Ashtanga; as an offshoot, Vinyasa took this rudimentary foundation and overlaid it with sequenced patterns according to each teacher's tastes, rather than the predetermined variety of series that Jois had developed according to his students' levels. That last idea was the hallmark of Krishnamacharya's fame: The ability to create a physical practice that meets the needs of each person, for whatever their body can handle. This would become even more important when he met the person who would transform his approach to yoga forever, Indra Devi.

Born in Latvia as Zhenia Labunskaia, this young woman challenged Krishnamacharya on two deeply engrained levels when asking him to be her teacher. Firstly, she was female; secondly, a foreigner. He balked. She persisted. He gave in, prescribing (and indeed, attempting to dissuade) her with a tormenting schedule and dietary restrictions. The latter was not in vain; Krishnamacharya was a master of Ayurveda—an ancient science, translated as "knowledge of life," predominantly focused on balancing internal energies and nutrition in pursuing a healthy and sustainable lifestyle—and knew that this system played a crucial role in yoga. Within a year of her apprenticeship, Devi endeared Krishnamacharya to her, and they became lifelong friends. Her 1953 book *Forever Young, Forever Healthy* was the breakthrough to the world that yoga needed. She lived to be 102 years old, and her schools remain open in Buenos Aires, Argentina, where she became

something of a local saint, again showing the global appeal
of yoga. Her creation of Sai yoga, the chanting and prayerful
aspects, continues to influence styles today. Demonstrative of
her mutual influence, Krishnamacharya incorporated Sanskrit
mantras into asana practice during his later years.

The last of the four great teachers Krishnamacharya
influenced may have, in some respects, been his most
challenging. His son T.K.V. Desikachar initially had no interest
in yoga. Father would tie up his son in postures and leave him
there for hours, something that only increased his loathing of it.
An encounter with another female would again alter the future
of yoga. Having graduated with a degree in engineering, son
was sitting outside when father was approached by a European
woman, who ecstatically jumped out of her car to hug him. For
a Brahman to be embraced by a woman in public was a no-no.
Desikachar asked his father what that was all about. He replied
that the woman hadn't been able to sleep without the assistance
of drugs for twenty years. Thanks to his yoga prescription, the
previous evening had been her first in two decades that she slept
peacefully and drug-free. This epiphany struck Desikachar, and
the young man begged his father for instruction. He gave up
a new job post in engineering to persuade Krishnamacharya,
who was more than reluctant. To be certain of his son's
devotion, they awoke at 3:30 every morning. Determined, a
comparably vigorous schedule continued for twenty-eight
years. Desikachar took his father's knowledge and created a
Vinyasa system known as Viniyoga, a style that is practiced by
millions worldwide, though virtually unknown in America.

Time and again we see how this towering figure of
yoga was continually humbled. His reluctance to teach the
physically unfit Iyengar, the foreign female Devi, and his once-
undisciplined son transformed the man into the legendary
healer he would become. Oftentimes we need to heal ourselves
of our own biases before we can cure others, whether it be of
ailments physical, mental or emotional. Being humbled seems
part and parcel of Krishnamacharya's life, especially in 1947
when his *yogashala* was shut down due to poor attendance.
While his students became highly demanded teachers with

international stardom, Krishnamacharya never left India, nor sought fame by any stretch of the imagination. He found work at the Vivekananda College in Chennai, where pranayama became the central focus of his teachings. The use of props continued as he encountered more students with physical ailments. The basis of his yoga was a style that helped, according to journalist Fernando Pagés Ruiz, "students more from a yoga that adapted to their limitations to a yoga that stretched their abilities." That seemingly small linguistic jump is a huge psychological boost to unfit or injured individuals who aren't looking to wrap their legs behind their head as much as simply feel better during the course of the day. While today there are dozens upon dozens of well-known styles, and possibly hundreds of lesser-known offshoots circulating in studios and gyms, it is this one man's devotion to both revitalizing and evolving yoga that we have to thank.

I can only think of Krishnamacharya while flipping through the pages of *Yoga Journal*, *Yogi Times*, *Elephant*, *Alternative Medicine* and the rest of the publications next to my desk. Most of these magazines offer a wonderful selection of yoga's varied benefits and applications, ranging from advanced postural sequencing to meditation guides and therapeutic advice. It's not the content of editorial that astonishes me, but the vagrant negligence of moral choices by advertisers. Teachers like Krishnamacharya and the lineage of students he inspired, and whom they in turn inspired, have devoted their lives to creating a system of yoga that is healing and community building. Now that it's become popular beyond what any of these originators could have imagined, we witness women who look like outtakes from Cirque du Soleil and Vogue photo shoots, advertising clothing, cereal, DVDs, spa-focused retreats and online networking websites. I've seen similar marketing approaches to making watches, pharmaceutical drugs, banks, and public transportation more alluring, using svelte women in tight clothing to sell their product or service.

That yoga went from a devotional connection and a

bridge between the individual and a community to becoming a sales tool to pimp someone's newest gadget is not surprising. It often happens in one's introduction to the practice. For example: Recently a woman was practicing next to me at Jivamukti Yoga School. During the class she noticed a floating technique that I have learned to transition between Crow pose and Chaturanga, and told me after class that she had always wanted to learn how to do it. I showed her the basic idea behind it, and mentioned that I teach. It turned out that she is a member of Equinox, where I hold my classes. She began attending.

After the third class, she approached me to mention how much she enjoyed the sequencing. Then she recommended that I take the Jivamukti certification program, so that I could "be more spiritual like them, you know, with all the chanting and such." I had to laugh a little. I told her that I was well aware of that style and enjoy taking those classes; that's why I go so often. But it's also not how I teach. The concept of spirituality is abstract to me. Over the years, I've noticed that teachers who talk about spirit and God and love over and over often stumble through the actual sequencing, forgetting to do poses on one side, rushing through another, and so on. Being focused on something "out there" does nothing to help the student "in here," which is both the actual room they are practicing inside of, as well as their own psychology. Sure, it's nice to theorize about a universal energy that binds all of us with love and joy, and if I pray to it, I too will receive abundance. At the moment, however, if I'm not being taught how to properly place my hands underneath my shoulders in Plank pose, or what muscles to engage and open in Triangle, how am I ever going to learn the foundational "seat" of each posture? How many times do I have to imagine something outside of myself before coming out of the esoteric and into the real work? All those lessons that the merging of Samkhya and Yoga philosophy accomplished are so frequently lost in translation. To go beyond the dualistic tendencies of mind-stuff, one mustn't linger in the ideologies of lordship and divinity. That is but a temporary stop on the path, and yet is often treated as the definitive goal.

I realize that it's hard to separate yoga from these

images, as that is how it has saturated in the public image. It is interesting that yoga has been given such an affirmative nod in modern culture. This can only be because it is treated as a stress-relief and muscle-toning and –strengthening program. Currently it is assessed as a three-billion-dollar-a-year industry. With figures like that no one is going to complain. Long gone are the days when yoga was perceived as a threat to the sanity and safety of our nation. The entire system, which is so linked to the exercise fascination in America, is perceived as the most non-threatening discipline imaginable, while in reality, the reverse is true. When the keys to yoga are unlocked, they are completely antithetical to the ways that Americans live. This is not to say *against*, however. Let us say, rather, that America is part of the global play, and the reason for yoga's popularity was established some time back in the Industrial Age when our machinery began tearing apart the natural connections we had to the land. While Iyengar's sudden vacation thanks to Menuhin was the spark that opened doors, he was not the first to introduce the practice to the country. He was the one who helped build a popular audience for it, however.

An early fascination with the literature of India was made possible in 1805 when William Emerson published translations of Sanskrit texts. His son, Ralph Waldo, and friend Henry David Thoreau, became fascinated with the ideas behind works like the *Bhagavad Gita*, incorporating symbols and metaphors into their own transcendental and nature-based writings. They were witnessing a widening rift between technology and the soil and trees around them, and used these mythologies towards their own end. Mere decades later, thinkers like Madame Blavatsky, the founder of the still-functioning Theosophical Society, integrated Hindu and Buddhist texts with Christian mysticism and Kabbalah and Sufi philosophies. Beginning with her founding of the society in 1875, she published thick volumes of encyclopedic learning, including *Isis Unveiled* and her pivotal two-volume *The Secret Doctrine*. In these works she proposed such ideas as the yogic underpinnings of men like Jesus and Mohammed, showing how various forms of mysticism from any culture could be related on a common ground—similar to the work of Evelyn Underhill, who was born the year the foundation was founded. Theosophy has been criticized for its attempt at synthesizing everything and anything (in much the same way that Ken Wilber's more recent *A Theory of Everything* does). While Blavatsky's work can occasionally seem like a bit of a stretch, the integrity of her research and her attempts at uniting global philosophies are certainly commendable.

The first citing of yoga in the West is granted to a thin and spindly sage named Swami Vivekananda, who at the World's Parliament of Religions in Chicago in 1893 gave a lecture and demonstration that made him a conference highlight. During the talk he spoke of the easy distractions of the Western world, and how the inability to focus on one thing at a time, as well as a disconnection to the body has created excess amounts of anxiety not only on people themselves, but also on the rest of the world. To prove his point, he went from his seated position into a handstand effortlessly, which astonished the audience. Ironically, he was viewed on the streets as a vagrant, adorned in a simple robe and sandals and begging for money. Even when the spotlight was turned onto him, he never left his dedication to spreading the teachings of his guru, Sri Ramakrishna, in both speech and behavior.

Twenty-five years later an Englishman who had been living in India since 1890 produced what would become the first comprehensive yoga book for the inquisitive Western eye to gaze upon. Sir John Woodroffe published all of his works on Indology under the pseudonym Arthur Avalon, and with the dispersion of *The Serpent Power: The Secrets of Tantric and Shaktic Yoga*, audiences in Europe and America were exposed to the foundation of this "ancient" practice. It is a scholarly and thoroughly researched work, certainly, and having lived and worked inside of the culture for so long—and becoming an early Sanskrit translator in the process—he was well aware that everlasting bliss and eternal salvation were not the superior states of humankind. "Yogis are not concerned with the 'heaven world,' but seek to surpass it; otherwise they are not Yogis at all."

By this time, however, yoga was being attacked in the

media and at churches. It had been deemed a cult, and even now, certain biased connotations from those days linger. Between 1870 and 1900, a million immigrants came to call America home; the following decade saw another one million gain entry annually. The country which deemed itself a melting pot began to deny its supposedly open-minded heritage. Having chased Native Americans into small encampments over the last few centuries, the original foreigners became not visitors, but regulars. The last thing they wanted was more of "them," i.e. anyone not of their cultural background, invading the land—another very modern anxiety, with immigration being an important topic during the 2008 presidential elections. (Interesting that another two topics—the war in Iraq and healthcare—are also concerned with territorial issues, albeit of differing forms.) Brightly clad, long-bearded men with matted hair and dark complexions speaking about the inherent unity of all creatures and functions of the universe were certainly dangerous to the tarrying strains of Victorian ideologies in vogue (then and now). The American media, even then so good at creating controversies where none exist, concocted tales about "white slavery" as daughters were being abducted by these sage-demons in disguise. Congress jumped aboard in 1910 by passing the Mann Act (aka the White Slavery Act), which dissuaded would-be abductors. By 1912 the government was promising the public that they were doing everything possible to stop the spread of these "Orientalist religions." Not surprisingly, some of the many targets of publishing magnate William Randolph Hearst were yogis.

This battle was never one-sided. If anything, it became more heated as many people were opening their minds with pranayama and asanas. Although men like Parahamansa Yogananda, author of the widely circulated *Autobiography of a Yogi* and founder of the Self-Realization Fellowship, were being questioned for running a "love cult," this skepticism was to be expected in a Christian society trying to maintain a clean image, especially in the spaces between World War I and what would become the Depression. Even the epitome of the Roaring Twenties, jazz music, was idolized and accepted only *after* the case. In the following decade, yoga found what it needed to target the general population: a poster boy. No one could deny Theos Bernard's good looks and steeled body, or his devotion to Tibet and yoga. He was introduced to the latter after a near-fatal illness had sent him to a family friend who happened to be an Indian sage. After returning from a trip overseas in 1937, he published two books, *Heaven Lies Within Us* and *Penthouse of the Gods*, dedicating the rest of his life to the path of yoga and philosophy. His uncle, Pierre Bernard, had already founded the New York Sanskrit College in Manhattan, and these two men, while occasionally hassled by the police (Pierre more than Theos), gained a loyal following.

Today little has changed in our handling of international relationships. It seems ironic that war and yoga continue to be entwined. Every time a skirmish or full-blown initiative takes place, American media announces that anything produced by foreigners is dangerous—including and most often the people themselves. In the 1950s India's Prime Minister, Jawarharlal Nehru, denied accusations that his nation was supplying yogis to Russia to help instruct astronauts in how to breathe more easily in outer space. This was the same decade that Iyengar embarked on his first overseas trip, and journalists like *Hartford Courant* columnist Jack Zaiman exposed the beneficial aspects of yoga to the public. While Krishnamacharya's students built their studios and brands across the planet, yoga began to move away from the love-cult stigma and into YMCAs and YWCAs. Celebrities were coming out of the closet with their yoga allegiance, something that still turns large audiences on, proven by Christy Turlington's 2001 *Time* magazine cover where the supermodel is shown balanced in a floating lotus posture. It would take a juggernaut of forms, however, to allow this beast to awaken and emerge from the sleeping global consciousness. Like all movements, there is no one single factor that incites them, but rather a symphony of influences raining down upon a nation to transform it. And symphony is exactly what it was, as the music of India properly opened our collective psyche to accept the arrival of yoga.

....

"If you look at the yoga of sound, that's what it is, we try to find that perfect note or that perfect sound that drops all the worries and hang-ups and all of this and that into that state where we get a little taste. It doesn't stay because you have to cultivate it. But you try to get a little taste of what could be pure sound. It takes practice. You could take years practicing one *raga* and then you hit that right note. Well when you hit that right note, you'll know it and the listener will know it because the listener will also hit that right note. It's not just you that hits the right note and you're so great and blah blah. No, the point is that the listener also gets it when the right note is hit. That's what makes you be aware that there is something divine about music; there is something that crosses the border and is universal. But I think it's more that perfect note. The whole idea behind *qawwali* is to get that note or that sense it is divine and yeah, we are all united and are all children of God, no matter where we're from, what we speak, all of that, because it transcends. If the universe was created with sound, then it's all there. We have to go to the source: What is that sound."

During an interview with Algerian-born DJ Cheb i Sabbah, he dropped this bit of science while discussing his electronic homage to the classical music of North and South India. His turntabling addiction began in 1964 in Paris, and still continues strong, over four decades later. His extensive knowledge of the various music forms of the planet have led to some of the most creative electronic albums ever created— gorgeous takes on the classical traditions of India, as well as devotional forms such as *bhajan*s and kirtan, all spread over tasteful beats. A certified veteran in the industry, he attributes his success to that sound, the source of all creation, also known as Nada Brahma.

How is it that a philosophical system which holds that the universe is endlessly cycling, and therefore unable to have a creation, can claim a source? While earth may have no absolute beginning in time, it does not imply that time does not have a soundtrack. The universe is in a constant state of vibration, known as *spanda*. While purusha is the meditator within, all forms of movement are resonant on some level. We mentioned Pythagoras, and here his "Music of the Spheres" applies. The Samos-born philosopher was turned onto Eastern theory after moving to Italy in 530 BCE, and developed his mathematical astuteness in tune with the laws of karma, promoting a strict vegetarian diet, heralding the wonders of ahimsa, and immersing himself in a form of jnana yoga that focused on science and math. The highest divinity, he reckoned, was in the proper vibratory state of the human body when it was attuned to the resonance of the universe. This dawning came to him walking by a blacksmith's shop when, upon hearing the pounding of an anvil upon metal, he noted the varying frequencies and estimated the harmonies and discords embedded with each tone. The entire cosmos, he figured, was strung together like the notes of a lyre, and with that notion he submerged himself into the idea of his *tetractys*, a "pyramid of dots" that repetitiously revealed the inner workings of the universe.

Most of us don't ponder arithmetic or physics while listening to the music that moves us. Nor is there any particular reason to do so. Thanks to philosophers of this magnitude, however, we can trace and discuss underlying principles of sound in an attempt to make sense out of our experiences while enraptured within it. Contemplation does not detract from enjoyment. By understanding the sway between the "good" and "bad" within the structure of sound, a stable philosophy of life unfolds. That which is rhythmic and harmonically pleasant is "good," while discord and arrhythmic tones are "bad." This notion can be applied and integrated into all mental and emotional states of being, which is how theory converges with reality. The idea is to first tune the frequencies to "good" by living a sattvic life, and then through meditation and a transformation of psychology, go beyond even that into the silence at the end of the resonating strings—Nada Brahma. When we talk about losing ourselves in music, it is better understood as being found.

"A *mantra*," writes Georg Feuerstein, "is that which saves the mind from itself, or which leads to salvation through the concentration of the mind." As the bhakti movement gained credibility and numbers, and the idea that a ritual or temple is necessary for ablution was discarded, individuals and small collectives employed the power of mantra recitation as a means of connecting with their notion of a divine source. The root of mantra is *man*, which means "to think" or "to be intent." The suffix, *tra*, is usually recognized as implying "instrumentality," though an esoteric translation of *trâna* renders the term "saving." Both meanings work in this context, in that a sacred word or phrase is repetitiously uttered to launch the yogi into heightened states, to bring one back to an "original state," which is not necessarily "good"—a constant mistranslation by peace-seeking dualists. Through the recitation of names, the yogi separates the distance between one who is being chanted and that which is chanting, so that, with success, the two become the same thing. (To put it another way, the two *always were* the same thing, and it is now being recognized.) The god or deva is embodied in the individual, quite similar to the global ritual associated with masking, where the human who dons the mask of a deity is transformed into the deity itself. Both practices are mentally and emotionally stimulating, in that the heightened state of awareness *is* the god they are "activating." Remember, gods represent situations and emotional states of being just as much as they do weather patterns and soil fertility. The processes that unfold through a life lived out of ritual are divine in their very action. Singer and listener alike are elevated when performing in a group setting, which in the bhakti yoga tradition is called kirtan.

The recitation of a chant such as "Om Namah Shivaya," translates as "He who is Bliss, the Lord of Destruction. Shiva liberates through change and upheaval. He is benevolent." This popular mantra is at the basic and fundamental root of Shaivite devotion, and when it is sung, the yogi assumes the responsibility for the creative and destructive forces of existence. By recognizing that they too are part of this process, they train themselves to not be upset when something is destroyed, for that which comes to pass will come again, albeit in a different form. At the same time, they are not overjoyed when something beneficial enters their life, as it too will pass—and emerge again, remixed. The "Middle Way," to borrow the Buddhist idea, is to enjoy each moment fully, and for what it is. The act of chanting offers gratitude for the opportunity to embody human form and even for being able to express such praises through song. While it is sometimes promoted as a means of achieving an end—if you chant this many times for so many days, etc., you will receive plentiful bounties—the act of reciting mantra is complete unto itself. It is the circle that subsumes and surpasses the Alpha and the Omega, to be enjoyed for the purpose of enjoyment itself.

The Sufi poet and *veena* player Hazrat Inayat Khan, born in the late 19th century to a princely Muslim Indian lineage, beautifully captures the spirit of music in his master work, *The Mysticism of Sound and Music.* Putting forth ideas like Shiva utilizing the "science of breath," Khan's meticulous understanding of the inner tunings of the human spirit reads like a song itself. In this prose-like book he highlights what he feels to be "two aspects of life": "The first is that man is tuned by his surroundings, and the second is that man can tune himself in spite of his surroundings." The first, then, would be anyone who enjoys music and uses it to set an aura in the surrounding environment. The latter is the work of the yogi, who manipulates the environment and their own inner space to vibrate on a refined and universal frequency. The forms of music that are most appealing and reach large audiences—and not, this must be added, through another form of manipulation accomplished by the media—are those resonating on the highest strings of "good," enabling the observant meditator to integrate, and then to even surpass, such songs.

Yehudi Menuhin's invitation to Ravi Shankar to play overseas, resulting in an inspired performance at a festival in Monterrey, California in 1967, sent tens of thousands of hippies and potheads into a frenzy that remains biblical to this day. Indian culture had been percolating at the fringes of American society for over a century. Now four decades later, Shankar continues to play in America annually, often with his daughter, Anoushka. Still, no one would top the Beatles, whose short-lived, though celebrated relationship with Maharishi Mahesh Yogi and his Transcendental meditation techniques inspired millions to tune in. Any fan of their *Lonely Hearts Club* and *Revolver* records knows how deeply Shankar's tutelage of a voracious George Harrison exposed America to the slithering sounds of the sitar. A large number of sudden adherents believed their drug-induced states rivaled the possibilities of enlightenment proposed by yoga, an idea that was rejected outright by Shankar (often to no avail). He was frustrated that Americans were tuning in to the "psychedelic" (i.e. drug-induced) sounds of his instrument, which caused him to not perform abroad for many years. He eventually realized that sound was more important than surroundings, and those who sought out his music for sonic reasons, and the inherent spirituality embedded in his interpretations of Indian ragas, would find their way through the drug-induced frenzy.

Both Indian music and yoga in America fizzled in the '70s and '80s, as hippie culture gave way to what would become the dominion of corporate control. As Shankar and others had feared, the "Indian craze" had come and gone, as all things in vogue do. (Eerily similar was the "bhangra craze" that came and went when Jay-Z rhymed over a Panjabi MC song in 2003.) There was never a time that people were not practicing yoga, or listening to the music of India, however. Longtime Grateful Dead percussionist Mickey Hart continued (and continues) to infuse his global grooves with *tablas*, and ex-Miles Davis guitarist John McLaughlin made valiant attempts at an East-West fusion with Shakti, and later, Remember Shakti. It was also a genre of music that brought together two people who would become crucial in the resurgence of yoga in America in the early '90s, David Life and Sharon Gannon.

In 1980, Life opened the Life Café in a small Manhattan storefront on 10th St and Ave B, which at the time nowhere near resembled the burgeoning wonderland of condos and eateries that it is today. Gannon, a Seattle resident, came to the café to perform with her band Audio Letter, a punk-based outfit partially inspired by Sanskrit chants. After her band moved to Manhattan and Life joined in, part of their act included teaching audience members call-and-response chants, bringing a new form of kirtan to unsuspecting rockers. Gannon, who had been suffering chronic back pain, was introduced to yoga by one of the café's waitresses, and Life was quick to sign up. They began to teach friends in their apartment, and in 1986, they traveled to India to meet their guru, Swami Nirmalanda, whom Gannon had been writing letters to over the past few years. Upon returning, they opened Jivamukti Yoga Center on 2nd Ave and 9th St. Today housed in Union Square on Broadway, and dubbed Jivamukti Yoga School, their joining together of numerous parts of the yogic tradition—including asanas, mantra, meditation, pranayama and philosophy—has come, directly or indirectly, to define how Hatha and Vinyasa yoga is taught and sequenced. Their special focus on ahimsa creates numerous opportunities for animal rights groups and the like to stage benefits, and informational packets and literature are always available to practitioners and visitors to the center. To say the least, they are the testament of living a sattvic life. When yoga was revitalized and began to reach large audiences, their integrity and passion fueled much of that fire.

Yoga has become as much an industry unto itself as it has a spiritual practice. I do not wish to dwell on what has shaped it over the past decade, as that is easily found in more comprehensive works, and not particularly the aim of this one. I did think it was important though, to briefly trace the emergence of yoga in America over the past two centuries to witness how an "ancient" practice is interpreted and created anew—sometimes with integrity, sometimes very loosely—from the original foundation. Today books on "yoga with weights" and a dictatorial sequence performed in a 100-plus-degree room are among the many "forms" that have borrowed some of the nomenclature of yoga, while retaining little (if any) of the initial intention: freedom from the bondage of duality. With designer mat bags retailing at $600 and downloadable podcasts to practice asanas while tuning in on your iPod, the gentrification of the yoga village is complete. These generalizations are indicative of heightened interest in any area where people realize money exists to be made—even Pet Rocks were big business for some time. The excuse that "if you really care about something, you'll spend money on it" is an unfortunate consequence of the shallow thinking that the creators of marketing plans in magazines and online ads have developed.

I have no fear of yoga "trending." It has become far too pivotal in the American consciousness and more widely, on the global level, to suffer such a fate. While I've been critical of the misinformed treatment of the "5,000-year-old" idea, I also recognize that yoga, in some form, is probably much older than that, if we understand it as meditation and as a tool in the quest for release from the bondage of suffering. Meditation does not mean the complete absence of thought. It is the ability to hold one thought in your mind for a sustained amount of time, so that when external stimuli or overbearing emotions seem to overtake your nervous system, you are able to wrap the mind back into itself and stay calm, poised and focused. You do not need to sit down in a quiet room with incense and soft music. While even that can prove quite challenging, the real integrity of meditation is much more instinctual. That is, it is a form of psychology that becomes so integrated into your own person that your initial reaction to any situation is one of pure meditative substance, being able to see the moment clearly for what it is and acting in accordance to your yogic path at the same time. I cannot describe in detail what this moment entails, for that would be to idolize a particular passage of time, whereas the entire idea is to celebrate each moment for its own sake—unbound by the notion that this moment here is really good, and that one over there is horrible.

Different countries offer various styles of yoga according to their own temperaments. While the aggressive and physically-oriented forms are not only found in America, they are certainly rampant here, given the all-or-nothing attitude of the daily workplace and our governing policies. In this way, "liberation" will be presented as something to be won and conquered, not as a state of being inherently inside of us that merely requires a quieting of the mind. We must subtract to multiply. Americans are reared as intellectual creatures from birth, a claim that I am not removed from, given the scope of this work and my general understanding of life. Even though I was never particularly gifted in terms of the educational system I was raised within, the patterns of my own thinking were molded and emblazoned with this system's ideologies. My biases are my own, partly as a result from this type of thinking, partly from personal inclinations. What remains vital to remember is that all systems offer only one—their own—take on reality, and none can be any more "right" than another. It has taken many years of yoga practice for this realization to dawn upon me, as well as for me to make sense of it in my personal life. Soon we'll take a look at how this affects the American understanding of yoga a bit more deeply, but first we must make one last pit stop, to contemplate how we think in general, and what the symbols of those thoughts really represent.

PART III

CREATING THE ABNORMAL

"The truth, as has been said countless times, will set you free. But what is said far less often is that sometimes it first will make you confront habits of behavior and thought that might be limiting you, so that you might attain the awareness to use your freedom for the benefit of your greater self and all of life."

John Robbins
The Food Revolution

CHAPTER 7

FUSING THE FULCRUM

Words, as stated, *are* mythologies. They serve as symbols pointing to something, without actually being the thing itself. Language is an indicator of reality, and can—and does—influence it a great deal. That is because the way we *express* reality is through words, and those words dictate the experiences we have. As cultural historian Richard Tarnas wrote, "World views create worlds." Word views create them too. For example, it is likely that a lifelong Buddhist in Tibet will not dream of Jesus, just as a devoted Christian rarely finds divine inspiration from within the circular folklore of a mandala. The key to everyone's spiritual understanding depends on the words and symbols they've become accustomed to. While transformations are completely possible, and new systems and symbols are considered and implemented, it is not the god who switches relevance, but rather your own way of experiencing the god through the language that you use. This is why Buddhists say many rivers lead to the same ocean. No matter how you define your version of ultimate reality, the ocean awaits your boat to set sail.

Mythologies have always served this function of expression, utilizing the symbols of cultures to tell their story. There are endless possibilities as to the telling of each of our stories, due more to nuances in language than to opportunities for actually experiencing the world. That is, experiences, while not limited, generally take on a limited number of forms and archetypes. It is the phrasing of these forms that is important and unique to each person and, by extension, the people of the particular culture who will understand the languaging. As noted psychologist Steven Pinker remarked, language is infinite, though the rules that govern it are finite. We all (hopefully) fall in love, yet the poetry describing this state can be continually fresh even if the underlying feeling is the same. If there is an infinite possibility of language, there is an infinite possibility for experiencing the world. Yet we tell the same stories time and again using different languages, and different language techniques. This occurs in the cosmic stories of ancient mythologies, as well as in our everyday sufferings and triumphs. We relate to one another through our pains as much as through our glories, making the best way to heal a broken heart through listening to sad songs. You relate to the singer and realize you are not alone in your suffering, a catharsis that is comforting.

In theory, different cultures appear extremely diverse. For all the incredible work Charles Darwin accomplished, the man proved to be overtly influenced by his Victorian English upbringing, carrying personal and cultural baggage with him wherever he traveled. Once he was able to cut through language and custom barriers, the traits he believed inherent to his own society proved universal. He encountered numerous social differences traveling along in the Beagle, and initially thought the native Indians of Tierra del Fuego were pure savages. As three of their members learned English and he settled into their culture, his original hypothesis changed. He recognized the altruistic friendships embedded in the core of their community, as well as their gracious extension to him. By the end of his trip he witnessed a fundamental similarity within this seemingly disparate group of people compared to his own nation, something, which, as odd as it sounds, was not the norm by any means—many people assumed different races were really different *species*. Through all the biological and environmental knowledge that he mastered during his life, Darwin's keen understanding of a global humanity was among his great accomplishments, especially given that we still hold on to a multitude of racial biases. While today we still cannot consider him to be a full-fledged "global citizen"—he retained many judgments until the end—his growing dismay at the treatment of Africans in Europe, for one, pointed toward a mind opening in numerous ways.

If we don't let go of biases, they remain with us indefinitely. As our companions, they affect our emotions and thoughts greatly, helping to formulate the way we experience reality. We can all understand this, as we know what it is like to have guilt or regret. It seems amazing how an unresolved issue can keep appearing, over and over in various forms, until confronted. This trend can last a lifetime, or if we ascribe to the notion of karma, lifetimes. They are, in a sense, our *negative mythologies*: mental, emotional, and sometimes communal tendencies that do not serve the freedom of the individual or society. These are also known as samskaras, psychic imprints that continue in perpetuity if unaddressed. While the negative tendencies of humans are rarely looked upon as mythologies, it is entirely appropriate to understand these underlying stories as such, for no mythology was ever produced about "pure good." Myths derive from the world of death, dis-ease and confusion, and are rarely concerned with "rightness" (even if their conclusion does set something right in the world). They are involved with *completion*. That is a different idea altogether. No mythology ever began without some form of struggle, so I consider the emotional and social ails of our day to be triggers of the current mythologies we are now living inside. Whether or not we choose to fulfill them is something to be decided upon, on an individual basis. Most importantly, it is a decision we are offered, and thus it is up to us to choose to take it.

When it was apparent that his passion for Native American folklore would turn into a lifelong career that spanned

176 of Sound Against Flame

every culture on earth, Joseph Campbell was amazed at the persistence of similar motifs that kept appearing across time and space. As we're now learning, much of this can be attributed to little-discussed cultural fusions (Africans in Mexico, Indians in Jamaica), yet there are many stories that cannot be explained by nomads or explorers. Carl Jung attributed this to the collective unconscious. The personal unconscious is comprised of events that have been experienced but then repressed or forgotten. They could then reappear after a period of latency to influence life in profound ways. If they are not openly realized, these "memories" turn up in dreams and, at times, manifest physically—hence, the seemingly unfounded inclination we display toward repetition when "stuck in a rut."

The collective unconscious, on the other hand, was never conscious. It is "acquired" through heredity (and not necessarily the heredity dictated by genes or DNA), and can influence our lives on an even more profound level because it has never been experienced. It is our psychic make-up. Yogis have their own expression of this, represented long before Jung's vast work on the psychology of dreams, in their fourth state—the one entwined in the symbol OM, turiya. The key to unlocking the inner doors of the collective unconscious is through the understanding (and integration) of symbols into our everyday lives. When symbols remain misunderstood—or, as was the case throughout the Crusades, and continues to be the case with our understanding of mass religion, interpreted egoistically and literally—they are worthless, and at times dangerous. Since it is essentially a latent state of being that has to work itself out in some manner, the repression of symbols and misunderstanding of doctrines sheds light on why global pharmaceutical sales were $643 billion in 2006—$290.1 billion in North America alone. By the same token, the U.S. antidepressant industry was estimated to surpass $20.5 billion in 2007. The disconnection to our roots appears, as Jung and others knew so well, in unconscious forms, and if we don't have the guidance to properly deal with these repressed reactions, the best we can hope to do is to further suppress them. Why else would pills with names like inhibitors and blockers "work?"

Can we attribute these monstrously large numbers to the repression of misunderstood mythologies? No, and yes. There are no pie charts to locate the root of every person's malaise. And of course, there are plenty of pharmaceuticals being sold to combat things like cancer, diabetes and AIDS, not to mention the majority of drug use, which is when chemicals are injected into farm animals to prevent disease and keep their weight up for slaughtering. Many human diseases can result from the inheritance of particular genes, and be exacerbated through environmental issues, as well as poor nutrition or the ingestion of numerous narcotics, predominantly nicotine, alcohol and caffeine. But to disassociate one's health from their mental state is one of the most confusing aspects of modern medicine. What we've gained in incredible treatment procedures and surgical techniques we've lost by depending heavily on specialists who focus so intently on one area of the process of being human that everything else is rarely considered. Granted, we probably would not want a podiatrist to operate on our heart, nor an ophthalmologist to remove our appendix. Specialism has benefits. The diagnosis of everyday ails, and of states that lead to massive bouts of disease, however, can often be attributed to the areas of our lives that remain in the dark. Illness rises from the unexplored regions of the collective consciousness that we each embody. The mythological hero begins his quest with an ailment or injury, often as much mental (such as egotism and pride) as physical. While one of the most common motifs of the hero involves sustaining a thigh injury, it is equally possible that a broken heart or fear of death can trigger the journey.

To contemplate dealing with these states of imbalance, we need to turn to our symbols. For the rest of this chapter I want to look at two examples of reading a mythology, and how these readings affect us here and now, not just in the annals of history and museums. In the final chapters we will discuss a fuller integration of these techniques more fully, and how an understanding of the foundations of yoga and atheism can similarly propel us not towards rightness, but rather, completion. That said, there seems to be only one place to start: the beginning.

The hero motif has made a lasting mark in literature. The ascension of the protagonist into cosmic or mythological time remains integral to great novels. It is a return to wholeness, the completed individual: Huraki Murakami's Toru Okada, Gregory David Robert's Linbaba, John Steinbeck's Cal Trask, Upton Sinclair's Jurgis Rudkus, Aldous Huxley's Will Farnaby, Thomas Mann's Hans Castorp, and José Saramago's Tertuliano Máximo Afonso are a few examples of how one's everyday existence can become extraordinary and mythic. Sometimes the hero consciously undertakes this path, while at others it is only when in the midst, or even at the aftermath, that they realize what is happening—*if* they realize what's happening. By condensing and crystallizing one's human experiences, the superhuman becomes apparent. We can say with confidence that this has *always* been the role of literature, as we have substantial proof: the story of Gilgamesh.

A complete retelling of the tale will not be necessary. Being the world's oldest piece of writing, it has been retold numerous times since its rediscovery in 1872. Like many ancient books, the texts were written by men who were scattered over a broad (for that time) geographical terrain, and over a number of centuries. Since then a credible, and rather beautiful, story has been pieced together, concerned with the coming-to-wholeness of the King of Uruk, Gilgamesh, who was promoted and provided for through the sacrifice of his confidante and best friend, Enkidu.

Before going further, we must note that wholeness does not imply "destiny." There is fulfillment, certainly, but the notion that a final stage awaits at the end of the path negates the fact that each step is necessary. Regardless of any ambition to reach it, "destiny" only exists in hindsight. For the tale that Gilgamesh learned was that he too would one day die—that his body was not eternal. While the text does not end with death, the implications for us, as readers, are clear: This is the story of everyone, a path we all walk, a reality we all confront. Through the understanding of the symbols of Gilgamesh we can know a richer, fuller meaning in life, for to contemplate death is to tap into the very essence of it. This knowledge helps us to cherish the moments that we do have, providing a basic outline of how to live morally and honestly, or at least realistically. Whether or not we take that advice is our choice.

Gilgamesh is a king beloved as much as he is feared. His physical prowess frightens everyone in his city, and he could be considered anything but moral. He makes a sport of sleeping with virgins on the night before their marriage, so that the lesser husbands will not be able to introduce their partners to this most intimate bond. His ability to party is insatiable, as is his appetite. He never loses any sort of game, and has the ego to match the ability. In fact, it is this quality that forces the gods to bring him down to earth by creating his second self, Enkidu, from dust. Thus begins the first of many symbols that will later be retold in the Bible. Upon close inspection of this particular text, it is astounding to see the parallels between those two tales, and perplexing that today's faithful believe biblical stories to be singular or unique. Mythological time is not concerned with historical events. The symbols *do* point to everyday existence, yet the stories themselves are just that—stories. We love and cherish them because we can relate to them, not because they may or may not have happened.

Besides biblical parallels, there are many insights to note. Firstly, the tale takes place in modern day Iraq. Secondly, Enkidu is an environmentalist, an ecologist of sorts. He is a vegetarian, running freely among wild animals in the forest. His diet consists of grass and water, the latter giving away his identity when being spotted by a hunter by a stream. Enkidu's size and stature match King Gilgamesh, only he is unkempt and beastlike. After fleeing, the hunter reports this to his king. Gilgamesh tells him to bring Shamhat to tame this beast-man through her "woman arts." Shamhat is what we could call a sacred prostitute, only that latter word does not translate well. The idea that a woman could make love to bring both herself and her partner to higher states of being is not justifiable in a world that has been dominated by patriarchy. Poets know better, as do the lovers of such women, not to mention these women themselves. Enkidu becomes one such lover to Shamhat, who awaits him naked by the stream. They unite for seven nights of passionate lovemaking (the number of days of creation in the Bible). At the end the beast is tamed, resting on the last day. As Joseph Campbell once remarked, woman is knowledge and it is man that is coming to such knowledge.

When Enkidu finishes his jaunt, he turns to rejoin his animal friends. They scatter. It is like the old Indian story about the lion cub raised by sheep, who believes these fuzzy ones are his true family. One day an adult lion finds him bleating among a pack while munching on grass, and has to shake the boy back to his senses. He takes him to his cave and force-feeds him meat, which at first sickens him. Once the taste of blood is inside, though, he awakens to his true nature; he becomes whole. He lets out a roar and recognizes the face in the stream the elder lion leads him to. As soon as Enkidu enters Shamhat, the same thing happens—Eve has fed Adam the apple. The consequences of wholeness, however, involve leaving the life you knew behind. After you cross the river in the ferryboat, there is no turning back. Once the garden is in the distance, the shrubbery grows to block the entrance.

This motif recurs in Gilgamesh, and has an important influence on the biblical tales that follow. While there is no sex in Eden (what a sham), the act is implied when Adam and Eve discover each other's "nakedness." More to the point is the symbolism behind the Tree of the Knowledge of Good and Evil. What the pair realize is not that a man and a woman should not be naked around each other. Rather, the realization is the notion of *duality*. By tasting the fruit of this tree, as Enkidu tasted the fruits of Shamhat, they obtain the knowledge that everything has two aspects. Adam and Eve recognize their nakedness, for before that moment *they saw no separation between them.* They were fully united, not just with one another; they were part of the entire garden, and nothing was unincluded in all of existence. Upon eating the fruit and becoming desirous of the knowledge of opposites, they left the realm of pure contemplation and begin to see two sides of everything, including themselves. The reason Adam "fell" is because he divided the world into halves, seeing one part "good," the other "evil." He was no longer whole. The entire natural world exists because of this distinction, but only humans partake in it: The distancing between reality and morals, between thinking *this is what is* and *this is the way it should be*. Adam, whose very name means "man," becomes a moral animal. When he saw things as divided—and, perhaps, began to make statements like "you're either with us or against us"—he was no longer complete. The number of people he has since roped into alignment with his misfortune has been tragic.

Enkidu is led near the kingdom to be "civilized." He's anointed with oil, has his matted hair (dreadlocks) sheared, and is fed bread and beer. His vegetarian diet will soon end. He will become as the others in the great city, who've built an exclusively urban civilization with high walls to protect themselves from the outside world. In one sense he is tamed; in another, he has lost contact with his natural self. He no longer sees everything as one process, and fear enters into his heart for the first time, just as fear entered Adam upon realizing his nakedness. This becomes even more apparent later in the tale, when Gilgamesh and Enkidu journey toward the Cedar Forest to defeat an evil guardian, and doubts about Gilgamesh's quest strip away his confidence. Before he meets these fears, though, he has to meet his double. When he does, sparks fly.

Since the days of Gilgamesh, the double is one of the most pervasive and insistent themes in writing, as well as in life. Take any of the great religious texts and you'll find parallels. Adam and Eve make a great starting point: Wholeness, then confusion and separation, continuing with exile, struggle and suffering. While there are moments of victory, and a shamanic leader who has the ability to transform reality by the name of Joseph, there is no general "coming together," or union— or so we translate it such. That the tales of the Bible are not complete unto themselves, and that prophecies are to manifest again in the form of past figures (such as Jesus) is the result of a politically oriented psychology. We'll address that theme in the next section. These Western texts treat exile as a divisive imposition, while the Eastern counterparts recognize ideas like exile as self-imposed. Home is a state of being, not a physical location. Sages were at home wherever they traveled. There are numerous characters in the Gilgamesh cycle, yet ultimately it is the story of one man's return to wholeness, to the home within himself. To experience the self-realization that he will arrive at, he must journey to, and return from, Utnapishtim—alone. Only then can he be complete.

In every hero cycle, there is separation followed by a quest. After Gilgamesh and Enkidu become best friends, seeing the "other" in each other—coming to recognize the separate halves of themselves—they party hard. Enkidu, no longer virgin nor vegetarian, partakes in human affairs, while the great Gilgamesh, one-third human, two-thirds divine, is no less tamed from his sensual and aggressive pleasures. If anything, he's more intent on fulfilling his egoistic lifestyle now that he has a partner-in-crime. Only: Something is not right inside of him. While the writer(s) never let us know why, Gilgamesh must travel to the Cedar Forest and slay "evil." Humbaba is an insatiable beast, true, but first and foremost he was given the duty of protecting the forest from human invasion by the great god Enlil. Again an ecological theme: To create civilization, man has to destroy the natural world. There must be protection or else consequences like global warming and depopulated forests will occur; species will become extinct; diversity will be gone from the wild. So while Humbaba may be horrendous and dreadful, he is not without purpose. He has to be stronger than the true evils that appear in the form of hunters and loggers if nature is to remain intact. When Gilgamesh pins him down and holds a sword to his throat, Humbaba begs for life, reminding the hero that if he slays the protector, the gods will display their wrath. The forest will be left open for gaming and construction, and all will be lost.

Gilgamesh considers. Interestingly it is Enkidu who encourages him to slit his throat, the same man who nearly turned back at the entrance of the Cedar Forest due to intense fear. Enkidu, beast turned man, turns his back on the very nature that provided for him for so long, much in the way that urbanites import lumber and metals without regard for their origins. He has lost his identity in succumbing to desires—and to desire is another translation of that Buddhist warning, dukkha. When his brother has the monster in his grips, Enkidu tells him to slay him, and quickly. How, exactly, a divinely ordained protector should fall at the hands of a (part) mortal requires an understanding of how the gods were viewed at this time. As we saw in Chapter 3, these deities were aspects of the natural world, as well as integral parts of the process of their existence. They were *part* of them, as likely to be influenced by their sacrifice—and there will be sacrifice in this tale—as they are to unleash sudden havoc on us unfaithful humans. What's more, they had what Alan Watts noted as being sorely lacking in the stories of the Western God: a sense of humor. Just like the playful aspects of Shiva, Ganesha and Krishna, as well as later Greek gods, they were able to laugh. Even though sometimes cited as omnipotent, with these deities events just kept slipping through the cracks. It seems doubly ironic that the divinely appointed Humbaba would be overthrown with the help of one of Enlil's partners, but if it were not for the divine Shamash blasting the beast with powerful winds, Gilgamesh would not have pinned him down. The gods of Olympus could never get over petty quarrels and jealousies, and neither could their ancestors. Neither can we.

This dual aspect of divinity was not lost in books like the Bible. It was the editing and focusing on translations of particular passages that made it into a battle of total good and evil. Even Satan was intended as a minor character, not the complete and horrific dark prince he has become today, and the word "sin" never even appears in the garden cycle of Genesis. So when Gilgamesh relents, slaying Humbaba and destroying total "evil," something inside of his heart still is not complete. He had thought that this one act would redeem him, only that idea proved false. The duo then brings "to earth the highest of the trees, the cedar whose top once pierced the sky." They construct a door "a hundred feet wide and thirty feet high" from the timber, and float it down the Euphrates to the temple of Enlil. They just murdered his protector after all, and have to make amends. Interesting that they destroy the natural world to do so, and make an idol for the gods with what they've destroyed. They've actually killed nature to appeal to nature.

Why would the legacy of the standing tree not serve as a fitting testament to the glory of a god who supposedly represents this aspect of nature? Why would they tear it down and carve it into innumerable pieces to pay respect to what it once was? This is a question we are still faced with, one that if not addressed will truly end our days of false idolatry … and everything else.

The jokes on the gods continue. Gilgamesh is tempted by the goddess Ishtar—a counterpart to the Indian Kali, in that she is both a ferocious lover and devourer of men. Gilgamesh is too smart for that game and sends the trickster on her way. In her anger she demands that her father Anu give her the Bull of Heaven with which to destroy Gilgamesh. Anu reminds his desire-stricken daughter that if he unleashes the bull, there will be seven years of famine in the city—another ecological trigger. She promises him that she has stored enough grain for the city, an assumption we cannot presume correct. Gilgamesh and Enkidu make quick work of the beast, though, and Ishtar is further enraged. As predicted, her jealousy causes a famine. In the context of the overall story this seems a sudden aside, though given the environmental slant, it makes sense. Once again, gods, like politicians, are playing war games, and the true victims are those suffering from a lack of grain and nourishment. Note that the biblical famine of Egypt, as told to Joseph, was seven years as well.

At the end of this chapter, while they're celebrating their victory over the bull, Enkidu has a vision. The gods have assembled. He asks Gilgamesh why, though the writer does not provide an answer. Book Seven opens with Enkidu revealing his dream to Gilgamesh. The gods have declared that it is time for him to die. The duo has slaughtered Humbaba and the Bull of Heaven, and therefore must pay a price. To overcome evil in the forest, Gilgamesh had indeed suffered a fee of sacrifice—his best friend, his double, the other half of himself who he thought had been complete. Evil was never truly destroyed because the evil inside of him remained. Enkidu dies after days of suffering miserably, and Gilgamesh puts forth a touching and emotional eulogy. Then he realizes what he must do. Gilgamesh prepares to become an ascetic, complete with the "matted hair" and "lion skin" we know from the proto-yogis of India. It is time for him to leave the kingdom, as Buddha left his, to overcome human suffering.

No story is written in a vacuum. This is why it is frustrating to hear fundamentalists talk of the Bible as "truth," and every other religious tradition as paganism and false idolatry. For the most part we have discussed the negative imprints that Christianity has left behind, but the literature of this religion is beautiful and rich in symbolism. It is the literalism that these words are interpreted with that is so frustrating. Soon we will look at these symbols and how they are much more universal in scope than assumed by people who take words at face value. Thus far we have witnessed numerous parallels between the Gilgamesh cycle and biblical folklore. Those stories were not "revealed" to a handful of writers. They are remixes of older tales that were crafted over the course of centuries before being edited and assembled. Each generation added their particular slant, to fashion the story to fit their time. Assuming that a book nearly 2,000 years old is the perfect and literal truth is anything but natural. Gilgamesh has made his sacrifice and must now go into exile to find himself—another motif that would set the path for the desert dwellers a few centuries down the road.

Gilgamesh sets out in search of Utnapishtim, the mortal who was granted eternal life by the gods. So there's the rub. It was death—most importantly, his own—that Gilgamesh had feared all along. He has to embark on a quest to find something beyond it. The death of his closest kin, his other half, awakened him to mortality. Witnessing it with his eyes was still not enough. He accomplishes a series of events that only someone granted the power of a god (or writer) could do, and sets sail across the Waters of Death on a journey three days and three nights long. He is resurrected; future usage of that motif need hardly be pointed out. Finally he reaches Utnapishtim, a man who was eternal because the gods had once sent a great flood and he survived by building an ark and gathering animals to sail to safety. Sounds suspiciously familiar.

After a long account of his adventures, and then telling Gilgamesh that the attainment of eternal life is only possible

if he is able to stay awake for seven days—the irony being
that as soon as he says that, Gilgamesh falls asleep for seven
instead. Utnapishtim offers him one last chance for perpetual
existence. He must swim to the bottom of the Great Deep and
pluck a certain flower. Gilgamesh bids him farewell, puts on his
goggles and chains rocks to his feet ... and down he goes. He
plucks the plant, returns to the surface, and then—more irony.
Instead of eating it, he decides that he will let an old man in his
city taste it first, and if it works, he will eat and then cultivate
it. (More agriculture.) Yet his suspicion of the gods makes itself
known, for why did he just not taste it right away? After all
that questing, you'd think he'd have acquired faith. He stops to
take a rest and a snake surfaces, snags the flower, and does not
question whether or not he should eat it. The serpent disappears,
and immortality is forever lost to Gilgamesh.

At the beginning of his quest, Gilgamesh is offered the
luxuries of life: fine, shaven hair, sweet oils, brilliant gold robes.
He is made to believe that these things are the signs of divinity.
It is a trick. Like the yogis of India, whose gurus first tell them
that the joys of eternal life are to be found in rich objects, it is a
test of sincerity. Gilgamesh has to deny these things and adopt
the costume of the ascetic to be initiated into the next stage of
education. When a seemingly well-intentioned student thinks
the fruits of material glamour are the benefits of divinity, they
have not made it past the very first step. This serves as a signal
to the teacher that they are not prepared. After the snake ate the
immortal plant from the bottom of the ocean, he shed his skin
and regenerated. This is the *same exact role* the snake played in
the Bible. His "temptation" to Eve in the garden was not evil.
He was playing the role of perpetuity, showing how human
mythology continues even after the spirit sheds its skin and
moves on to another body. Recall that Krishna offered Arjuna
the same advice regarding the changing of clothes. The snake
in India, *naga*, is the symbol of the sacred kundalini energy
that brings a human to completion. Before becoming complete,
however, they must understand that they are divided, and
they must comprehend the nature of the world, which *appears*
in duality even though it is always whole, which is maya and

samadhi at the same time.

Through such a symbolic reading of one mythology, we see how it translates across time and space to affect numerous peoples. In a naturalistic theology, the snake is the perfect representative of continuous life. Like the grain and seed of farming cycles, so the skin of this serpent denotes something that endures. The spirit of our own age lives on in the reading of these tales and the understanding that we, right now, are experiencing the same motifs as our ancestors did, thousands of years ago. The story of Gilgamesh predates biblical writers by centuries, yet the Bible became the basis of numerous religions while this king remains nothing but the subject of mythology. Why? For one reason, it is certainly due to it being "lost" for thousands of years, not to mention the time it took scholars to translate cuneiform before deciphering it. Yet the main reason has to do with marketing. The Bible is touted as the world's "most read book," which is not necessarily due to demand, but rather that it is very evidently in supply. If you print hundreds of millions of books and pass them out in every unsuspecting village and hotel room across the planet, what do you expect? When you take boats and airplanes to remote regions of the planet, carrying advanced technologies and helpful medicines, and declare the work of engineers and scientists to be produced by the God of Abraham, who wouldn't believe?

With missionary motives like this, it's not challenging to see why atheism has grown as a reaction to the deluge of forceful and uncompromising marketing techniques. Yet you don't have to believe in God, or the gods, to appreciate the rich textures of story embedded in our mythologies. For while the Gilgamesh cycle talks about divine beings, this is very much a story about being human, and the quest to overcome suffering. Even as the hero dove to the bottom of the ocean, Utnapishtim knew he would not find what he thought he was looking for. What he found, however, and what he returned to Uruk with, was a complete self. His "other half" was integrated. The story ends with the very lines that it opened with, a touching homage to the beauty and splendor of the city. It does not finish with any word on how Gilgamesh then ruled his citizens, or

what has changed inside the king. The details are left to our
imagination, much in the same way that we don't know who
we'll be in a year's time, although the opportunities for being
virtually anybody exist. We can only suspect that Gilgamesh
was humbled, even though some inner demons never perish.
Yet his symbolic life and death left a legacy for poets and
thinkers to contemplate 3,000 years later, so in some sense he
did attain eternal life—or at least a commendable chunk of it.
Remember, when Enkidu died, he was turned to clay. His story
was embodied on actual clay, the "paper" these writers carved
into. So it is the story that survives, not the flesh, and the words
that are now the mythology, triggering ideas and emotions
inside our own hearts and brains. This is even more apparent in
the tale we turn to next, a remix of the Gilgamesh cycle whose
name lives on in perpetual glory. As is the case with many such
tales, this name has been used in the murder of millions of nonbelievers in a continuation of the cosmic joke that we've been
laughing at, and crying to, for thousands of years.

E very story is written with prior influence, just as every
human has the advantage of his ancestors to build
upon. In the realm of faith, however, some rules are
suspended. Different religious traditions have tried to make
distinctions between "revealed" texts, i.e. scriptures that were
"divinely told" to an individual, and those that are merely
supplementary documents, supporting the foundation of the
religion without being direly necessary. The Vedic scriptures
that were supposedly recited by gods to mortals are called *Sruti*,
while the poetry of men is *Smrti*, the former obviously being
more valuable to their pantheon of letters. Readers of the Koran
believe that Allah spoke directly to Mohammad, and the words
inside are the exact messages given to this prophet. Religionists
of the Bible are certain that those stories are not mythologies,
but actual accounts of history.

In mythological terms, human or profane time, governed
by clocks and calendars and solar and lunar cycles, is on a
different plane than cosmic time, which is based in eternity. It is

important to recognize that eternity is not a *measure* of time; it is the *negation* of it. A concept that is perpetual exceeds time, and should be treated as a symbol and not quantitatively. It is also an idea exclusive to the mythological realm. It does not make sense to treat anything biological, anthropological, or chemical as eternal. Those are all involved with various measurements of time. The idea of eternity is confined to human patterns and processes, and when used denotes something that is continual through generations upon generations, like folklore and DNA. Anything involved in the cyclical process of samsara would fall into the measurement of time. The achievement of moksha, the state where opposites are psychologically and symbolically united in the sage's mind, denotes eternity.

Religious philosophy, for the most part, is bound by time. In Christian ideology, time is not eternal, for there was supposedly a moment when a man was chosen by God to represent his kingdom on earth, and that time is past. In a sense, time is not cyclical or linear in Christian theory; it moves *backwards*. It is constantly peering back with statements like "What would Jesus do?" and derives from the idea of a specific date of creation. Even though there is a backwards movement of time, the philosophy of eternity does appear: in hell. The damned are sentenced to the impossible imprisonment of eternity, which is an improbable judgment on any soul. Time, in the world of opposites, has to be temporal. The only way to access eternity is to go beyond opposites, and the placing of one group for some moral or ethical reason into a perpetual state of torture is yet another inconsistency in the understanding of scripture.

It is especially frustrating to witness such mistranslations when closer inspection of biblical motifs reveal it as an agricultural mythology, one that is completely dependent upon the cyclical nature of time. As we've noticed, the predominant spiritual traditions have utilized two major motifs: agriculture and warfare. The latter is still well publicized in the Christian world, with George Bush's erroneous call for a modern Crusade and the fundamental insistence on maintaining an Army of God. Agriculture, though, is rarely discussed. The most important season of the Christian story takes place between Christmas and Easter, and reveals numerous keys of a tradition rich in symbolism. To understand them we have to leave the realm of profane time—that is, stop treating biblical folklore as if were factual history—and journey beyond the dates and places associated with the stories to arrive at a place where we can delve deeper into their meaning.

As Richard Dawkins pointed out in *The Selfish Gene*, the translation from Hebrew to Greek rendered "young woman" as "virgin," and hence a disastrous series of biologically impossible misinterpretations ensued. Yet the virgin motif is not new—the Buddha too was born of a virgin in some stories. Recognizing the feat as symbolic in the Christian world, Mary was an updated equivalent of the Egyptian goddess Isis, who, as Manly P. Hall wrote, "although she gave birth to all living things—chief among them the Sun—still remained a virgin." As we will get to, Jesus *is* a solar deity, so the sun approximation is fitting. If we treat the word virginal as meaning pure, which would move us into the realm of ethics and away from biology, then the birth of her gifted son (sun) was due to her positive nature: she was pure of heart.

More to the point, and beyond morality to boot, is that Mary's virginity was representative of unplowed soil. Her son was born at midnight on the winter solstice, the time of year when the sun is weakest upon that particular hemisphere. This would correlate her as a lunar deity giving birth to the sun, a very old story indeed. At the point of total and complete darkness a light is born. This is why he is destined to be a "light unto all nations," for the star that beams into every nook of this planet, as well as what gives life to this planet, is the Sun—the Son, "light bearer," Christ. If there were any actual creator of life on this planet, this would most certainly be the source.

The Bible is ecologically inclined in numerous ways. Not only is it a tale of the barren soil (a motif fitting for Sarah as well as Mary), it is a folklore that begins, and ends, with trees. Trees are necessary for human existence: they provide oxygen for us to breathe; they attract and retain moisture, helping to prevent dehydration of soil; they provide shade, fruit and medicines;

they are, quite literally, what civilization is built by, in the ways of ships, houses and buildings, as well as assisting us in the transition from single-text doctrines on clay and papyrus to the mass production of books, so that the most sacred aspect of existence—the Word—could be passed down for thousands of years. We noticed in the last section that the Tree of the Knowledge of Good and Evil was the trigger of duality, and when mankind ate of this tree, consciousness came to be. This is the same tree that Christ was crucified on, completing a very important cycle: In Adam's time, as he was one who sinned upon earth (sin=ignorance), the tree served as the same instrument by which Christ, the redeemer, was enlightened upon. As the ultimate sacrifice, Jesus allowed himself to become merged with the tree, similarly to Gilgamesh in the Cedar Forest. Man's descent into darkness and subsequent rebirth is told through the ecology of trees.

Look at it another way. In the Bible, mankind was originally made from "clay." This is the exact substance that the Word which was God was inscribed upon, for it was clay that held language and was passed from man to man. The tree became the next step in this evolution; hence, the Word would be passed along on this substance. The tree is by no way exclusive to Adam and Christ, or Gilgamesh. It is seen in the pine tree that embalms Osiris in the palace of Byblos, another solar deity who "travels to the underworld" only to be resurrected by his divine consort after he is dismembered. The Buddha reaches enlightenment while seated underneath the bhodi tree; the Kabbalah bases its Ein Sof on the symbology of the Tree of Life; the Norse god Odin learned the wisdom of runes while immolated upon the World Tree; the Aztec hero Quetzalcoatl was formed when a hero shot an arrow of the *pochotl* tree into another *pochotl*, a sort of homeopathic creation tale. Moses's staff was also made from the Tree of Life, as was the consecrated rod of Hermes, the great Egyptian god of literature, athletics and poetry.

The tree is also indicative of the spine, the pillar upon which yogis raise the sacred kundalini energy. Kundalini is said to sleep at the base, coiled like a serpent, and reveals its knowledge by standing at attention as a sort of rod or antenna. The "roots" are embedded in the sacrum, as well as the sexual organs, while the "trunk" of the body is the map it passes through. Energy flows out through the crown of the head (as leaves are the head of branches), extending beyond profane time into that of the cosmic clock, blossoming like a thousand-petal lotus flower. The leaves that form at the end of each branch eventually blossom only to decay and die, leaving the tree on a downward spiral to regenerate soil. If the snake remains coiled at the base, he is "asleep" or "ignorant," just as mankind would have remained had not the snake awoken Eve, and then Adam, in the garden. The awakening occurred upon the first taste of duality, which required the union of male and female aspects of existence. It should be noted that in the yoga tradition, it is a *conscious* attempt of raising the energy that produces *unconscious* results. Through meditation and breathing techniques, the knowledge of unity is then integrated into the individual, who understands that the supposed fissure that separates was all part of a great illusion. Upon being awoken they never "sleep" again; they no longer partake in the game of "this" or "that," but understand cohesion between opposites.

In Gilgamesh's tale, the snake shedding its skin was representative of this knowledge—the king returned to his city neither dethroned, nor blissful. He was enlightened, to the mortality of human flesh, to the immortality of the process of existence. The snake motif, so important in revealing this knowledge to Gilgamesh, recurs in many traditions. Images of two snakes wrapped around a rod—the ida and pingala nadis coiled upon the sushumna—represent the union of opposites, today employed by numerous medical professionals who use this image of Hermes's caduceus as the ultimate symbol of healing: the balance of forces, like the Gorgon Medusa's blood, which exhibited the peculiar behavior of both poison and medicine. This motif is disarmingly similar to the logo of Christ, which features two fish on either side of one cross (and two doves above), one ascending (representing the Christ figure), the other descending (Lucifer). This motif is underexplored in contemporary Christianity, for it implies the necessity of both

Christ and Lucifer within the balance of wisdom—as indeed they are.

But as Alan Watts wrote, "One of the special distinctions of Christianity is that it takes evil more seriously than any other religion." Lucifer is a key figure representative of *enantiodromia*—that which turns into its opposite. His passion for God had been so substantive that he assumed the symbol to be greater than the reality, and he became "fallen." Every extreme turns into its opposite, which is the psychological apparatus that fuels such a love to turn faithful warriors—real or suburbanized—into agents of the very force they believe to be extinguishing. It's a vicious cycle. Suburban politicians are just as dangerous as national ones, for their votes keep certain figureheads in office. There is a trickle-down effect, where minor players mimic major ones in hopes of sharing the spotlight. Little can they be aware of another important meaning of sin: to miss the mark. Their arrows of righteousness are the flaming specters of corruption and egoism. It is little surprise that maya, the great illusion of separateness, is derived from *matr-*, to "measure," which also gave us the words "mother" and "matrix." The unity of the virgin field, the crops growing from it and the sun that gave it all life are parts of one process. Dividing them and giving more credence to one rather than another is to measure time, and thus create the illusion.

This form of dismemberment is coded into numerous religious traditions, as noticed in our previous discussions of cannibalism. The cure for dis-memberment is re-membering—recalling the original and complete knowledge of union. Our rituals have evolved, but the meanings behind them have not. The Vedic *rishis* were not interested in human sacrifice for its own sake, and thus began to formulate the spiritual significance of the action. The same is true for Christians, who transformed the body of Christ into wheat and blood into wine. Both wheat and grapes, of course, are parts of the agricultural process, and it took the dismemberment of Christ in the figure of the crucifixion to lead back to original knowledge, the complete man—Adam returned to the garden. This is the portion of the process that disturbs the part of us that believes there is a secret elixir at the bottom of the ocean that will one day bring us immortality, when the apparent truth is that each one of us right now is involved in this cycle, becoming our own sacrifice in the sequence of nature, fertilizing soil with the bacteria contained inside of our skin. When we grasp the meaning and tools provided to us by the Christ motif, we can certainly appreciate life more, but no matter how hard we try, we cannot use them to escape death.

To fear death is simply a way of saying that life frightens us. James Hillman, in *Suicide and the Soul*, reminds us of the great French philosopher Jean-Paul Sartre, who "maintains that we can never grasp death at all because it is always the death of someone else; we are always outside of it." Therefore it is not death that frustrates us, for we will come to know it in time. The fear of life, however, binds us to time, and we feel imprisoned because we don't understand mythological symbols. As Hillman goes on to write, "We are more often lived by than live our myth." This is most unfortunate, considering that those religious figures who we now honor with accolades, hymns, and t-shirts were attempting to help us access the latter.

Let us look at more symbols. On Holy Saturday during the Easter ceremonies, the priest lights the triple candle, a three-pronged waxen statue that is an iconographic parallel of Shiva's trident, and yet another representation of the caduceus. This trident would later be borrowed by Poseidon, god of the sea; later still it was given to the ever-expanding image of Satan. This makes logistical sense from the church's standpoint: use the imagery of those "other" gods against them, even if we will take it for ourselves. The priest continues with long liturgies centered on Christ's forthcoming judgment of the living and the dead, all by fire. This is a common motif in the religious world, as fire is the force which destroys, though it can heal as well. This is probably the most important symbol in the understanding of the play of opposites: *the fire that heals is the same fire that destroys*. This is why the Christian concept of hell is the exact same idea behind kundalini—it is not the substance that changes, but our psychology in regards to it. The destructive aspects of fire are obvious. A little less obvious are those that are healing: the use of flame through cooking, and the intestinal forces inside of us, resulting in what practitioners of Ayurveda called "cooking" (i.e. digestion); the innumerable important uses of electricity; lasers used by doctors to "burn" through internal disorders and cancers. This very mythology plays out in every moment of our lives, when we can use our breath to both heat, and cool, our bodies. Judgment through fire is the ability to utilize this element in its varied uses simultaneously and with an understanding of its dual tendencies. To be overwhelmed by one "side" is to be consumed by its opposite.

This concept is further enumerated in the Bible, Acts 2:3, when the author writes of *glossolalia*—speaking in tongues—as "cloven tongues like as of fire." The tongue of flame, which resides just above the head, is considerably similar to the raising of kundalini, brought about by tapas, the austerities or "inner heat" of the individual in meditation. The yogi is said to burn through karmas in the quest for enlightenment, and the ability to speak in tongues is to see beyond the supposed deception of Babel and into a universal language, one spoken through the rays of the sun god. This narrative is offered at the time of Pentecost, which falls seven weeks after Easter, either in mid-spring in the Northern Hemisphere or mid-autumn in the Southern, both times when the sun is near its annual apex. The destructive use of fire is elaborated upon in the mythology of Shiva and his Tandava, the cosmic dance of destruction. There is one further parallel from this dance, which correlates to Christian mythology. First, during Lent, the faithful receive ash on their forehead, which is also the *bindu* in Indian symbolism, representing the third eye center, where all opposites converge. One of Shiva's main stomping grounds is the cemetery, where he smears himself in the ashes of the dead, in honor of that which has passed and as a tribute to the process of life. Lent, occurring during the onset of spring, symbolizes the passage that the solar deity from the underworld makes in order to give life to the fields, to grain and grass and all the inhabitants within. Jesus, as life-giver, is a metaphoric return of the sun, bringing food to the fields. When the faithful consume his blood and body in sacrament, they are honoring the farm.

The final analysis we will address here is contained

within the very architecture of the church itself, where the ceremonies are held. When looked down upon from on high, the building represents a cross, with the nave being the body, the chapels flanking the sides like arms, and the choir and sanctuary at the head. This "head" faces east, the direction of sunrise; upon entering, individuals pass from the bottom of the nave (sacrum) to the altar (crown). The entire idea behind the blueprint of a church is the chakra system, the faithful moving from the foundation, or root, to liberation at the top of the head, the thousand-petal lotus, the solar deity who is eternal because he is no longer chained by the dualistic aspects of time and space. The mythology of Christianity is the story of yoga.

The writers of Sanskrit believed that language is not made of words, but that words *are* the things they represent. Muslims also recognize the importance of speech: the power of the Koran is in the recitation of the words, which lulls the speaker into a trance-like state—a trance being a meditative mode of consciousness where the rules of everyday logic are no longer dominant. The word Tao—today known as "the way"— originally meant "speech." Language is important in Christianity, and not only in the reciting of biblical phrases. The word Hallelujah does not have any inherent meaning. The relevance of it is in the expression of it, so that the choir chanting it would be able to access a state of trance, or beatitude, dissolving the distance between individual and cosmos—the very same trigger, in fact, as the syllable OM. This was further elaborated upon in the beautiful style of antiphon singing, in which the choir offered alternating call-and-response verses of psalms or canticles—again correlating to the Indian kirtan and Pakistani qawwali traditions. The community was connected through sound.

None of the above is meant to imply that Christianity "stole" or even "borrowed" the symbolism of India. Yet the Christian doctrines were assembled over many centuries, given the form we know it as today, in 1611—sixteen centuries after the birth of Christ. We have a tendency to treat much of the ancient world with suspicion, as a land of primitives who lacked the technology and sophistication of our modern world. But while the stories are not direct copies, it would be surprising if the folklore of India, passed along for generations through trade and conquest, did not influence biblical tales. What's more is that direct contact is not necessary to have expressed symbols through the collective unconscious. It's not hard to imagine the relevance of a snake shedding its skin, and with the regenerative power that implies, that it could be used for the same meaning, even if geography keeps the poets distant.

Regardless of exact historical interactions, what proves relevant are the constant themes of staying grounded in the present moment, of moving beyond profane time through an integration of opposites. This *has* to be expressed in a religious philosophy, for, once again, that is the meaning of the word religion. If a religion does not go beyond duality, it is not of significance and can have no meaning in the union of, well, anything that appears to be separated. This applies to time as well as space (and material objects in space, such as humans). There are events confined by the realm of time, and those not bound to it—sacred, or mythological, time versus profane time. The first is the archetype, the essence; the second, a manifestation of the archetype, the form. As Alan Watts wrote, "We must not mistake that which is beyond the future for that which is in the future." We also cannot assume that the historical past is merely a series of stories that are dependent upon exact times and people. Mythologies can stand alone—they do not lose power when personified; we do. When assuming that one specific figure embodied the archetype, or essence, for the entirety of humanity, we are eternally disempowered.

Christian mythologies rarely get such a reading. In fact, they are almost never treated as mythologies at all. Since this is the case, the stories of the Bible are museum pieces, treated as historical artifacts that once served a community and can no longer. This is why the only means of expression in modern Christianity is through a supposed Second Coming of Christ, an occurrence prophesied in every age, and yet slippery and deviant in that it has not yet transpired. That it will is highly unlikely, and not particularly relevant. What can manifest, though, is an integration of the philosophies of Christianity through mythological understanding. In such a case, these tales can be as relevant and meaningful today as they ever were. To find faith in Christ is to worship the sun and all the processes which that star helps to keep alive on our planet.

In Chinese philosophy, health is a balanced state and disease signifies an energetic imbalance. "To Western medicine, understanding an illness means uncovering a distinct entity that is separate from the patient's being; to Chinese medicine, understanding means perceiving the relationships among all the patient's signs and symptoms in the context of his or her life," wrote Ted J. Kaptchuk in *The Web That Has No Weaver*. Healing is a *holistic* exercise—it is concerned with the whole person. The strains of the either/or philosophy expounded upon in our religious past can be seen in modern medicine, with both its Cartesian split between cause and effect with humans and illness, as well as the capitalist posturing of making a patient believe they are unhealthy in order for them to ensure insurance rates are kept at a premium. A good doctor is concerned with healing a patient so that they *won't* have to return, and is more apt to offer techniques of prevention rather than waiting for a problem to manifest, which must then be cured. As Pico Iyer wrote, "The most important thing we ask of a doctor is that he not hide the truth from us, out of kindness or sympathy, not dress it up in euphemisms or periphrases, but just tell it to us straight, so we know where we stand." The same truth should be evident to our religious leaders. If a person arrives with a metaphysical problem, then offer a solution—not an unsolvable equation to perplex and confuse them. The solutions are as numerous as the questions. There is a balance between them, though that does not mean we will find it. The path towards the end is like a camel passing through the eye of a needle, as one memorable person phrased it. In the final chapters we will look at possible solutions, concerning ourselves with what would help us in the here and now, not the forever after and never before.

CHAPTER 8

EMBODYING THE SURVIVAL MACHINE

Attempting to discern the starting point of time is a speculation that will always baffle humans. Albert Einstein showed that you cannot separate time from space, as well as that neither entity moves in a straight line, like the linear diagrams in high school history textbooks. When his relativity theory blew asunder the notion of Newtonian gravity, the scientific world was given the opportunity to move beyond the simple cause-and-effect mentality produced and dictated by religious psychology for hundreds of years. Gravity was no longer dictated by force, but rather by space-time curvature. Time was once again circular; no, that's not quite right: time was *always* circular, and mathematicians, physicists, and philosophers stopped fearing the grain that church and governmental leaders had sanded; with circularity, they took a more realistic view of what was going on around them. What they found was that their sciences correlated amazingly with primitive agricultural ideas, not to mention Hindu, Buddhist, and Taoist musings. These ideas were not discovered; they were *remembered*. Today, this is continuously being realized across a diverse range of subjects, from bioecology and ecodesign to physics and genetics. The form and focus is rearranged—the essence, the same.

In China, the term "10,000 years" was a symbol used to denote eternity. When sages used that figure, they weren't literally implying that this or that event took place ten millennia ago. In the same way, the term "In the Beginning" at the outset of Genesis served a similar function: God was not *not* there one moment, suddenly there the next. This god, the ultimate ground of being, existed in perpetuity, and through the process of life all things manifested. (Note: I did not write, "through the process of life all things *were* manifested.") To claim that 10,000 years is a fixed amount of time—which isn't a calendar but part of the process of existence—or that someone or -thing waved a magic wand and "poof!" all of existence came to be, is to place a pinpoint on a map and start a line. What Einstein showed by drawing a square on the surface of the earth (as you would laying a wash cloth atop a globe) is that you will not produce four ninety-degree angles—hence any or no line can be straight, depending on where you're standing. Space is curved, and time, being inseparable from space, cannot move in a strictly linear fashion. To put a starting point on it is to imply that time, and space, are not continuous. This idea has no basis in any reality we experience, yet it has been doctrine to the Intelligent Design movement. They claim that "In the Beginning" was an actual, historical event, and in doing so, they miss the symbolism—the beginningless time—behind the poetry.

If read as a historical novel, the Bible is unabashedly unrealistic, which is why "believers" have to constantly cut-and-paste according to whatever they're trying to argue at that moment. As we saw in the last chapter, when read as a symbolic guide, it offers profound insights that help the individual move beyond the notion of opposites, and can promote individual freedom and social cohesion without contradictions. There is beauty throughout its numerous pages of poetry. The sciences developed by westerners influenced by linear, biblical thinking, however, were clear on one point: spirit is separate from matter; the individual observes life without interfering with the process. This was never the case in Asia, where *koans* like "Who is the observer observing the observed?" had already been in circulation for centuries. Einstein's relativity theory put the observer into the position of being observed and observing simultaneously, a scientific movement that was recycling a very old notion: karma. When individuals become disconnected from the oneness of the universe, they become bound to karmic laws. The Indians knew that there was a way out of the circling of time, and practiced numerous austerities and meditations to find it. Many are still doing so today, continuing an unbroken thread of consciousness that exceeds time while embodying numerous different human bodies.

In 1976, when contemplating the lifespan of a gene, Richard Dawkins wrote, "It leaps from body to body down the generations, manipulating body after body in its own way and for its own ends, abandoning a succession of mortal bodies before they sink into senility and death." He notes that genes are "replicators," and that we are their "survival machines." While the combination of genes is unique to each individual, "One gene may be regarded as a unit that survives through a large number of successive individual bodies." Dawkins and other biologists have made it clear that genes are not responsible for our moral or religious beliefs, and should not be discussed in such terms. Journalist Robert Wright dedicated an entire book to the question of morality and genes, declaring that there is a percentage of our makeup that dictates the latter (one-third), while the environment we grow up within will (two-thirds) influence our outlooks and perceptions. I'm not arguing that genes "carry" spiritual significance or that they "destine" us into one direction or the other. As Richard Tarnas points out in *Cosmos and Psyche*, regarding the astrological movement of planets in relationship to how it manifests in our human existence on earth: "Radically different embodiments of a given archetypal complex appeared to be equally possible, as multiple potentialities and 'tendencies to exist' (to use the phrase familiar from quantum physics), while they still remained faithful in underlying ways to the deeper principles involved." To highlight this, he uses the examples of Adolf Hitler and Charlie Chaplin, who both exhibited numerous comparative tendencies while remaining obviously varied in their experiences.

Potentiality and tendencies to exist are important, for as Tarnas shows, that while the planets may line up in certain directions to promote specific situations, this does not imply that the human will embody the function—or that the function will be "good." In one example, he shows how Charles Darwin and Abraham Lincoln, both born on the same day, embodied parallel realities in their lifetimes while accomplishing vastly different goals. The example of Chaplin and Hitler seems even more varied. Born four days apart but retaining numerous planetary alignments, these two men shared many qualities even though their paths unfold as differently as imaginable. Like Wright, Tarnas points out that social conditions are highly significant in the manifestation process, not to mention that having a particular quality (passionate, stubborn, driven, romantic) can express itself in numerous ways.

In the realm of biology, research is being conducted in search of a "God gene," to be able to pinpoint some sort of spiraling DNA that signifies who may or may not believe in a divine being. This sort of research is distracting us from the point. What's important about observations like that of Dawkins's above resides in language. When the writer of the *Bhagavad Gita* used the symbolic figure of the ground of all being, Krishna, to describe life as a continuous process, whereby the spirit sheds bodies like humans change their clothes, he was not aware of genes, or DNA. He had, though, been observant of the cyclical process of life, and since grain and animals die and are reborn, he assumed the same happened to humans. If we remove ourselves from this process and pretend that humans observe life without being involved, then the replication of genes from lifetime to lifetime will not produce any mental or emotional effect. Yet through physics (not to mention common sense), we know that this is not the case. Our bodies, ideas, beliefs, and morals are all passed on, be it in the form of genetics—which is nearly invisible and assumes the form of bodies—or through words—which are invisible but assume the shape of ideas. There is *something* that is continuous and self-perpetuating— that does not have to be created, but is constantly creating itself through time and space; that did not need an originator, but is a continuous process of replication that circles back and feeds upon its own tail.

Yogis define this process as samsara. The world is comprised of layer upon layer of maya, usually translated as "illusion," though it originally meant something like "magic creative power." The play (lila) of the world is not false; the magic is the illusion that the parts are separate from the whole, or that you can extract fragments to make it such. This is why the Buddha understood that our acute and lasting suffering is created solely by the mind, not external circumstances: dukkha. This affects our reactions and emotions regarding any external phenomena, even if they appear "random" or "destined." We do not need the world to change; we need to reorient our psychology to adjust to the ways of the world. Much of the history we've learned, as we've seen in the examples of this book, has been passed to us through generations of people who viewed the world, and our place in it, through the singular lens of a biased mind. That God was creator of the universe and blessed humans with life was no more uncertain than the fact that negroes and primitives were not humans, but sub-humans, and that Muslims were meant to be destroyed by Christians in a battle of righteousness. Different circumstances called for different takes on the omnipotent. In one view, a Christian victory signified that God is on their side, while in another a loss is God's way of humbling them, as well as offering them courage for the next battle. Either viewpoint is an excuse. Regardless of which outcome is experienced, it can only be applied in hindsight. The very notion of destiny allows us to fool ourselves into not taking responsibility for our actions. The individual trapped in the play of victories and losses will continue to be engaged by this game until she is able to see the totality of her circumstances, which, to the yogi, could very well take lifetimes. When the yogi does take responsibility for her actions—and, more importantly, her reactions—a state of inner calm is embodied. This is the state the yogi then exists within, the place where his or her perspective is governed. It is a much more appropriate definition of enlightenment than the usual connotation, which is a quasi-mystical rapture. The "blowing out" might be ecstatic, but to maintain such a state is where the real discipline occurs.

Part of Carl Jung's genius rested in his theories of the archetype and collective unconscious—the idea that recurring motifs appear and reappear until consciously dealt with, even if their origins were from an unnamable and self-perpetuating source. Just as the individual is a survival machine passing down physical genes, so the biases, thoughts, and emotions are passed on as well. This does not imply a direct link, or that they have to be to members of the same family. Let us consider the electromagnetic spectrum, of which visible light is only a partial fraction. We can see light—or, better put, light is what enables us to see—yet we cannot detect radio waves, x-rays, or cosmic rays without the help of machinery. The invention of our machines did not coincide with the invention of those rays. The rays had always existed, and over time we were able to harness the beneficial aspects of their properties in our technology, be it by projecting music through space or inspecting the internal infrastructure of the body. In the same way we can audibly project sound through space (and thus time), it is more than possible that we project emotions, ideas, and perceptions in the same manner, and that some individuals are more "tuned in" to those frequencies than others. In yoga the spinal cord is one such antenna. Through the tuning of chakras, via practices such as meditation and chanting, such states are consciously cultivated—the yogi is turning "on" to the waves, with practices and perceptions that create a high frequency connection.

We are all operating on some channel, for the most part unconsciously. We ingest different waves from across space and time, all of which influence our everyday realities in ways we would never suspect. Only upon bringing these states to light—by essentially becoming so assimilated with the light that there is no difference between us and it—can we tune the channel how we see fit. We cannot tune in if we don't even know where the dial is, however. This state of being tuned in, samadhi, is often advertised as the "goal" of yoga. Instead, let us consider it as a highly attuned state of being. To be absorbed into this state one must expel the ego, as prescribed by Siddhartha. Without irony, this makes perfect sense on a genetic level, for now we can recognize a similar platform espoused by biologists—the very point where religious believers load their ammunition against the "amoral" scientists. Whereas the frequencies passed along from person to person do have varying oscillations—Pythagoras may have stated that harmonized melody was "good" while discord was "evil"—genes do not. Genes do not "care" whether the individual is compassionate or self-serving. Ironically, in many ways, that second state is much more beneficial to the survival of the gene. As Robert Wright, ahem, writes, "natural selection never promised us a rose garden. It doesn't 'want' us to be happy. It 'wants' us to be genetically prolific." This is perfectly in line with the state of samadhi, which, like Gilgamesh returning to his city after the snake shed its skin, is concerned with *wholeness*. A completed individual does not choose to be good over bad, right over wrong. They will move accordingly and with compassion in their actions, which are triggered by instinct more than they are informed by flipping through the pages of a book. Most of all, samadhi is a state concerned with pure observation—not observation + this moral demand + this particular belief in an eternal deity. To embody this state of being is to see beyond the constrictions of duality, eating from the Tree of the Knowledge of Good and Evil and recognizing that both of those ideas are rooted in the same fundamental reality. You cannot simply pluck a branch and expect the tree to remain whole, just as you cannot pluck evil from the world and expect it to remain operational. In fact, you can never remove evil from good, for they balance the scales of one another.

When religious believers consistently circumvent the mythology of their doctrines by claiming that it is literal truth, they are perpetuating a paradox that cannot be resolved. They are trying to *prove* something as a basis for *belief*. That is, quite literally, absurd! If a scientist gathers enough evidence for a hypothesis, and tests it over and again, and acquires the

consensus of peers, it becomes a theory. If over time that theory is
refuted, it is done away with and the new hypothesis is explored
in depth, until that too becomes theory, and eventually a law,
which can also be overturned if enough evidence is presented.
It is impossible to work the other way around. We cannot start
with something that is true to prove a belief. As stated in the
opening line of this book, belief is a lack of experience. We
cannot afford to live on beliefs. We need the experience of life to
fulfill a rich, meaningful existence. Speculation does us no good
if we are going to stop without following through, and claim
that our hypothesis is an infallible fact.

There is certainly a paradoxical nature to evolution. We
are evolving in a particular direction, one suited for our continued
survival—and that does move forward, even if influenced from
the past in so many ways. The problem is that our morals are
moving in the opposite direction, or more precisely, they're not
moving at all. During the time of the Crusades this can at least
(partly) be understood. If you never saw the culture you were
planning to wage war against, it is easy to consider the people
of that culture as being of another species, or as the wicked
devils of the earth. As we've seen, once the battles were over
and foreigners settled into new homes, they quickly realized
that their neighbors were human after all. Interbreeding began,
and new cultures were formed. The only people this bothered
were those far removed from the scene, such as those on the first
Crusade who had never visited the land of the unrighteous. This
trend is not unique to the Crusades, and has occurred whenever
new people come into contact with other new people. It's called
being human.

Today, within reason, there are no longer any inaccessible
regions left undiscovered, no cultures we cannot educate
ourselves about, either in approximate theory or by actually
visiting. We are afforded the opportunity to learn about each
culture from their own historical perspective, not the "primitive"
rendering painted by anthropologists and sociologists a half-
century ago. We can tune in wirelessly and experience the
sounds, sights, and visions of distant lands, and recognize that
outside of the differences in clothing and skin pigmentation,

"they" are as human as "us." That is a dividing line that needs to be dissolved, and the sooner the better. Knowledge, however, is paralyzed without the behavior to match it. The plight of the Crusades continues this very day as the Christian descendants create their Army of God to slay infidels ... and, of course, drain their resources. How much the intent is purely material and how much is defined by long-standing and unresolved grudges cannot be measured, nor does it particularly matter. What is evident is that the process of greed and guilt has lingered for thousands of years and shows little signs of abating, at least in the images proposed by mainstream media and governance.

With such a rapid advance of technologies overtaking us, we are witnessing the same double-edged sword that appears with any new cultural transformation. Every day in New York City I witness hundreds of people texting or chatting on cell phones, oblivious that there are actual people they bump into, or ignore completely. What is supposed to bring us closer is forcing us apart. At the same time that we are creating a global community, we are returning to tribal mentality, with specialized media appealing to our peers and ourselves, and specialized friends who fall within our own belief system. Playing the edge between global and local will be the continual challenge for generations to come, especially given the ecological demands of the former that will trickle down and affect all aspects of the latter. To that urgent message we now turn, for it is one that our religious traditions have been built on, and if there is any such thing as true evil in this world, the culprits can only be ourselves. Fortunately, if we are going to dip into ethics and choices, we are equally capable of goodness.

Throughout this work we have spent much time discussing the concept of moving beyond duality, but what actual application does this fulfill? We have said that the silence beyond sound is the essence of sound itself, but how do we listen in a world full of noise? How do we *hear* the space between words, the moment between inhale and exhale? If the world is a play of constantly enfolding and enduring opposites, what happens when we have to choose a side? These are all challenging questions that, to my mind, retain power by remaining unanswered. This does not mean we avoid them, however. It simply implies that there is no definitive answer. The assumption that there will be one eventually creates a dogma. In the creation of any dogma, individuals, cultures, and entire generations become fixated by a past that, for them, never was. In contrast, meditating on each question reveals not as much an intellectual response that can be written and distributed as an internal quieting of the chattering of the mind—one that, when practiced and focused upon, results in incredible clarity.

In his lecture at the 2004 TED conference, Buddhist monk and author Matthieu Ricard, when discussing the nature of happiness, stated, "No one wakes up in the morning and says, 'May I suffer all day.'" He then delved into the essence of mindfulness training, a way of consciously triggering your mind to notice its patterns and cycles, and willfully redirecting them into patterns that are more conducive to happiness. Essentially you are exchanging negative habits for positive ones. The same pattern occurs in the physical practice of yoga. As the yogi lessens a certain tension (anxiety), he or she strengthens another tension (muscular strength). This practice, of course, simultaneously boosts mental clarity, emotional focus and general well being. True, there is a state where opposites converge—when the snake uncoils, or sheds its skin—and the distinction between the two is seen as the ultimate illusion. Yet, for most people, it does not come instantly (unless you subscribe to a practice like *satori*, instant enlightenment, which is not conscious as much as intuited). The reality for most of the population, especially those living in urbanized, industrialized societies, is that a strong and concerted effort needs to be made.

In Chapter 4 we briefly mentioned the gunas, or the three states of existence that are considered in the system of yoga: sattva, rajas and tamas. The word guna literally means "strand," though its definitions are broad. Tamas is a state of inertia and laziness; rajas, an excited state akin to frenetic and nervous energy; sattva implies balance. Physically we can define them in context by the asana *paschimottanasana* (seated forward bend). For a person with a tamasic practice, he or she might spend his or her time in this posture playing with the toes, or constantly looking around the room at other people, or at the clock. In a rajasic practice, the yogi will stay folded over the entire time, though will keep shifting the seat and adjusting the shoulders, essentially fidgeting through most of the allotted time, or be so distracted by thoughts that he or she forgets they are in a posture. The yogi in a sattvic state will focus on the pose itself, making minor adjustments when necessary, and predominantly remain unmoved until the next posture arrives.

The gunas are not reserved for asana practice. The concept affects all areas of life, and is used as the basis for the Ayurveda system of nutrition and internal balancing. In *Yoga: Freedom and Immortality*, Mircea Eliade defines sattva as "modality of luminosity and intelligence," rajas as "modality of motor energy and mental activity," and tamas as "modality of static inertia and psychic obscurity." With that definition we can dissect the various aspects of our life to find what we are more "obscure" in, and what we shine within. You are rarely only one of these states. Balance occurs when focusing the more frenetic and unfocused energies into the luminous aspects that define your most beneficial qualities. Perhaps you are an amazing accountant but horrible at familial relations, or an inspired lover with no grasp of nutritive health. When all the aspects of your life become sattvic, the conditions are set for experiencing a sublime state beyond this duality. It takes time, discipline and preparation. While the state beyond opposites may not have any defining qualities, I would have to agree with the Buddha, who stated that what was essential to develop in every aspect of life is compassion. This is the highest frequency vibration we can reside within, for it is free of judgment and over-moralizing. It sets the stage for experiencing yoga.

In *The Moral Animal*, Robert Wright cited parsimony as a decisive factor in groundbreaking science, which basically states that "the simpler a theory, and the more varied and numerous things it explains, the more 'parsimonious' it is." Time and again Sam Harris has argued that this is exactly what Christianity is failing at, with their theorizing about virgin births and resurrections, concepts that on a physical level are impossible. Buddhism, however, is extremely parsimonious, accounting for its ever-growing popularity in the Western world. There is no abstract theorizing, and there are no gods. It is entirely based on the experiences of life itself, and like the yogis, Buddhists attempt to exist on a sattvic, or balanced, plane. To say that "Jesus Christ is the Son of God and we must bow to him" is an opinion, and cannot affect people who have no emotional connection to the figure. Saying something like "All life is suffering, and there is a way beyond it" will quickly resonate with a much broader audience, and thus in essence is a lot more meaningful.

In his book *The Hidden Connections*, Fritjof Capra expands his theory of organization from three components—form, matter and process—to include a fourth: meaning. He uses this skeleton key to unlock the innumerable social constructions that human beings experience, and offers numerous ways that we can include meaning in our ecological and social understanding of life. As he argued twenty-seven years earlier in his groundbreaking *The Tao of Physics*, the web of life is intricate and perpetual. Our actions, from the very large to the subtlest, not only affect others, but also the world around us. In the more recent work, he cites Norwegian philosopher Arne Næss's distinction between "shallow" and "deep" ecology, the former focusing on the ecology of humans alone, the latter considering humanity as an integral part of the process of *all* aspects of life. Given the recent turmoil around carbon emissions, global warming, changing weather patterns, oil consumption and genetically modified foods (and animals), Capra's insightful survey into the environmental state of the world is both courageous and necessary.

In the same way that Karen Armstrong noticed that it is behavior and not belief that reveals a person's true religious intent, Capra believes we need to optimize, not maximize, the environment. Since the dawn of the Industrial Age companies have relied more and more upon the bottom line, which is why today numerous progressive organizations are focusing on a "triple bottom line": one that is economical, environmental and social. It has been challenging for scientists, farmers, and geneticists to thrive in a system where government is focused on taxation for defense, and corporations underwrite research in order to secure patents on technologies. Major corporations are engaged in a scenario conspicuously similar to the blatant paradoxes investigated in religious belief. Concerning food companies that claim GMO products are not genetically different than other crops, Capra writes, "On the one hand, the industry claims that its crops are substantially equivalent to traditional crops and hence do not need to be labeled, or tested; on the other hand, it insists that they are novel and therefore can be patented."

This patent race has wreaked major havoc on modern agriculture. In the 1930s over thirty million farms existed; today less than two million are left, and the largest of them control the distribution market, both to chain grocery stores as well as governmental subsidies. In the period between 1995-2003, the US government offered $131 billion dollars in subsidies. $30.5 billion of this money went to roughly one percent of the market: 30,500 farms. The bigger the farm, the more money it received, which is completely counterintuitive. Arkansas-based Riceland Foods Inc., the largest rice miller and marketer in the world, collected $110 million over that time, while Producers Rice Mill Inc., whose annual sales top $300 million, was awarded $83 million. This is even more baffling when compared to the average median subsidy for all other farms: $5,194. To add insult to injury, corporations that exist in other sectors and who just happen to own farmland also received payola: Chevron Oil collected $427,000 while Ted Turner made $206,948. Offering the media mogul this amount of money while local farms received roughly two-and-a-half percent clearly shows where the government's focus is.

More disturbing is mono-cropping—the re-planting of single crops over and over on the same soil, year after year—an action that depletes soil *and* vegetables of nutrients, eventually rendering the land impotent. Whereas farmers would naturally grow one cycle of crops in a season, and then switch to other crops or just let the soil rest, they must now plant three or four cycles of the same crop—predominantly corn or soybeans—to keep buyers—predominantly resellers—happy. This focus on single plants has caused us to lose a great diversity of plant life. Instead of 158 types of cauliflower, as traditional societies knew, we now harvest 9; carrots, from 287 to 21; tomatoes, 408 to 79; 7,089 varieties of apples have dwindled to 878. In general, the world now eats four foods: corn, wheat, rice and potatoes. All four have potential and real hazards, both in the manner in which they're grown as well as in their relation to our bodies. Many people have developed wheat allergies, and potatoes, a starchy root tuber, are not exactly nutritionally beneficial. Rice has fed nations for centuries, though it too is a high-carbohydrate, low-protein food. Perhaps the most perplexing of these, corn, has become the most ubiquitous additive in a boggling range of foodstuffs, spanning the forms of corn starch, dextrin, xanthan gum and, of course, high fructose corn syrup.

When the Green Revolution of the 1950s fired massive amounts of fertilizer onto American soil, the annual use of nitrogen increased to over eighty million annual tons. A six-state region known as the "corn belt"—predominantly Iowa, Indiana, Illinois and Ohio—is responsible for seventy percent of the nitrogen in the Mississippi River. While that cannot be good news for the surrounding area, the real crises occurred hundreds of miles south in a region currently referred to by ecologists as the "Dead Zone," once a fertile fishing area the size of New Jersey that now lies barren. Nitrogen pollution has created genocide on large populations of fish and shellfish, especially shrimp, in the Gulf of Mexico. We have lost a substantial portion of a protein-rich food, for a low quality, over-subsidized crop.

This is just one of numerous examples of how the drive to maximize profits is *always* at the expense of some fraction of the totality. This is also how, on a very real level, enantiodromia takes place: the attempt to become so much of one thing turns into the opposite. This is rarely noticed in a corporate environment, where executives retain over-inflated incomes and lower level workers, not to mention those unknowingly affected hundreds or thousands of miles away, not only do not benefit in the slightest but often lose. If we continue to keep ourselves distant from those "others," our economics, and not just our ecology, will remain shallow.

That many of our great religious traditions, based on seasonal cycles which prompted the writing of agricultural mythologies, have been degraded as mere means (foodstuff) to an end (money) is indicative of a psychology steeped in an egoistic spell of maya. Greed is certainly not new, but the global damage currently happening is truly overwhelming. There is something to be said about self-fulfilling prophecies, which may justify the religious fear of an "end of the world." When the actions taken by individuals contribute to the progress of greed and division, things will certainly feel doomed. When this cycle is passed down generation after generation, it is very challenging to change such long-ingrained habits. Richard Dawkins has argued that it is simply wrong to assign a child to be a certain religion, for they never had any say in the matter. That is one way that the karma of the parents is transmitted. It's little surprise that children, when taking communion, for example, must admit their "sins." The very idea that a child is born into such a state where those admissions are expected is understandable though, when the word "sin" retains its original meaning: ignorance. The parents, themselves under the spell, assign it to their child when declaring they are of this or that faith. The web continues to be woven. In place of the diamond in the belt is a kernel of corn.

Of course it is not the world that will end, but our place in it. The process of the planet was occurring for billions of years before the slightest sign of us appeared. Extinction is a word that we've applied to numerous species, and we should be wary of excluding our own. If this happens, history does indeed end, as the very word is a construction exclusively designed by and for our minds. Having worked with many brilliant people in a variety of occupations who are doing incredible work, many of them creating—recreating—a sustainable planet, it is hard to discount such passionate impact this will have over time. Whether we are discussing the survival of genes or the quest for liberation, humans are resilient and enduring creatures. It would be a shame if the actual and tangible possibility of global warming is the trigger that awakens us to the greater good of the planet, and each other, and all the amazing qualities and cultures we have yet to experience. Still, it would almost seem poetic if it were really this intense "heat" that causes a "purifying" process in the next stage of our cultural evolution. It's very challenging to war against each other when the sun, our "creator," is warring on us.

In *The Omnivore's Dilemma*, journalist Michael Pollan reconstructs four meals in ways few of us ever will, tracing every single ingredient back to its source. His facts and research are impeccable, and while the book is incisively critical of the population who does not think at all about what their food contains or where it comes from, he portrays numerous positive figures. One of them is Joel Salatin, a self-described "Christian-conservative-libertarian-environmentalist-lunatic farmer," not to mention owner of one of the most successful alternative farms in America, Virginia's Polyface Inc. People travel for miles and hours to purchase his eggs, chickens, tomatoes, rabbits and sweet corn, mostly due to the philosophies of natural farming that he embodies, in every sense of that phrase.

Following a scrupulously detailed rotation schedule, Salatin does not use any sort of chemical or fertilizer. Instead, he lets each animal and plant do what it does best: be itself. Calling himself a "grass farmer," he uses the most influential member of the chain—the sun—as the catalyst for his meticulous cycling techniques. He constantly moves his cattle from area to area so they do not exhaust the quantities and qualities of the grasses, and uses their output (feces) to feed chickens. These birds feed on the grubs in the cowpats, creating a more effective fertilizer (by eliminating parasites) while finding their nutrition, and without needing antibiotics or corn-based feed. He lets all the animals roam freely, unlike many so-called organic farms that keep their chickens cooped up for the first five weeks of their life (so they will not become sick and spread illness) and then offer them two weeks of vacation by opening one door at the end of the warehouse that leads to a small strip of grass—an option they rarely, if ever, choose. Like any animal, chickens develop habits quickly, and if all you know is one life and are suddenly offered another with no known creature comforts, chances are you'll stay put—which is probably why most Americans have never applied for passports.

"All agriculture is at its heart a business of capturing free solar energy in a food product that can then be turned into high-value human energy," Salatin wrote in one of his regular columns on the farming industry. His approach is completely parsimonious: cows eating grass that ate the sun, which then feeds the rest of the farm in an intricate yet simple chain. In fact, it only *seems* intricate because we've moved so far away from these techniques, as megafarms turn cows into cannibals and wreak havoc on the land that farmers once respected. In our attempts to maximize the environment, we've overtaxed the soil, water and animals, not to mention ourselves. It's no surprise that the cattle call of megachurches—more concerned with membership numbers than quality of the members involved—exhibit like tendencies. Salatin, a devoted Christian, feels that farming is part of natural theology, and puts his beliefs into his behavior, every step on the path.

These processes of recycling, redistribution, decay, and life are much older than we—after all, they produced us! This is why Pollan keeps reminding us that while we think we're domesticating crops like corn, the probability is that *they* are domesticating *us*. While we are damaging the environment on an unprecedented level, corn—once an inedible plant that produced a mutant gene that an ancestor stumbled upon, ate, and didn't die from—is thriving like never before. From an evolutionary standpoint, humans may be destroying the ecosystem (and ourselves), but corn is doing great! Salatin's story is an example of how utilizing the natural cycles of the earth not only feeds many mouths, but also replenishes the earth and soil in the process. It's not even a win-win situation, for that implies that there was a contest in the first place. Living according to nature should never be a contest, for if it is, then we forsake the essence of life itself. Kicking and screaming the whole way down the evolutionary warpath is the special reservation for the self-defeated.

Signs that smaller companies and even large corporations are beginning to awaken to the power of natural energy are, fortunately, becoming apparent. It's nearly baffling that the idea of solar energy surprises us, so dependent upon our machines have we become. The day that I'm writing this page, one shy of Thanksgiving 2007, an article appeared in a local newspaper about solar panels installed in Rockefeller Center to help power the lights on the famed Christmas tree. Actions like this are being taken by organizations worldwide, and the more the "greening" of the planet is no longer presented as a hippie, granola throwback—but rather a viable, thriving, and economically progressive platform—the more people will join in. Interestingly, for as much flack as oil receives in creating carbon emissions, Fritjof Capra points out that its predecessors—wood and coal—were much more hazardous to the environment. The practice of burning trees for fuel, an evolutionary adaptation of Prometheus's kindling, appears to have been the onset of what today would be called global warming. For every molecule of hydrogen released, ten molecules of carbon follow. In comparison, the ratio when burning oil is 1:2, meaning only one carbon molecule is released for every two hydrogen. Natural gas is a step further (1:4), but it will not be until we harness the power of pure sunlight, which does not release any carbon, that we will see drastic changes. More poetic justice: To save us from sunlight, we need to use sunlight. The blood of Medusa is still fresh.

In *The Labyrinth of Solitude*, Octavio Paz reminds us that, "No one can know the final outcome of history because its end is also that of mankind." Until then, we have plenty of history to make, and certainly more will be discovered, or remembered, as time progresses. The study of history is a constant process of reflection. Today, we have reached an important junction. Never before has so much of the world's history, and present, been so readily accessible. Yet when is it *not* an important junction? Every moment offers opportunities for introspection, on an individual basis, as well as on a social, national, and international level.

To be in a constant state of reflection, while simultaneously engaged in the moment, is one of those seeming paradoxes in the discipline of yoga that is not a paradox at all.

Paz knew this well. While *Labyrinth* is a meditation on Mexican identity, he spent six years in India as his country's ambassador. He recognized the cross-pollinating relationship between politics and spirituality and infused his masterful books and essays with a sense of the transcendental possibilities of both of those subjects. Through his work, one reads of the inner social struggles both Indians and Mexicans face in their endeavors for freedom, be it from the realms of time and space or the oppressive dictates of a tyrannical ruler. For him, a thin line is trodden by the figure of Natraj. "Creation and destruction are antithetical notions to man, but identical to the gods: all is play. In their games—which are wars which are dances—the gods create, destroy, and, sometimes, destroy themselves. After their self-immolation they re-create the world. The game of the gods is a bloody game culminating in a sacrifice that is the creation of the world."

The bloody game of humans is no different. Thus far we've treated human sacrifice as an archaic remnant of our forgettable and unforgivable history, yet the reality of these rites lives on during warfare. We no longer push our kin and children into *xenotes* or from temple steps. Instead they sign forms and pack into planes. It's all a matter of phrasing. If we put it this way—"The time has come to sacrifice yourself for your country, young man"—it comes across as patriotic, not ritualistic; a duty to your country and its ideals. That's more of a literary ploy than anything else. When you see a cadet hanging one-handed from a cliff before "meeting the challenge" and wielding a sword on a television commercial, that sword will one day enter the body of another—or his own, if he's not careful. In the twentieth century alone, over 105 million people were sacrificed to the gods of war and, even more sadly, 62 million of these were civilians.

In two unrelated books, war journalist Chris Hedges and psychologist James Hillman affirmed the notion that war is, as Hedges's title reads, a force that gives us meaning. This topic is a constant battle in any culture that features both supporters and opponents of war, which is to say, every culture. When dealing with the culture of yoga, the pendulum definitively swings to one side. One of the main aspects of the practice is ahimsa. It is bedrock in modern yoga philosophy, essential to cultivating a sattvic lifestyle. But practicing ahimsa does not mean we can turn a blind eye to the reality of war, or claim it as something inherently "evil." Doing so would debunk the entire premise of seeing beyond opposites. War is, as Hillman suggests, a "mythical happening." It is also constant (when was a war *not* happening somewhere?) and ubiquitous (what country has not hosted one?). Neither author states that war is necessarily justified, but here we move past the realm of morals and beliefs. Both men are able to see the mental and emotional factors of battle with carefully crafted insight, Hedges as a war journalist and Hillman as a former war psychologist. Helping soldiers comprehend and integrate the psychic imprints of battle is no easy occupation.

There is good reason that war is set against love, and many gods and goddesses of past lore governed both. Love is indescribable and does not need the justification of the intellect, or so poets and those in love claim. If war is its opposite, it must share similar qualities. This non-justification of *why* is one of them. I feel a resonance when yoga teachers talk about universal compassion, as it is something I strive to cultivate. I have to cringe, however, when they speak about the cessation of war because of some righteous indignation, or that "peace is our original nature." If we want to understand our original nature, we have to turn to the very moment that we were born. And the process of birthing is anything but peaceful, for mother and child alike. The only recognizable quality a human baby possesses is helplessness. Put another way: dependence. There is poetic justice in this too. Every child is born into this world relying upon others. This process of interdependence never stops, until the day he returns to the soil that birthed him. This is something we can witness and observe. A statement about "peace" or "compassion" being our original nature is morally loaded, and while there is great benefit to cultivating such qualities, we should not confuse the process that created us with what we are consciously attempting to create. It is to put the cart before the horse, and then complain when we get kicked in the rear.

Regarding cultural history, warfare was even more necessary for humans prior to the dawn of urban civilizations, before it was questioned as ethically or morally correct. Sure, the cessation of war is a nice dream, but yoga is essentially about seeing through the layered veil of dreams to uproot essence. And it is this: humans are warring creatures as much as loving ones. There is balance in this, although it cannot be seen if you're standing on one side. As mentioned earlier, there may be greater wars we have to face which will require a widespread unity as never seen to our species. In many ways, it seems that this may be the catalyst that will elicit camaraderie between nations. Sometimes we only learn through substitution, by trading one habit for another. I'd have to agree with Hillman's assessment, that "Even those who know history are doomed to repeat it because, though it may be easy to kill the living, it is hard to kill the dead." Those past figures he speaks of include religious icons who we quote and mold into the current righteous justification of why we're invading this or that country.

In his groundbreaking work *Re-Visioning Psychology*, Hillman wrote about how the soul defines us—that although we may not possess its "inhuman" reaches, we are able to reflect upon them. This is the same recurring motif appearing in Pollan's domestication of plants: There is a process investigating us as diligently as we investigate it, and perhaps even more so, as it is not bound by language, morals and ethics. It does not need to reflect anything, for every action is a reflection of everything else. At every turn—in psychology, religion, anthropology, botany, ecology, economics and so on—it appears again. As Hillman phrased it, regarding war, "The god does not stand above or behind the scene directing what happens. He *is* what happens." We are at the disposal of life much more than life is at the disposal of us. Gods are not mega-people with superhero skills. They are the reflective quality inside of us documenting the process.

In his book *2012: The Return of Quetzalcoatl*, Daniel Pinchbeck investigates the archetypal nature of the plumed serpent king. The mythology of 2012 is based on an intricate calendric system developed by the Mayans which supposedly ends (or continues to another phase) in that year. Like their cross-continental neighbors, the Aztecs created a cyclical calendar called the *Tonalpohualli*, or Day Count, system, with each year (cycle) lasting 260 days. (The annual Mayan Long Count is of equal length.) Agricultural societies believed they could portend forthcoming events through the understanding of cycles, which caused the Aztecs to state that Abubakari the Second's arrival in 1311, sailing from the direction of the sun, was the return of Quetzalcoatl. Four cycles later in the year 1519, Hernán Cortés washed ashore, with a visit that would prove much more destructive. What this next cycle beginning in 2012 will yield remains open for speculation. Pessimists declare it the end of the world, although that has already been anticipated in their minds many times over, to no avail. Given the current ecological situation at hand, it would be little surprise if this forthcoming cycle spawned a greater awareness of both our role in and our effect on nature, hopefully before any more irreversible damage to the environment is done.

Regarding the famed bird/serpent deity, as well as the Mayan cyclical counting system, Pinchbeck states that, "Their underlying meaning points toward a shift in the nature of the psyche." Quetzalcoatl's original citations in Mexican culture date back to roughly 980-999 CE, when he was born to Mixcoatl, chief of the Toltecs. Ivan Van Sertima argues that the *imagery* is far older, denoting a kindred remixing in the psyche of two countries separated by thousands of miles. This play between the bird and snake is an important symbol. The snake guarded the well of life, as well as the life-giving moisture contained within. The bird nested in a giant tree, with water needed to sustain the foliage, as well as to release the rains that would raise the crops. In order to do so, he had to devour the snake, which would, of course, regenerate. Interestingly, as Van Sertima notes, there is only one successful hunter of serpents: the African secretary bird. Equipped with an eagle-like frame and growing to over four feet tall, this bird was unique in that few other fliers could ever contend with the vicious bites of snakes. In the observation of this majestic bird, and the symbolism manifested through its struggle against the snake, a mythology was born, similar to the well-known Asian motif of a tiger battling a dragon.

Whether or not direct contact occurred with Africans to influence the creation of Quetzalcoatl (the basic motif in Mexican folklore dates many centuries before Abubakari), or whether this is another tale told by the collective unconscious spiraling invisibly through the generations, is irrelevant. All of the essentials appear: death, dismemberment and rebirthing. It's the significance of these archetypes that Pinchbeck investigates throughout his elucidating work, as he secures modern man's place within the context of these fascinating stories. All cultures have been built on oral histories, at least until writing was introduced and widespread. For some, letters came to replace oratorical arts, yet it still remains of primary importance *how the tale is told*. That is the realm where the archetype can be *felt* instead of intellectualized. And as many writers—with another seeming paradox on the way—have commented, it is in language itself, through the process of bookbinding and distribution and dependence on visual information *instead of* seeing, that we have lost so much contact with the natural world, and where we find that our relationship with the process of existence has faltered and become stuck. You can read about a savannah or experience one. The difference between those two approaches is crucial to our understanding of how religions are born and spread. As David Abram so eloquently stated in *The Spell of the Sensuous*, "It is only when a culture shifts its participation to these printed letters that the stones fall silent. Only as our senses transfer their animating magic to the written word do the trees become mute, the other animals dumb."

So much inspection of hunter-gatherer cultures has taken place over the last two centuries because it is believed that they are a prototype of what mankind would later become: agriculturists. Even this, however, is partly fabrication. As Colin Tudge points out in *Neanderthals, Bandits & Farmers: How Agriculture Really Began*, "Human beings virtually throughout their two million year history have not merely been 'hunters and gatherers,' in the way that these terms are generally understood but have always manipulated their environment in various ways that increased their food supply." The idea that humans suddenly jumped from hunting and gathering into agriculture is an easy way to compartmentalize time periods, but just like the 5,000-year history of yoga, it is imprecise. Even if the transition took a few thousand years, in evolutionary time that would be startling. Such a leap not only requires a change in food production, but also requires adaptability to new nutrients, diseases and calories, which would not simply happen overnight. What's worse with such easy scholarship is what Richard Dawkins warned us about regarding evolution: history has *not* been happening for 4.5 billion years just to produce us. As Tudge puts it, "Still less should we entertain some weird quasi-mystical concept of human evolution, envisaging that the ability to farm is a 'stage' that human beings are somehow predestined to achieve."

Still, the dominance of agriculture did sprout in the Fertile Crescent, thanks to climate conditions, weather patterns, air quality and soil nutrients. As agriculture became widespread and available to growing populations, our rituals associated with animals changed drastically. Indian sages began looking for alternatives to human sacrifice as their diets switched to plant energy and then proceeded to shift the philosophy to discourage the practice. Finally, they ceased condoning the consumption of any meat, indicative of a culture no longer dependent on eating another species in order to survive. The domestication of plants domesticated us. If our regular meals were bison and lamb, of course our gods craved those to be appeased. As maize and rice became the foodstuff of choice, the gods would most certainly want the same.

Yet our Fall dictates the opposite: We are not of the earth, we are Providence's special subject, and have been given dominion to rule over lands and animals and everything else with a name. If it doesn't have a name, we'll invent one and claim ownership of it as well. We bring an apple for Teacher and become His pet. This sense of separateness is exactly that:

it separates us. After Indians inspired Africans in Jamaica to expand upon their original spiritual practices, they dreamed of returning home to Ethiopia. Some did. When they arrived, they realized that what they were looking for was not a physical land, but a state of mind. Understanding that crucial knowledge, many turned back and returned to Jamaica. Their ignorance had been lifted. The same thing occurred in Jaffa when European Jews arrived after the British declaration and saw fellow pilgrims standing on the docks. It appeared as if they were there to welcome them. In actuality they were leaving, disgusted by the state of affairs and living conditions. To this day the Jewish state, well outnumbered in Israel by Muslims, continues massive outreach programs to beef up their presence, and has to rely on their army, which all Israelis must serve in, to keep their power intact. For both Rastas and Jews, the veil of maya was torn away when they realized that physical land is *not* the key to salvation. Such an idea is a political, and not spiritual, invention.

This feeling of separation, or at least the idea that you are separated from something, is a powerful marketing tool, one that works in an unbelievable range of contexts. Governments enforce tribal warfare with it, and corporate executives would not be where they are today if they hadn't made you feel that you *need* their product. Loyalty to a political group, loyalty to a brand, and loyalty to a religion are all differing emotional states with a common denominator. Because, as stated in the outset, what we're dealing with is not so much the innumerable forms a process can take, but rather the process itself—this one being loyalty. The last thing anybody who wields control or influence over your life and the decisions you make wants is for you to realize that loyalty to yourself is the most important allegiance a human can have. To avoid this realization they'll tailor their products and philosophies to make you feel that they are necessary and relevant to you. It's an amazing game of smoke and mirrors, and people fall into it—for lifetimes.

The more samskaras we carry, the harder it is to sift through verbiage and get to the essence of words. When we cannot integrate the teachings of our faiths and leaders on an instinctual and heartfelt level, we remain separated from the meaning of the message. We feel incomplete, for completion and liberation are sold as ideas akin to meditating Buddhas. And this is not in reference to the state the Buddha was in, or men on crosses, because that one cross is considered to be an actual construction and not a symbol for unfettering ourselves here and now. There is never enough money, never enough time, never enough enough. Prescriptions for these crises come in pill form, and as Barry Schwartz, author of *The Paradox of Choice*, reminds us, since pharmaceutical companies are not allowed to directly sell you their medicine, they sell you on the idea that you may have an illness analogous to what they can cure. The ubiquitous term "Ask your doctor about XXX" is their not-so-subliminal marketing technique to make you feel that their product can help. Because, as you know, once you get your hands on it, you will be free. As journalist Melody Petersen reminds us in *Our Daily Meds*, "The tragedy lies not with the medicines but with the marketing and the unprecedented power these companies now have over the practice of medicine. We've come to a time when decisions on how to treat a disease have as great a chance of being hatched in a corporate marketing department as by a group of independent doctors working to improve the public's health."

The pharmaceutical executive board had great and effective role models: clergy. In contrast, if you set out to find a guru in yoga, you would have to be prepared for a long and arduous path of abiding by his disciplinary nature. Yet if enlightenment came, and the guru was true, he would have led you on a path to realizing that you were never unenlightened. You just had not awoken to that knowledge yet. While the yogic techniques involved can be drastically different in form, there is always the opportunity for recognizing your individual divine nature, one that is part of the entire process of existence. A yogi needs no gods to understand this. What he or she needs (if anything) is the friendship and trust of other humans, for that is what a *sangha*, community, is. What we need is each other, like the endless diamond web strung together by Indra.

No such possibility exists in the way we view modern

religion. The basic understanding is that eventually we can be free because someone else after death decides that we will enjoy an afterlife of bliss and comfort. *That's the best we can hope for.* Not only Christians buy into this idea of a perpetual "in the future," either. The philosophy is so vitally integrated into every aspect of our lives and culture, from our earliest educational experiences (when we are taught that each grade leads to another grade, which will lead to another school, and so on) to our last breaths (when the 401Ks are cashed and we have to worry about preparing for the afterlife, whatever that means), that it is nearly impossible to escape. It's easy to see why critics of religion are so dumbfounded by the claims of fundamentalists. There's no logic in their belief system—you cannot cultivate presence while perpetually striving towards a future that may or may not exist. In fact, the future cannot exist, because all we have is the present. What's worse than this, though, is that there's no heart. A compassionate person would never judge a fellow man's character on the basis of the word that he uses to express something beyond, or behind, himself. And that is key to understanding our mythologies: what is beyond is really behind. The relevance of mythology as being "past," as Alan Watts wrote, is symbolic only. In reality it is *"behind* us, not as time past is behind us, but as the brain which cannot be seen is behind the eyes which see, as behind memory is that which remembers and cannot *be* remembered." He concludes with another appropriate twist of language, offering "that we do not understand it because it under-stands us."

It. A very good word indeed: genderless, unbiased, and applicable to species, chemicals, ideas and processes. Defined as referring to a thing previously mentioned or—and this is key—something "easily identified." For that which is beyond or behind us to be noticed, all we must do is open our eyes and look. "It" is capable of being a very parsimonious idea, much better than that ego-driven "I am that I am," a statement of shallow theology. What we want to do is to go deep, and going deep is nothing more than picking out the patterns that affect all of us, all the time. It does. As long as we refrain from posting stick-It notes of title, deed, and inheritance to the word—"My It is not your It" or "It is a he" or "You just don't get It"—we'll be fine. And it would take nothing more than closing your eyes and taking a few deep breaths to contact It. There's little coincidence that the great mysteries of many cultures share a common root: *atman* (Sanskrit), *ruah* (Hebrew), *pneuma* and *psyche* (Greek), *anima* and *spiritus* (Latin) all mean "breath." By contacting this quality that is with us every moment of every hour of our lives, we are assimilated with It. And there needn't be any defined method of doing so. While yogis may do so in seated meditation, what is prayer but another form of this? Closing your eyes and focusing on one thing and one thing alone; prayer is a form of directed mediation. And meditation is not an escape into nothingness. It is the ability to hold and sustain one thought in your mind indefinitely. What this does is create focus, dispels distractions, and fuses your thought processes with that of a state of the mind that is relaxed, clear and receptive. Kneeling to pray is a similar exercise. By tuning in to one thought and putting your efforts into the cultivation of this thought, you are, essentially, meditating. Most importantly, you are connecting with your breath, the spirit of life. Remember that to kneel on the pew at church and place your elbows over the seat in front of you is to straighten your spine and focus—to extend the psychic antenna of the body and breathe from bottom to top.

When quieting the mind, the internal warfare being waged by thoughts, ethics, emotions, and ideas settles, as the Taoists say, like the ripples on the surface of a lake. When those have calmed and you are able to hold one thought for extended periods of time, you are liberated. No one comes and unlocks the invisible shackles around your wrists and ankles because, in truth, you had been holding the key all along. This knowledge is innate. You do not pull it from the atmosphere; you *reclaim* it as a way of being, a means to exist. It is completely natural, for these are words we know and crave, words we sing along to without pausing to think of the meaning. Take one of the most well-known and cherished reggae songs of all time: Bob Marley's "Get Up, Stand Up." Stop the easy slide of syllables from Nesta's voice and reflect on the words passing through your lips:

Preacher man don't tell me heaven is under the earth/I know you don't know what life is really worth/It's not all that glitters is gold, half the story has never been told/So now you see the light, stand up for your rights/Most people think great God will come from the skies/Take away everything and make everybody feel high/But if you know what life is worth, you will look for yours on earth/And now you see the light, you stand up for your rights

And if that didn't settle the issue, co-songwriter Peter Tosh ends the inquiry:

We sick and tired of your bullshit games, dying to go to heaven in-a Jesus name, lord/We know and we understand, almighty God is a living man/You can fool some people sometimes, but you can't fool all the people all the time/So now we see the light, we gonna stand up for our rights

Almighty God is a living man. Can't be much more straightforward than that. How have we strayed so far from this knowledge? Why have churches and governments called this idea blasphemous and heretical, and even murdered those whose tongues have let slip these very basic and fundamental words? If the entirety of existence is engaged in one process, and that process extends to include everything in one continuous dance, how could we not be gods? And, more to the point, if everything is divine, why do we even need the concept of divinity?

A faithful person needs no justification for the experience of life, for the experience is the process unfolding and reflecting simultaneously. It is the unfaithful who proselytize, who demand subjugation and obedience, who promote wars and foster ideals such as sexism, racism and speciesism. They have not understood that mythologies are constructed *unconsciously*, and the more you try to mold and form them into your own liking, the more you are alienating everybody but the small group of people who happen to agree with you. What we need is to write new history books, ones that are not dependant on the biased claims of one culture or religion in seeing others as primitive; ones that place the modern world inside the unfolding process of the rest of time, and do away with those constant timelines marking every date as episodes meant to lead to us; ones that rid themselves of abstract thinking and focus on the here and now, and the history that is here and now, and the future that is here and now.

As Alan Watts wrote, "The true artist does not rebel against the limitations of his media, but rejoices in the possibilities of how much can be expressed *with* such limitations." There is so much life to be experienced on the earth that it's simply a shame that we look any further than our everyday lives for the magic of mythology. The hero is every one of us fully experiencing ourselves in a manner akin to our cultural and genetic evolution. And to keep evolving, we must take into consideration the processes of the species and ecosystems that sustain us. We have to optimize, not maximize: each other, what we put inside ourselves, what we allow to leave our community, and the words that leave our mouth. When you take full responsibility for your actions and stop letting dreams of cosmic schemes poorly influence decisions made, there is no longer any quest for liberation. No one else can free you from yourself. No secret words, esoteric clubs, or political leaders are going to make everything better. The world never promised us anything, but by letting go and taking part in the process of life, we gain the world.

CHAPTER 9

THE END OF BEGINNINGLESS TIME BEGINS

During the summer of 2007, I ran into a close friend, *ghazal* singer Vishal Vaid, in the East Village. I had not seen him for some time due to his recent fatherhood, and together we walked down University Ave. to Washington Square Park, joined by a few friends and his son, Ashar. When we entered the park, he put down his chai and began telling me about an upcoming trip to India. He was recounting a beautiful story from Hindu mythology about a child's first haircut, and what it represents—essentially, that it is a letting go of past karmas in hopes that the child will be spared suffering for this life ahead. Ashar, nearing two years in age with gorgeous silky brown hair, was running around the park, happily chasing squirrels and invisible animals only children can see. Then Vishal's face turned sullen. I looked up.

Walking past was an elderly woman with long white hair holding a sign in front of her chest that read, "Only Roman Catholics Go To Heaven." At first I couldn't tell if it was some sort of performance art, but given the despairing look on her face, I got the sense that she was serious. When I see such inane displays of "devotion," I usually laugh it off, but this particular laughter turned to sadness. Here we were, having just discussed an uplifting example of mythological storytelling, how the symbolic shearing of hair represents something that linked Ashar to the rest of the world, and then walks by the downside of belief, which isn't belief as much as it is fear.

There is no proof that cutting a child's hair to absolve him of karmic debt is real. In fact, there is no reliable proof that reincarnation exists, although it is hard to discredit tales like the birth and rise to power of the current Dalai Lama. At the same time, there is absolutely no truth to the notion that only Roman Catholics go to heaven, just as there is no substantive evidence that heaven is a place we good folk get to live after we die. The difference between the two approaches is that the first recognizes the ritual as symbolic, while the latter believes the literality of their message. That's the heart of danger, an element with no heart.

In the year that it took to research and write this book, the work has changed me as much as I have changed the work. I couldn't help but notice the connections between members of the yoga community unapologetically proselytizing ideas like vegetarianism and ultimate bliss with the same egoistic reverence and ethical demands as those of religious fanatics wielding bibles and Korans. Wherever I turned, the concept of neti-neti appeared: not this, not that. At the same time that yoga has stormed America as a supposed cure-all to hate, racism, bigotry and stress, among other off-kilter symptoms, books on atheism were topping bestsellers list and the hands behind those books were giving important speeches around the planet. While some were direly pessimistic, the importance of the human connection was stressed. Within these two camps one common factor became apparent: both are building communities based on turning progressive ideas into sustainable realities. Successes were, and continue to be, dependent on factors too numerous to list. Most importantly, the attempts are there, and continue to evolve us in a direction that will hopefully be beneficial to as broad a population as possible.

I agree with men like Richard Dawkins and Sam Harris in the sentiment that the idea of God is outdated. Yet as Karen Armstrong and Huston Smith have pointed out, religion is necessary, if not in the reality of logic, then in the hearts of countless people who whole-heartedly believe there is "something else." These theories do not have to be incompatible. Yoga, for one, offers us that something else, without ever leaving our own bodies, and without any need for a god. As I intimated last chapter, it takes a lot of responsibility, and a multitude of focus and discipline. What's most confusing is that there is no definitive path to self-realization, and yet people like to compartmentalize their spiritual understanding into an easy, one-answer-fits-all paradigm. Within that small percentage of biology that separates individuals is an insurmountable array of possibilities for variation. When overthinking the choice of any definitive course, I always recall the important words of D.T. Suzuki: "Since beginningless time there have never been Buddhas attached to form. If you wish to attain Buddhahood by practicing the six virtues of perfection and all the ten-thousand deeds of goodness, this is prescribing a course, and since beginningless time there have never been Buddhas graduating from a prescribed course."

It is understandable that we want to give form to what is beyond/behind us. That's why mandalas were created, circular representations of the totality of reality that serve as focal points for meditation. The idea is that you sit and contemplate this one image, one thought alone, and eventually that thought becomes the totality of thoughts. The inter-/inner-connectedness of existence becomes apparent. The symbol provokes you to move beyond the symbol, as all great mythologies do. When you become stuck in the symbol, you are trapped in the circle that encases it. The rat race continues.

At the outset of this work I would have never expected it to be as entrenched in politics as it is. My own ideas about political issues tend to be more Taoist (self-governance) than Confucian (state government). The more I researched and wrote, the more I realized how important it is to highlight the political ties that

governments have had, and still have, to religious institutions—
essentially, how the creation of any organization that is going to
"speak for the people" follows the same process, and cannot
truly be separated. Those lines continue to be blurred today,
as religious fundamentalists actively support the politicians
who offer lip service to God's work, and universities such as
Patrick Henry College in Purcellville, Virginia, are focused on
training young Christians for a public life fifty miles away in
Washington D.C. Ironically, the gavel often does not swing
both ways. Conservative politicians certainly love the support
of ambitious, eager twenty-somethings on their campaign
trail, but do not like the possibility of churches influencing
their members, as evidenced in the case of All Saints Episcopal
Church in Pasadena, California. Two days prior to the 2004
election, a guest preacher delivered a heated sermon regarding
the current war, and concluded, "I don't tell you how to vote ...
you go your way, and I'll go God's way." The undertone, saying
it without saying it, was that Bush was not the lever to pull.
Turns out that since 1954 the government holds the right to call
into question a church's non-taxable status if they take sides in
political issues, a convenient way for Washington to check and
balance their clergy. All Saints found itself in a media spotlight
(albeit nearly a year after the sermon), with the government
hanging this obscure and dated law over the church's head.

     The taxability and accountability of the church's power
becomes more dangerous when moving into the realm of
megachurches. Defined by having congregations of 2,000+
people, since 2001 the number of these institutions in America
has grown to more than 1,200. Whereas malls used to host
churches, churches now house malls. The church no longer has
need to hide its corporate ethics, as Frank Santora's Faith Church
in New Milford, Connecticut, includes a green-and-white Jesus
logo-bearing Son Bucks—the church's "faithful" version of
Starbucks—as one of the attractions. Joel Osteen, who leads
the largest congregation in the country and purchased an old
basketball stadium in Houston to house his Lakewood Church,
claimed donations upwards of $73 million dollars in 2006. This
is outside of his $13 million book advance, the largest ever by

Simon & Schuster, topping the paltry $12 million paid to Bill Clinton. Granted, Osteen passed on his annual $200,000 salary at the church (though those donations do pay for his touring expenses), and running a stadium-sized concert every week is no small strain on the wallet. But considering that money is also pumped into advertising and missionary outreach, we again see how the Word of God is not separated from the money put behind the media campaign. These men and churches are spending tens of thousands of dollars weekly, when that money could be used for efforts that religion is more commonly supposed to be about: feeding the poor, housing the homeless, purchasing medicines and water for nations that do not have easy access to these essential items. Jumping up and down and saying that faith in the Lord will find you a good parking spot is a sad display of supposed spirituality.

Men like Osteen and Santora are criticized for their brand of religion-lite, which is closer to a self-help program than old-school religious service. For one, Osteen promises that prayers to the Almighty can help you in the most basic of circumstances (like parking lots). While there is something to be said for his ability to entwine the divine with the everyday, this constant focus on the goodness of a higher power while completely excluding the shadow is dangerous. There's something suspect in seeing an author's face as the cover image of a book, with the subtitle promising seven steps to a better anything (refer to the Suzuki quote above). While optimism is never a bad quality to cultivate, this sort of thinking sets the believer up for failed expectations and righteous bigotry. Add to this Santora's running joke that "I just want fifty thousand—split up the rest" in reference to his growing congregation, and we see over and over the not-so-hidden strains of egoism at every turn. A leader, as the Taoists liked to say, leads by staying behind.

When dealing with the realms of social power, there will always be a push and pull. Recall that as Christians claimed Israel by the sword, and no longer needed to fight external enemies, they turned on one another. Some believers became "more Christian" than others; converts were treated with a watchful eye; insistent divisions caused a progressively downward spiral. Today church and state may be separated on certain levels, but the psychological constructions supporting them remain the same. Just look at the recent presidential bid by former Massachusetts Governor Mitt Romney. Knowing full well his Mormon faith would be a hindrance to securing the Republican bid (they are the black sheep of Christianity), he gave a heart-wrenching speech in front of an important Washington crowd in December 2007. While he cloaked his languaging in the verbiage of universal religionism, the reality was that he is speaking of religious freedom *if* you are a believer in God, most notably Christian. This is the tendency among the disparate sects of one religion—to say they can get along with the strains of their own faith while not even acknowledging that others exist. (He briefly mentions Jews and Muslims.) More telling were the immediate attacks (as well as support) moments after the speech coming from Christians on all sides, dissecting the integrity of his religion. Yet another case of "My God is better than yours" all over CNN. We really haven't evolved as much as we'd like to believe.

This habit occurs in the yoga community, showing how an imported philosophy cannot do without the weight of cultural biases—which is why Carl Jung proclaimed yoga to be dangerous to Westerners, who he believed will never fully appreciate the intricacies that the discipline entails, and will continue to apply their either/or psychology to ideas not inherently chained to that form of reasoning. Hence certain schools are considered "more legitimate" or "more yogic" than others (by the practitioners of said school, of course). I often encounter this bias, as I predominantly teach in gyms; hence I teach "gym yoga" (i.e. non-spiritual, aerobically-inclined movement). Members of particular lineages will claim things like knowing the "true" yoga, much in the same way that Protestants battle Catholics over their brand of righteousness. When expressed aloud, the absurdness of this becomes clear. Yoga, like religion, is the art of union. Every action and thought that moves towards division and away from unity is counterproductive. To divide is to be confused about forms, to not grasp the essence.

The yoga mat is a microscope for observing your own processes. If treated as a means to a purely physical workout, you will certainly get that. The real advantage comes by noticing your psychological reactions during movement. How you express your body is a reflection of your inner state. If your movement is constricted and jagged, will the movement of your thoughts be any different? If you are constantly distracted, fidgeting around, concerned more with your pedicure than relaxing your hamstrings, what can you really expect from the practice? I often tell my students that it's not whether you can perform a pose or not that's important. It's how you react to whether or not you can do a pose. If you are easily frustrated by what you cannot do, that is a microcosm of how you treat the world and the challenges that you face. The most important reaction to cultivate is laughter, an extension of humility. At the same time, if you are really strong and flexible and can accomplish postures with grace and ease, what does it matter if you spend the entire time showing off your abilities? This is the reason promotional items like yoga calendars are so unfortunate. Sure, there is beauty to a well-performed posture, but too many people treat that as *the* essence of yoga. In reality that is the first, and not even necessary, step. Asanas were never believed to be the epitome of yoga until its popularity soared in America, predominantly over the last two decades. This focus on the body is indicative of the culture which has birthed it.

The roots of this physical emphasis are reminiscent of the same patterns that birthed democracy. From the polis that informed modern politics we trace ethnocentric divinities: Greeks were the first to draw human images as totems of mythic gods. Prior to their time, gods were either seen as pure essence (wind, water, earth), animal or half-human/half-animal creations. The Greeks carved them into extra-humans, and millennia later comic books that feature mythological deities in human and extra-human form are big business. As we evolved as nations equipped with ever-growing technologies to carry our languages to the distant reaches of the planet, we became the gods that nature used to provide. Religious prophets who once spoke for all of existence now championed the human cause alone, and bestowing honor, we placed them on pedestals. This focus on the human led to the demise of our relationship with the rest of nature. Windows that once let in fresh air became shielded by glass; chiefs that lived within their tribe became presidents residing on armed ranches; local cuisines became global, and the regeneration of soil and species slowly ceased to be.

These are the "hidden" connections, the multifarious layers that inform our everyday life that are not readily apparent. Michael Pollan is unparalleled in uncovering such links between the way we eat and how it arrives on our table. Currently, one-fifth of American petroleum usage goes to producing and transporting our food. On an even more subtle level, it can take up to ten calories of work to create one calorie of food. That is not the product of a sustainable industry. Sustainability is a key component to evolution, for it promotes the continued success of our species. If we are eating petroleum-dependent, low-energy foods steeped in innumerable mutations of corn, how can we expect to think clearly at all? The annual corn harvest—roughly 530 million bushels—is used in the production of 17.5 billion pounds of high fructose corn syrup. A child born in 2000 now has a one-in-three chance of developing diabetes. How can we miss such an obvious link? Worse still, how can we not do anything about it? Even more despairing is nutritionist Dr. T. Colin Campbell's assessment that casein-rich cow's milk is perhaps the single most dangerous liquid to put inside of a child's body, leading to this onslaught of diabetes. When a mother denies her child milk created by her own body specifically for the purpose of nourishing her young, and relies on the milk of chemical- and antibiotic-fed cows, the results could—and are proving to—be disastrous.

This is not the time to sit back and contemplate Jesus's return on a chariot of fire, to overlook our responsibilities because a supposed Eden awaits us at the end of the tunnel. This is no place to invoke "God's will" when we fall sick with disease, unease and unrest. The true fires burning are inside of our intestines and brains. As gastroneurologist Michael Gershon wittily put it, "Where primitive peoples use a variety of gods to explain the inexplicable, modern humans use psychiatric illness. When all else fails, invoke a psychoneurosis." Or, as James Hillman expressed when quoting Carl Jung during his keynote lecture at the 2004 Mythic Journeys conference, "The gods have become diseases; Zeus no longer rules Olympus, but rather the solar plexus, and produces curious specimens for the doctor's consulting room, and disorders of the brains of politicians and journalists who unwittingly let loose psychic epidemics in the world."

Obviously there is much being done, although a bit of research and a trip beyond your local supermarket may be required. Sustainable food industries are becoming more prominent, and more profitable, by the day. While there is no way around the heavy costs of transportation as of yet, the intention is there, and a lot of change can be created from that alone. Let us put aside the industrial food platform for a moment, and focus on the people who are actually attempting progressive ideas, and how their good intentions are sometimes as ego-based and misunderstood as the industries they rail against. The burgeoning yoga industry is stuck on one idea that it uses as righteous fuel in many campaigns, a topic I deal very personally with: vegetarianism, often in the form of veganism, and at its extreme, raw foodism. I have not eaten meat in eleven years (save a brief stint in 2007 while dealing with uncertain health issues), although I am, by definition, not fully vegetarian—I occasionally eat seafood. For the most part, I am 98% vegan, though. It has taken some time, but I have found a diet that works well for my temperament and health. This too is not uncommon—Ayurveda treats dietary requirements as a process, one which changes over time. While there have been numerous reasons as to why I don't eat meat, upon reintroducing it into my diet for a stretch of three months, I realized that the most basic reason for my choice is the most honest: I don't like it. Perhaps that is the result of having lived over a decade without it, but to me that is irrelevant. I cannot say I will remain so for the rest of my days, but as of now there is no room for meat in my foreseeable future.

Now as I said, this diet works for me. If I were to then

go on and state that it is the diet that must work for everybody, a problem arises. Sadly, this is what a portion of the yoga community is focused on, and if there is any one reason I think the practice has not reached a larger audience in America, it is that. (The other is chanting, which a number of people feel is hokey; granted, most naysayers have never even tried it.) In the last few decades, vegetarianism has gone from being the culinary choice of a fringe community to garnering mainstream attention. Yogis will claim that it is part of a great awakening of a more morally conscious society. While that may be the case to some degree, we should not write off eating meat blindly. It is the *type* of meat that should be considered—how it's handled, grown and killed, and how it reaches our tables. It seems rather unreasonable that as a species we've been eating meat for hundreds of thousands of years, and within forty we should suddenly abandon the practice entirely. Obscure references about tooth shapes and digestive systems aside, there is little reason humans would need to do so.

When defending animal rights, proponents cite many grievances, and one of the most notable is also among the most preposterous. They claim domestication is unnatural. As Pollan points out, for many of these species, domestication is the *best* thing that could have happened. Remember, our very basic and primordial drive is to survive and perpetuate as a species. So while any number of individual animals may be killed for consumption, their numbers have increased dramatically, thus fulfilling their genetic intent. What Pollan shows is that although they may eventually be slaughtered, most often their lifespans are *longer* in captivity than they would be in the wild, where they are at the mercy of predators much less humane than our kind. Thus it is the method of killing, and how they are allowed to live, that are really the issues. The romanticized notion that they will prosper in their natural settings is fallacious and idyllic. By taking part in the human food cycle there is a greater chance of sustainability for all parties involved, but this only happens if they live on grass-fed farms and are treated like living beings, as they are at Polyface.

Evolution is a dauntingly slow process if measured in

human time, which is why massive changes in any part of the cycle cannot occur during one generation. It is highly improbable that our hunting and gathering ancestors ever questioned the ethics of eating meat, yet for most of our evolution "they" were who we were. Early agriculturists prepared their meals in conjunction with bison, pigs and cattle. Then two strategies— widespread farming and writing—evolved, and the entire way that we lived was altered, including how we perceived the world. As mentioned, when humans were no longer dependent on hunting as a means of sustenance, only then were morals introduced into the picture. Even then, it was human sacrifice that was first done away with; other forms of sacrifice— cannibalism and infanticide—took centuries more. Animals were sacrificed still—whether the ritual intent was geared toward appeasing gods or to quiet pangs of guilt will probably remain a mystery, though a bit of both is not a bad answer. One of Pollan's conclusions is extremely important: Once humans stopped making personal contact, especially eye contact, with the animals being eaten, the mysterious distance between "us" and "them" grew. It's much easier to dine on an already-cooked steak that smells of sauce and pan than it is to put a blade to the heifer yourself.

While watching a documentary on the National Geographic channel, I was struck by a clip of a mother lion training her cub to hunt. They had found a fawn; junior was chasing it down while mama jogged behind to ensure it wouldn't escape. The youngster did its job, though, taking down the baby deer by wrapping its jaws around the hind and dragging it to the ground. Then there was a moment of silence that we see often in nature. Both mother and son knew the prey was caught, and so did the fawn. She was not seriously injured, yet once surrounded, she just lay there on all fours, staring blankly into a horizon we can only imagine. There was nothing she could do, and had to flounder as both lions ripped the flesh and muscle from her body. Death was certainly not instantaneous. So here is the puzzle: If the activist call to arms is that eating animals is taking part in speciesism (favoring humans over all other species), and humans should be treated on equal footing as all other forms of life, why are we not waving banners against the horrendous assaults these lions are performing on deer? If all species are created equally, then why do we not cry in outrage when a whale consumes billions of krill every day? If these seem like outrageous questions (and to me, they do), we have to realize that the claims of activism for animal rights are equally outlandish, from an evolutionary standpoint, in many of their assertions. Treating animals more humanely is certainly a noble deed. Supporting regional farms and businesses to acknowledge the source of your nutrition is of primary importance. Banishing meat from the human food cycle for good, however, would create an imbalance in nature both to vegetation and to animals that is not even considered.

For example, consider the sacredness of the cow in India. This is often treated as the *sine qua non* of modern vegetarianism. The cow, Krishna's playmate and divine supplier of culturally essential products such as ghee and milk, is gazed upon with symbolic reverence in American yoga circles. As we saw in Chapter 4, this vegetarian trend was not always the abstention of choice in India. Bones of all sorts were found in the kitchens of the Mohenjo-Daro digs. Until at least 1000 BCE, cows were regularly consumed, and early Vedic texts were inconsistent on the topic for centuries after. Circa 600 BCE, things started to change, albeit not due to any spiritual reasoning. Rather, they were running out of meat. As would occur in non-sustainable hunting and gathering societies that killed too much game too quickly, priests could not afford to slaughter and distribute these animals. Meat eating became the cuisine of Brahmans. The "spiritual" idea was a clever way for clergy to explain to the lower castes that meat was not necessary for their livelihood, even though Brahmans continued to sacrifice and feast. As the economic rift widened, and sects such as Buddhism and Jainism recognized this social gulf and responded with ideas of universal compassion, the once-forced vegetarianism became *reinforced* to lift the morals of the lower economic strata. The ping-pong of ethical meat eating became more prominent, but as recently as 350 CE it was still part of the Brahman diet, and probably until 700 CE when Muslims rolled into town. From there unfolded an interesting situation: Muslims had no problem eating beef, so the widespread ban and fully accepted "sacredness" of the cow didn't actually take over Indian consciousness until this *reaction* came into play, with a movement to protect this important symbol—one sacred to some (lower castes) and ritualistic to others (Brahmans). This sort of dietary code is not unique. Consider why it is appropriate to fast during Lent, the days leading up to the resurrection of Christ. Nearing the end of winter, when the new harvests are nowhere in sight and saved food supplies dwindle, it makes economic sense to create a ritual to keep supplies guarded. If there is a figurehead to attach to the idea, all the better.

It is not rare for the "spiritual" to appear *after* the social reality sets in. While Hindus were preserving their identity as separate from Muslims (who, as just mentioned, were not especially dogmatic about their religion as much as their social prowess), the priestly class soon had another issue to contend with. Oxen were important for another reason in India: they plowed the fields. With such population density and widespread hunger, and a growing season dependent on annual floods, these beasts became a crucial part of the workforce. Killing them for meat would have been disastrous to the growing number of people dependent upon grains and vegetables to survive. The creation of the sacred cow was a way to prevent farmers or others from killing these valuable helpers. It was not God's law; it was resource management. In a sense, the oxen were even more important than female cows, which are allowed to roam freely around the towns. The females do offer milk and dairy products, but their real worth comes in reproduction. The oxen are needed to stay in prime shape for fieldwork. Both need ritual protection so that they can stay employed. Making something sacred is the surest way to ensure that humans remain domesticated.

When performed with an acknowledgement to the interconnectedness of life, slaughter is not an inherently "evil" occupation. It is more "natural" than abstaining from meat, for it follows the death and birth motif that all religions have been founded upon. The more distant we grow from our food, and food sources, the more we are open to the ever-growing intervention of businesses who are intent on maximizing profits. We need to shed the idea that large corporations with giant marketing budgets are looking out for our best interests. Instead, we need to look out for ourselves, a process that begins with self-observation. If the statement that we are what we eat (and, as Pollan puts it, we are what what we eat eats) still holds any weight—and it should—then digesting low-energy, highly processed foodstuffs is going to continue to turn our stomachs inside out. Better it is to understand the metaphysical lesson of the wafer and wine. Through the embodiment of the harvest we are creating the regenerative cycles within ourselves, fine tuning our lives to the recurrent cycles of nature. Try to control the ride, and crashing is inevitable. Working with the elements is a much more suitable, not to mention sustainable, way to exist.

The counter-argument is equally treacherous, however. Carnivores like to cite that all humans were hunters and gatherers. This is most likely true. Yet the amount of meat that they consumed was nowhere near the daily (or twice daily, or even three times daily) diet of meat that modern Americans consume. As we noted earlier, women supplied the most essential part of the diet: seeds, nuts and plants. Meat was a luxury. The person today who does not go a day without eating or drinking some form of animal product is, from an evolutionary standpoint, an anomaly. As T. Colin Campbell points out in *The China Study*, the chances of being afflicted by the "diseases of affluence" by which many Americans die from—heart disease, certain forms of cancer and the medical system itself (the third highest killer in our country)—are enhanced by the eating of animal products. His massive research projects have uncovered the fact that roughly 2-3% of our illnesses are completely genetic, which is in contradiction to the derisive anthem of those who fall sick and blame it "on my genes." Genes need a trigger to turn them on, and time and again Campbell has scientifically shown that those triggers are meat and dairy products. This is not a belief; it is the results of over fifty years of dedicated research.

So why the billboards with milk mustaches—an

especially disturbing phenomenon, especially to the African-American community, as there is no actual proof that milk helps ward off osteoporosis; in fact, milk drinkers have the worst bone health and highest fracture rates in the world—and research saying meat is necessary for our wellbeing? Simple: big money is at stake. Can you imagine our political leaders coming to the podium to announce that a low-fat, low-protein, high-carbohydrate diet of plant-based whole foods can actually turn our health and economy around? Sadly they'd be laughed from their job. And this is exactly the spell that the meat and dairy boards have created with their "research." Today one of every seven of our dollars is spent on healthcare, and by 2030 it is predicted that the American healthcare system could cost 16 trillion dollars a year. Even more urgently, Melody Petersen writes that by 2015, "America is expected to send 20 percent of all it produces on health care." A recent U.S. Surgeon General's Report on Nutrition and Health stated that two-thirds of our mortality rate is related to dietary choices. Yet diet books promoting quick weight loss through high-fat, high-protein cuisines are making tens of millions of dollars. Why? Because they confirm our laziness and tell us things we want to hear. Meanwhile the FDA is turning much of the "scientific" work onto the companies themselves, allowing the corporations to tell us whether or not their products are safe for consumption. As John Robbins writes in *The Food Revolution*, "Thus we have a situation where the very companies that stand to profit are the ones that decide whether or not their products are hazardous." Time and again, it is the consumer that pays the full price for their trickery, and with much more than money.

Is the sudden rush toward going green part of an ever-growing moralism on the planet, one where humanity will do away with the consumption of all animals and processed foods for the betterment of everything? If it suits the survival of our species, it is a possibility. Yet I have to agree with Pollan when he writes that such activist ideologies "could only thrive in a world where people have lost contact with the natural world." Just as Karen Armstrong noted about monotheistic religious traditions—that they take root in urban civilizations—so it is within the city that many of these modern traditions have started. The further away from nature you are, and the more removed from the realities of food production and management you become, the more unrealistic your philosophies grow. You then begin to think in terms of grids and squares instead of the curves and flows of nature. This current activism is, like the Indians defending their culture against Muslim invaders, a reaction to the brute and uncaring force of industry, to the distance created between food source and food store. While I applaud the efforts that some organizations have made in attempting to balance the scales, to tip them too far to their side would not address the overall problem, which essentially has to do with imbalance in the first place. Again, I see the key word here to be sustainability, a means of coexistence, with each other as well as all the forces surrounding us, for they are inside of us too—*they were what created us.* Is it really difficult to understand why our religious traditions were agriculturally based, ostensibly concerned with purity of soil and regeneration? That the gods were embedded inside of the soil, as well as in the rains and sun nourishing that which grew from the earth? That their very names, which gave them actual life, were synonymous with the process it produced? What good is an abstract god who is invisible and does not take part in human affairs, yet has the ability to judge us at the end of our lives?

Our technology, once the realm of artistic creation, is now focused purely on economics. This trend is diseasing every market, be it "spiritual" or not. We don't need more information; we need less of it. We need to unclutter our minds, to become the empty vessel that Buddhism speaks of, a fleshy container that can hold everything while holding on to nothing. Unused, and unusable, information is not going to help. We have the entire history of the world at our fingertips, and need only to cultivate all the knowledge and insights that have been passed through the generations. We need to let go of certain habits and ideas, certainly. Yet this is not to forget everything. Like Joel Salatin's chickens, we need to pick out the rubbish from the nourishment, digest and filter it back into our environment. We need to read authors like John Robbins and T. Colin Campbell to remind us of our responsibilities—to ourselves, our children and each other. Yet these men are not going to tell you what you want to hear; as heart specialist Dr. Dean Ornish wrote of his own research, "The point of our study was to determine what is true, not what is practicable." This requires work; it requires not taking everything at face value and believing all the labels on what we feed ourselves with, be it from a supermarket shelf or the daily newspaper. Most of all, it requires those qualities that prophets and sages of past times have always put emphasis on: compassion, charity, and the cultivation of inner quietude.

     Undoubtedly this all forces us to change. As Campbell wrote,

> If changing your diet is expensive, I don't know what they would say about being bedridden and incapacitated. As far as altering the "normal nutritional balance" is concerned, what is normal? Does this mean the diet that we now eat is "normal"—the diet that is largely responsible for diseases that cripple, kill and make profoundly miserable millions of Americans every year? Are massive rates of heart disease, cancer, autoimmune diseases, obesity and diabetes "normal?" If this is normal, I propose we start seriously considering the abnormal.

And this advice does not only apply to food—our entire cultural philosophy, one based on the idea that the world is ready to abide by our ideals, needs to become seriously abnormal. There are no gods about make this change for us. It is one we must activate ourselves.

     I began this book with an example of one of my students, and will close full circle. This particular student was in her mid-sixties and had three metal plates in her back. She could barely bend over to touch her knees, let alone her toes. Every week she took my open level class, which is challenging for someone even in good shape. Needless to say, she moved a bit slower than everyone else, as she had to take extra time doing seemingly simple tasks, like sitting down and standing up. Yet I will never forget her, for two important reasons. Firstly, she never moved out of a posture until the next pose was called for. While her version of that pose always appeared "lesser" than the more flexible and stronger students surrounding her, she was far superior in her ability to do whatever she could do in the moment and not be distracted by her toes, her thoughts, or the people staring in from outside the glass window. While many of the students in the room were working out, she was practicing yoga.

Secondly, the thing I will never forget about her: the expression on her face every time she looked up to see the next pose. She smiled. A big, white shimmering gaze that revealed no sign of complaint or regret. She took her media and worked within it to the fullest of her potential, and, what's more, *she enjoyed it*. What more can we ask of ourselves and the world that birthed us?

ACKNOWLEDGEMENTS

Throughout the writing of this work, I was fortunate enough to have my best friend and business partner, Dax-Devlon Ross, living just one floor above my studio in Jersey City. During this time he has also written his first philosophy book, *The Nightmare and The Dream*, and while the subject matters are worlds apart, the underlying similarities are startling. Our constant late-night talks—provoking and rebuking—and enthusiastic cheerleading on both ends has been invaluable—as has been this entire publishing endeavor.

A very large thanks to Sasha Dmochowski, who patiently edited this manuscript, providing advice where it was most needed, and most importantly reminding me that not everyone is inside of my own head—a space I find tough enough to navigate on my own. Equal gratitude goes to William Doty, who has offered many important points and edits to the original manuscript. More thanks to my InnerContinental partner, Jill Ettinger, whose patience during my ramblings about the topics covered inside these pages during evening rides home from New York City is highly appreciated. And to Jeff Benjamin and Mike Hull, who both kindled the flame of this work with generous offerings of books, which subsequently opened my eyes to viewing my own discipline in new and innovative ways.

Having taught yoga for over four years, innumerable teachers, colleagues, and students fill the pages of this work in ways that I cannot explain. In a special way, this book is for anybody who dedicates themselves so devotedly to a practice like yoga. I feel honored to have a made a career in this form of movement, one that is not only physically challenging and enlivening, but emotionally and mentally stimulating and engaging. Thanks to all of you for sharing the ride, and to the staff and members of Equinox Fitness, where I have had the opportunity to make their facilities my playground. A few teachers have been special to me well beyond our time in the studio, and I'd like to personally thank Stephanie Culen, Sadie Nardini, Marc Coronel and Adam David for all the help, love and friendship.

A final thank you to my good friend and amazing artist, Craig Anthony Miller, who once again caught your eye with the cover artwork. And of course, to my family, who has shown nothing but love over the decade since I began working on this chaotic island to learn, grow and experience. When I first arrived in 1998, I used to say New York City is a battlefield of the soul. The forms have constantly rearranged, but the essence of that statement remains true today.

SOURCES

1. MOVING BEYOND BELIEF

Altemeyer, Bob and Hunsberger, Bruce E. *Atheists: A Groundbreaking Study of America's Nonbelievers* (Prometheus Books, 2006)

Alter, Joseph S. *Yoga in Modern India: The Body Between Science and Philosophy* (Princeton Paperbacks, 2004)

Crowe, David M. *A History of the Gypsies of Eastern Europe and Russia* (St. Martin's Griffin, 1996)

Dennett, Daniel. *Breaking the Spell: Religion as a Natural Phenomenon* (Penguin, Non-Classics, 2007)

Harris, Sam. *The End of Faith: Religion, Terror, and the Future of Reason* (W.W. Norton, 2005)

Hedges, Chris. *War is a Force That Gives Us Meaning* (Anchor, 2002)

Hillman, James. *A Terrible Love of War* (Penguin Press, 2004)

Love, Robert. "Fear of Yoga," *Utne Reader* reprinted from *Columbia Journalism Review*, March/April 2007

McGrath, Alister. *The Twilight of Atheism: The Rise and Fall of Disbelief in the Modern World* (Galilee/Doubleday, 2006)

Pinker, Steven. *The Blank Slate: The Modern Denial of Human Nature* (Penguin, 2002)

Stephen, Leslie. "An Agnostic's Apology," *Atheism: A Reader*, [S.T. Joshi, editor] (Prometheus, 2000)

Thompson, Emma. "The Philosophy of Atheism," *Atheism: A Reader*, S.T. Joshi, editor (Prometheus, 2000)

Warren, Rick. http://www.rickwarren.com, August 2007
Watts, Alan. *The Wisdom of Insecurity: A Message For An Age of Anxiety* (Vintage, 1951)
Wilber, Ken. *A Theory of Everything* (Shambhala, 2000)
Wolf, Gary. "The Church of Non-Believers," *Wired*, November 2006

2. REDEMPTION SONG

Information on anxiety found at http://www.l-theanine.com/intro.htm. Information regarding passport percentage at http://www.lonelyplanet.com/passport.

Diamond, Jared. *Guns, Germs, and Steel: The Fates of Human Societies* (W.W. Norton, 1999)
Lee, Hélène. *The First Rasta: Leonard Howell and the Rise of Rastafarianism* (Lawrence Hill, 1999)
Mansingh, Laxmi and Ajai. *Home Away From Home: 150 Years of Indian Presence in Jamaica 1845-1995* (Ian Randle, 1999)
Van Sertima, Ivan. *They Came Before Columbus: The African Presence in Ancient America* (Random House, 1975)

3. THE UNWISDOM OF HINDSIGHT

Biblical passages are taken from the Holy Bible, King James Version, printed by Zondervan Publishing House, 1962.

Cassirer, Ernest. *Language and Myth* (Dover, 1946)
Dawkins, Richard. *The God Delusion* (Houghton Mifflin, 2006)
Diamond, Jared. *Guns, Germs, and Steel: The Fates of Human Societies* (W.W. Norton, 1999)
Florida, Richard. *The Rise of the Creative Class: ...and how it's transforming work, leisure, community, & everyday life* (Basic, 2002)
Fortey, Richard. *Life: A Natural History of the First Four Billion Years of Life on Earth* (Vintage, 1997)

Frankfort, H.A. and Henri. *The Intellectual Adventure of Ancient Man: An Essay on Speculative Thought in the Ancient Near East* (University of Chicago Press, 1977)
Harris, Marvin. *Cannibals and Kings: The Origins of Cultures* (Vintage, 1977)
Harris, Marvin. *Our Kind: Who We Are, Where We Came From & Where We Are Going* (HarperPerennial, 1989)
Kapleau, Philip [editor]. *The Wheel of Death: A Collection of Zen Buddhist and Other Sources on Death, Rebirth, Dying* (Colophon, 1971)
Pierce, Charles P. "Greetings From Idiot America," *Esquire*, November 2005
Postman, Neil. *Amusing Ourselves to Death: Public Discourse in the Age of Show Business* (Penguin, 2005)
Russell, Bertrand. "Is There a God," *Atheism: A Reader*, S.T. Joshi, editor (Prometheus, 2000)
Wolf, Naomi. *The End of America: Letter of Warning to a Young Patriot* (Chelsea Green, 2007)
Zinn, Howard. *A People's History of the United States 1492-Present* (Perennial, 1999)

4. THE PLIGHT OF PROTO-SHIVA

Armstrong, Karen. *The Great Transformation: The Beginning of Our Religious Traditions* (Anchor, 2006)
Bae, James C. and Sharma, Indra. *In A World of Gods and Goddesses: The Mystic Art of Indra Sharma* (Mandala, 2003)
Campbell, Joseph. *The Hero With a Thousand Faces* (Bollingen, 1968)
Campbell, Joseph and Moyers, Bill. *The Power of Myth* (Anchor, 1988)
Coomaraswamy, Ananda K. *The Dance of Siva: Essays on Indian Art and Culture* (Dover, 1985)
Easwaran, Eknath [translator]. *The Bhagavad Gita* (Vintage, 2000)
Eliade, Mircea. *Yoga: Immortality and Freedom* (Bollingen, 1969)
Feuerstein, Georg and Miller, Jeanine. *The Essence of Yoga: Essays*

on the Development of Yogic Philosophy from the Vedas to Modern Times (Inner Traditions, 1988)

Feuerstein, Georg. *The Yoga Tradition: Its History, Literature, Philosophy and Practice* (Hohm Press, 2001)

Keay, John. *India: A History* (Grove, 2000)

Mishra, Ramamurti S. *The Textbook of Yoga Psychology: The Definitive Translation and Interpretation of Patanjali's Yoga Sutras* (Baba Bhagavandas Publication Trust, 1997)

Neumann, Erich. *The Origins and History of Consciousness* (Princeton/Bollingen, 1954)

O'Flaherty, Wendy Doniger. *Siva: The Erotic Ascetic* (Oxford, 1981)

Watts, Alan. *The Wisdom of Insecurity: A Message For An Age of Anxiety* (Vintage, 1951)

5. THE FIFTIETH SECOND COMING

The Sam Harris article that is referenced is available at http://www.newsweek.washingtonpost.com/onfaith/sam_harris/2007/10/the_problem_with_atheism.html. The Intelligent Design Network website referenced is http://www.intelligentdesignnetwork.org.

Altemeyer, Bob and Hunsberger, Bruce E. *Atheists: A Groundbreaking Study of America's Nonbelievers* (Prometheus Books, 2006)

Armstrong, Karen. *A History of God: The 4,000-Year Quest of Judaism, Christianity and Islam* (Anchor, 1993)

Armstrong, Karen. *Holy War: The Crusades and Their Impact on Today's World* (Anchor, 2001)

Armstrong, Karen. *The Great Transformation: The Beginning of Our Religious Traditions* (Anchor, 2006)

Cantor, Norman F. *Antiquity: From the Birth of Sumerian Civilization to the Fall of the Roman Empire* (Perennial, 2003)

Coyne, Jerry A. "Intelligent Design: The Faith That Dare Not Speak Its Name," *Intelligent Thought: Science Versus the Intelligent Design Movement* (Vintage, 2006)

Dennett, Daniel. *Breaking the Spell: Religion as a Natural*

Phenomenon (Penguin, Non-Classics, 2007)

Harris, Sam. *The End of Faith: Religion, Terror, and the Future of Reason* (W.W. Norton, 2005)

Keay, John. *India: A History* (Grove, 2000)

Krakauer, John. *Under the Banner of Heaven: A Story of Violent Faith* (Anchor, 2004)

Krishna, Gopi. *Kundalini: The Evolutionary Energy in Man* (Shambhala, 1997)

McKenna, Terence. *Food of the Gods: The Search for the Original Tree of Knowledge* (Bantam New Age, 1992)

McGrath, Alister. *The Twilight of Atheism: The Rise and Fall of Disbelief in the Modern World* (Doubleday, 2006)

Miller, Kenneth R. *Finding Darwin's God: A Scientist's Search for Common Ground Between God and Evolution* (Harper Perennial, 1999)

Prothero, Stephen. *American Jesus: How the Son of God Became a National Icon* (Farrar, Straus & Giroux, 2003)

Ratliff, Evan. "The Crusade Against Evolution," *Wired*, October 2004.

Susskind, Leonard. "The Good Fight," *Intelligent Thought: Science Versus the Intelligent Design Movement* (Vintage, 2006)

Wright, Robert. *The Moral Animal: Why We Are the Way We Are: The New Science of Evolutionary Psychology* (Vintage, 1994)

Zuckerman, Phil. "Contemporary Numbers and Patterns," *The Cambridge Guide to Atheism* (Cambridge University Press, 2007)

6. INTEGRATION IS GLOBALIZATION

The translation of the chant to Shiva is found in the *Jivamukti Chant Book*.

Avalon, Arthur. *The Serpent Power: The Secrets of Tantric and Shaktic Yoga* (Dover, 1974)

Beres, Derek. *Global Beat Fusion: The History of the Future of Music* (Outside the Box, 2005)

Feuerstein, Georg. *The Yoga Tradition: Its History, Literature, Philosophy and Practice* (Hohm Press, 2001)

Gannon, Sharon and Life, David. *Jivamukti Yoga: Practices for Liberating Body and Soul* (Ballantine, 2002)

Hall, Manly P. *The Secret Teachings of All Ages [Reader's Edition]* (Tarcher/Penguin, 2003)

Iyengar, B.K.S. *The Tree of Yoga* (Shambhala, 1988)

Khan, Hazrat Inayat. *The Mysticism of Sound and Music* (Shambhala, 1991)

Larsen, Stephen. *The Mythic Imagination: Your Quest for Meaning Through Personal Mythology* (Bantam, 1990)

Lavezzoli, Peter. *The Dawn of Indian Music in the West* (Continuum, 2007)

Love, Robert. "Fear of Yoga," *Utne Reader* reprinted from *Columbia Journalism Review*, March/April 2007

Ruiz, Fernando Pagés. "Krishnamacharya's Legacy," *Yoga Journal*, http://www.yogajournal.com/wisdom/465

Shankar, Ravi. *Raga Mala: An Autobiography* (Welcome Rain, 1999)

7. FUSING THE FULCRUM

Campbell, Joseph and Moyers, Bill. *The Power of Myth* (Anchor, 1988)

Dawkins, Richard. *The Selfish Gene* (Oxford University Press, 2006)

Hall, Manly P. *The Secret Teachings of All Ages [Reader's Edition]* (Tarcher/Penguin, 2003)

Iyer, Pico. *The Open Road: The Global Journey of the Fourteenth Dalai Lama* (Alfred A. Knopf, 2008)

Jung, Carl. *The Portable Jung* [Joseph Campbell, editor] (Viking, 1976)

Kaptchuk, Ted. *The Web That Has No Weaver: Understanding Chinese Medicine* (McGraw-Hill, 2000)

Mitchell, Steven. *Gilgamesh* (Free Press, 2004)

Moyers, Bill. *Genesis: A Living Conversation* (Doubleday, 1996)

Pinker, Steven. *The Language Instinct: How the Mind Creates Language* (Perennial, 2000)

Tarnas, Richard. *Cosmos and Psyche: Intimations of a New World*

View (Plume, 2006)
Watts, Alan. *Myth and Ritual in Christianity* (Beacon, 1968)
Wright, Robert. *The Moral Animal: Why We Are the Way We Are: The New Science of Evolutionary Psychology* (Vintage, 1994)

8. EMBODYING THE SURVIVAL MACHINE

The conferences I cite and many more lectures from the TED conference are available at www.ted.com.

Abram, David. *The Spell of the Sensuous* (Random House, 1997)
Armstrong, Karen. *The Great Transformation: The Beginning of Our Religious Traditions* (Anchor, 2006)
Capra, Fritjof. *The Hidden Connection: A Science for Sustainable Living* (Anchor, 2002)
Capra, Fritjof. *The Tao of Physics: An Exploration of the Parallels Between Modern Physics and Eastern Mysticism* (Shambhala, 1999)
Chan, Wing-Tsit [translator/compiler]. *A Source Book in Chinese Philosophy* (Princeton Paperbacks, 1979)
Charles, Daniel. *Lords of the Harvest: Biotech, Big Money, and the Future of Food* (Perseus, 2001)
Dawkins, Richard. *The Selfish Gene* (Oxford University Press, 2006)
Eliade, Mircea. *Yoga: Freedom and Immortality* (Bollingen, 1969)
Harris, Sam. *Letter to a Christian Nation* (Vintage, 2007)
Hillman, James. *Re-Visioning Psychology* (HarperPerrenial, 1992)
Kimbrell, Andrew [editor]. *The Fatal Harvest Reader: The Tragedy of Industrial Agriculture* (Island Press, 2002)
Manning, Richard. *Against the Grain: How Agriculture Has Hijacked Civilization* (North Point Press, 2004)
Paz, Octavio. *In Light of India* (Harvest, 1995)
Paz, Octavio. *The Labyrinth of Solitude and Other Writings* (Grove, 1985)
Petersen, Melody. *Our Daily Meds: How the Pharmaceutical Companies Transformed Themselves into Slick Marketing Machines*

and Hooked the Nation on Prescription Drugs (Sarah Crichton Books, 2008)

Pinchbeck, Daniel. *2012: The Return of Quetzalcoatl* (Jeremy P. Tarcher/Penguin, 2006)

Pollan, Michael. *The Omnivore's Dilemma: A Natural History of Four Meals* (Penguin, 2006)

Pringle, Peter. *Food, Inc.: Mendel to Monsanto—The Promises and Perils of the Biotech Harvest* (Simon & Schuster, 2003)

Pyle, George. *Raising Less Corn, More Hell: The Case for the Independent Farm and Against Industrial Food* (Public Affairs, 2005)

Tarnas, Richard. *Cosmos and Psyche: Intimations of a New World View* (Plume, 2006)

Tudge, Colin. *Neanderthals, Bandits & Farmers: How Agriculture Really Began* (Yale University Press, 1998)

Van Sertima, Ivan. *They Came Before Columbus: The African Presence in Ancient America* (Random House, 1975)

Watts, Alan. *Beyond Theology: The Art of Godmanship* (Meridian, 1967)

Wright, Robert. *The Moral Animal: Why We Are the Way We Are: The New Science of Evolutionary Psychology* (Vintage, 1994)

9. THE END OF BEGINNINGLESS TIME BEGINS

Campbell, T. Colin and Thomas M. *The China Study: Startling Implications for Diet, Weight Loss and Long-Term Health* (Benbella, 2006)

Fitzgerald, Francis. "Come One, Come All," *The New Yorker*, December 3, 2007

Gershon, Michael. *The Second Brain: Your Gut Has a Mind of its Own* (Quill, 2003)

Golianopoulos, Thomas. "God, Without the Fuss," *GOOD*, Jan/Feb 2008

Gross, Michael Joseph. "Render Unto Caesar?," *GOOD*, Jan/Feb 2007

Hillman, James. "The Gods, Disease, and Politics." *Parabola*, Winter 2004

Jung, Carl. *The Psychology of Kundalini Yoga* (Bollingen, 1996)

Petersen, Melody. *Our Daily Meds: How the Pharmaceutical Companies Transformed Themselves into Slick Marketing Machines and Hooked the Nation on Prescription Drugs* (Sarah Crichton Books, 2008)

Pollan, Michael. *The Omnivore's Dilemma: A Natural History of Four Meals* (Penguin, 2006)

Robbins, John. *The Food Revolution: How Your Diet Can Help Save Your Life and Our World* (Conari, 2001)

Rosin, Hannah. "God and Country," *The New Yorker*, June 27, 2005

Suzuki, D.T. *Zen Buddhism: Selected Writings of D.T. Suzuki* [William Barrett, editor] (Image Books, 1996)

About the Author

Derek Beres is the author of four books, including *Global Beat Fusion: The History of the Future of Music*. He has been working in various forms of journalism for 15 years, the same length of time that he's been studying world religions, cultures, music and mythologies. He is the creator of EarthRise Yoga, and teaches and lectures internationally. In 2005 he co-founded Outside the Box Publishing with Dax-Devlon Ross, and continues to strive in creating high quality and inventive literature and thought. He lives in Jersey City, NJ. For more information visit www.derekberes.com.

About Outside the Box Publishing

This publishing endeavor is the latest in a long-time literary collaboration between friends who have experienced enough together to consider themselves family. It is an important and valuable way for us – perhaps more than anyone else – to continue believing in the written word. It seems only fitting in a cyberworld so accessible, so democratic in its way, that companies like ours are a natural outgrowth. Publishing books nowadays isn't that difficult. So many alternative avenues have opened that anyone can write and publish efficiently. The difficult part is finding people that believe in and support your work. That makes a big difference in whether we move ahead or stand still. If we don't have someone, that one person besides us, how can we expect the best of ourselves? In many ways, our commitment to literature is an extension of our commitment to fellowship. We have been fortunate enough to have one another to keep us creatively and philosophically alive, despite the setbacks and detours and plain old realities of modern existence. Outside the Box Publishing is our way of opening up the conversation and allowing other serious writers into the fold. - Derek Beres & Dax-Devlon Ross

LaVergne, TN USA
18 September 2009
158317LV00001B/104/P